The Great Age of Sail

Illustrated from the Picture Collections of the National Maritime Museum, Greenwich

THE GREAT

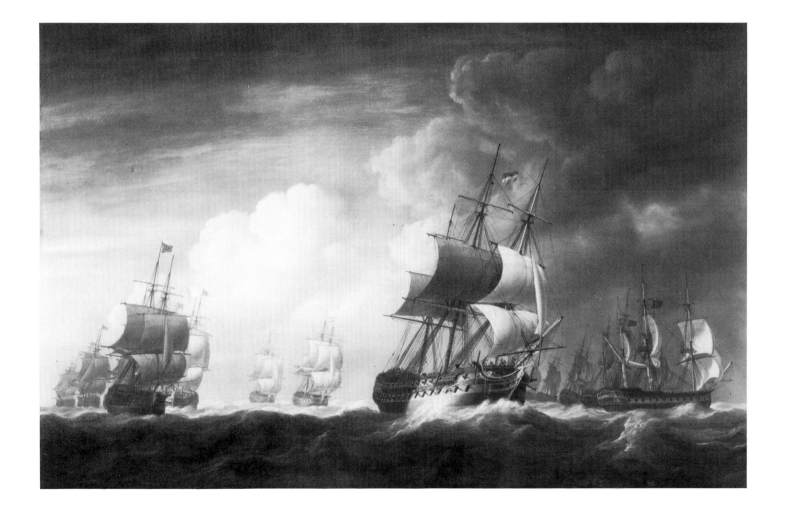

PETER KEMP AND RICHARD ORMOND

AGE OF SAIL

Maritime Art and Photography

PHAIDON · OXFORD

Contributors : Chapters 4, 7, 12 and 20 on marine painting are written by
Richard Ormond; the remaining chapters and the glossary are by Peter Kemp.
The captions are the work of Erica Davies, Stephen Deuchar, Joan Dormer,
Richard Ormond, Roger Quarm and Dennis Stonham of the National
Maritime Museum.

Phaidon Press Limited, Littlegate House, St. Ebbe's Street, Oxford OXI ISQ

First published 1986
© Phaidon Press Limited, 1986

British Library Cataloguing in Publication Data

Kemp, Peter, *1904–*
    The great age of sail.
    1. Marine painting, European   2. Ships in art
    I. Title   II. Ormond, Richard
    758'.2   ND1373.E/
    ISBN 0-7148-2423-2

Design by James Campus

Typeset in Monophoto Baskerville by BAS Printers Limited, Over Wallop,
Hampshire

Printed in Great Britain by Jolly & Barber Limited, Rugby, Warwickshire

Frontispiece. The 'Hindostan' (A Fleet of Indiamen at Sea)
Nicholas Pocock, 1803
This atmospheric painting was exhibited at the Royal Academy in 1803.
Pocock's own title for the picture was 'The Hindoostan, G. Millet,
Commander, and Senior Officer of 18 sail of East Indiamen, with the signal
to wear, sternmost and leewardmost ships first'. It was possibly commissioned
to commemorate Captain Millet's voyage to Cochin, China, between March
1801 and June 1802.

Contents

Preface

The National Maritime Museum holds the largest and most comprehensive collection of marine paintings anywhere in the world. Its holding of 500 Dutch marines is unrivalled, including great masterpieces by the Van de Veldes and their contemporaries. The English School is represented in depth, from early seascapes by Charles Brooking to the high pinnacles of Romantic painting in the work of J. M. W. Turner and Philippe de Loutherbourg. Apart from sea-pieces and battle scenes, the Museum owns more than 500 portraits of famous seamen throughout the ages, a representative group of port and coastal scenes, and a wide range of ship portraits which are of particular interest to nautical specialists and maritime historians. While the primary function of the collection is to document the story of maritime Britain in all its aspects, and to provide a visual context for the other collections in the Museum, its value in terms of art should not be underestimated. It would be impossible to chart the history of British landscape painting without reference to the marine tradition, though the subject has never received the attention it deserves. The collections at Greenwich include some memorable works of art that will give pleasure and inspiration to those who know little of the subjects which are represented.

Most large maritime museums collect pictures but on a modest scale and chiefly as documentary records. The scale of the collections at Greenwich is quite exceptional and places it in the league of major art galleries. There are two primary reasons for this. At the time of the Museum's foundation in 1934, the historic collection of pictures from Greenwich Hospital was placed on permanent loan. This included Sir Peter Lely's famous set of 'Flagmen', commissioned by James II when Duke of York, Turner's *Trafalgar*, and a selection of over 200 naval actions and portraits. On this foundation, Sir James Caird, the Museum's greatest benefactor, proceeded rapidly to build up the collection. He had already bought the Macpherson collection, which forms the basis of the present-day print-room, and with it a number of oils. In the years following, he and Sir Geoffrey Callender, the Museum's first director, secured many of the finest marine paintings, which were then coming on to the market in such numbers. Callender the historian could assess the significance of subject-matter, while Caird seems to have had a genuine appreciation for their quality as works of art. Price presented few problems, for marine pictures were still relatively inexpensive, and Caird's generosity was inexhaustible. By 1945 the collection numbered some 1,500 works, and already included many of the masterpieces now at Greenwich.

Since the time of Caird and Callender the collection has expanded to approximately 4,000 pictures, though nearly 1,000 of these are represented by the studio sketches of the twentieth-century marine painter John Everett. In spite of restricted funds, a steady stream of distinguished works has been added to the collection, and these have been supplemented by gifts and bequests. The most notable of these was the bequest in 1963 of thirty Dutch and early English marine pictures of high quality from the collection of Sir Bruce Ingram; he had previously presented his magnificent collection of 700 Van de Velde drawings to the Museum in 1957. Together with the Palmer collection, purchased *en bloc* in 1962, the Museum's survey of the Dutch marine school is now unrivalled.

The primary purpose of the present book is to make the collection of paintings at Greenwich more widely known and appreciated. Over 200 works have been reproduced, sixty-five in colour, accompanied by descriptive captions. When the project for the book was first discussed with Phaidon Press, it was agreed that the pictures must be accompanied by a text, covering the chief events and developments of maritime history, which would set them in context. We were very fortunate in persuading the distinguished naval historian Peter Kemp to undertake the daunting task of condensing several centuries of maritime history into 30,000 words. He has successfully accomplished the task, writing of battles, ship design and seamanship with notable verve and aplomb. His general historical survey is complemented by a sequence of chapters written by myself, which cover the main schools and artists of Dutch and British maritime art. We hope that the resulting mix of history and art will help to explain the significance of the pictures themselves. The advent of photography helped to undercut the market for marine pictures and ship portraits, and the last chapter has, therefore, been devoted to a selection of illustrations from the Museum's vast holding of historic photographs.

I am grateful to my colleagues in the Picture Department for writing the succinct captions, many of which incorporate new research, under considerable pressure of time. I must also thank Dr Alan McGowan, Head of Ships Department, Dr Roger Knight, Head of the Information Project Group, Dr Sean McGrail, Head of the Archaeological Research Centre, and Dr Ian Friel of the same department, for their invaluable help and advice. The book would never have happened without the enthusiastic collaboration of Roger Sears, the commissioning editor of Phaidon Press, and it has been seen through the press with painstaking care by his colleague, David Morgenstern. We owe a special debt of thanks to the designer James Campus for so happily combining picture and text, and producing such an elegant result.

Richard Ormond
DIRECTOR
National Maritime Museum

1. EARLY YEARS

The cradle of man's use of the sea is lost in prehistory; all we know for certain from the evidence of rock carvings and pottery decoration is that ships and boats were widely used in the eastern Mediterranean and the Arabian Sea more than 6,000 years ago.

The oldest ship still in existence is the funeral ship of the Pharaoh Cheops [fig. 1], which dates from around 2,600 BC. That she has been preserved intact is something of a miracle; even more remarkable is the evidence she provides of the skill of Egyptian shipwrights in their ability to build ships of such a size all those years ago. She is 133 feet long with a maximum beam of 26 feet.

Although we know that the Egyptians built large fleets of merchant ships and of warships to protect them, it was the Phoenicians who made the first real impact on the growth of the ship and of maritime trade. Their trading empire, based on the city states of Tyre and Sidon, flourished between about 1,000 BC and 333 BC and owed its wealth in part to the excellence of the ships the Phoenicians designed and built but more to the skill of their seamen. Alone among sailors they knew that the Pole-star at night pointed to the north and that the sun at noon by day pointed to the south. They used a rudimentary compass, the wind-rose, to give them a course to steer, and with these beginnings of navigation they made voyages which took them beyond the borders of the Mediterranean and possibly as far as southern England and the Canary Islands. To protect their ships from pirates, mainly Greek, who infested the Mediterranean, they built war galleys with two banks of oars and equipped with a bronze beak or ram. These galleys became the model for the later Greek bireme and were the true forerunners of the principal type of Mediterranean warship for the next 2,000 years.

The multiplicity of Phoenician trade made Tyre the richest city in the world, a great clearing house for the produce of east and west. The wealth engendered by this trade was the impetus that called for continuous improvements in design and strength in the ships that were built and in the knowledge and skill of the seamen. The Phoenicians were the first to build ships with a continuous deck, made possible by transverse beams at deck level; they were the first, too, to add a second mast to the ship's rig to enable it to point higher towards the wind. Before their maritime dominion of the Mediterranean came to an end they had achieved the basic ship design of keel, stempiece, sternpost, ribs and deckbeams, which gives the vessel her strength and is still accepted today as the only way in which a large ship can be built if she is to withstand the rigours of the sea.

It was, perhaps, inevitable that so much success should attract the envy of other Mediterranean nations. As the Phoenician ships ventured further and further into hitherto unknown waters, they set up new city states along the routes of their trade. It all grew too large to defend against the envy of other nations. Ezekiel, the Old Testament prophet, brought captive to Babylon

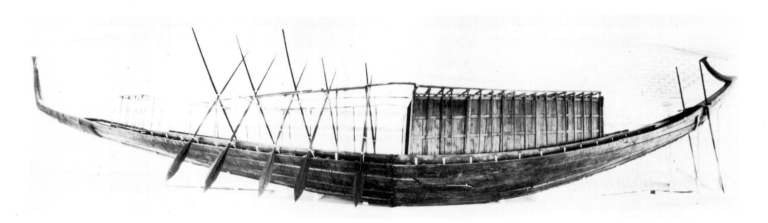

1. The Cheops Ship

This ship was found in perfect condition (albeit in a dismantled state) in a sealed pit at the base of the pyramid of the Pharaoh Cheops in 1954. It is the earliest known example of a planked boat, probably taking its distinctive papyriform shape from earlier reed craft. It is unclear whether the ship had been used on the Nile before its burial, or whether it was a 'sun boat' for use in the King's afterlife.

by Nebuchadnezzar in 597 BC, prophesied the end of the Phoenician city states in blood-curdling detail. Eventually, in 333 BC, Ezekiel's prophecy came true when Alexander the Great destroyed the city of Tyre and sold the 30,000 survivors into slavery.

The sudden and complete downfall of the Phoenician trading empire opened the way for 300 years of grumbling war as the Mediterranean nations fought to seize the mastery of that inland sea and inherit the Phoenician wealth. For a few years Carthage attempted to carry on the seaborne trade but it was the Greeks, relying on their fleets of war galleys, who finally won control of the Mediterranean.

Over the course of years the Greeks, like the Phoenicians before them, over-extended their empire until the drain of attempting to defend it became too great. This left the Greek dominion of the Mediterranean open to challenge, first from Carthage and then from Rome. Great battles of massed galley fleets were fought until at the battle of Mylae in 260 BC the navy of Rome shattered the navy of Carthage to establish Roman sea power in the whole of the western Mediterranean. Control of the eastern Mediterranean followed in 67 BC when a Roman fleet of over 500 galleys destroyed the Greek challenge to Roman sea supremacy led by Philip of Macedon. With the defeat of Philip, Rome ruled supreme throughout the entire Mediterranean.

Knowledge of the size of the Roman ships was established when Lake Nemi, in the Alban hills, was drained in 1932 and two full-sized hulls, one modelled on a war galley and the other on a merchant ship, were discovered in the mud [fig. 2]. The galley was 235 feet long with a maximum beam of 110 feet, a trireme with probably fifteen men pulling on each oar. She was almost certainly two-decked, the rowers accommodated on the lower deck and the marines carried on the upper deck. The merchant ship, less well preserved than the galley, was about 240 feet long with a beam of 47 feet. There was no evidence of her rig, but with that length of keel she would certainly have had two masts, each carrying a square sail. A few years later the Roman designers added a third mast to their merchant ships and lengthened the mainmast to carry two triangular topsails above the square mainsail.

We get the best description of a Roman merchant ship from Lucian, writing from the port of Piraeus during the second century AD. 'What a tremendous vessel it was, 120 cubits [180 feet] long, as the ship's carpenter told me, and more than 30 cubits [45 feet] across the beam, and 29 cubits [44 feet] from the deck to the deepest part of the hold. And the height of the mast and the yard it bore, and the forestays that were necessary to keep it upright. And how the stern rose in a graceful curve ending in a gilt goosehead, in harmony with the equal curve of the bow and the forepost with its picture of Isis, the goddess who had given the ship her name. All was unbelievable, the decoration, paintings, red topsail, the anchors with their windlasses, and the cabins in the stern. The crew was like an army. They told me she could carry enough grain to satisfy every mouth in Athens for a whole year. And the whole fortune of the ship is in the hands of a little old man who moves the great rudders [steering oars] with a tiller no thicker than a stick. They pointed him out to me, a little, white-haired, almost bald fellow: I think they called him Heron.'

The development of the ship in northern European waters owed nothing to the much earlier designs and building methods of the Mediterranean. It evolved from its crude beginnings of hides stitched across a wooden frame, not unlike the modern Irish curragh, into a vessel designed to stand up to the turbulent waters of the northern seas. Rock carvings in Norway, Sweden and Denmark, some dating back into the Stone Age, can give us an idea of the earliest designs of northern boats and it can be seen from them that already they were leading into the traditional longship design with a long, straight keel to give needed stability in the rough seas so frequently met in the waters in which they had to operate.

The real longship came into being with what we now call the Vikings: individual bands of Norwegians, Swedes, Danes, Jutes and Angles. They were ferocious groups of marauders, as local chief fought local chief for mastery of his area of sea and for loot and women. Kings were those who emerged victorious in the long series of small battles with their neighbours, and by about 800 AD they had grown strong enough to venture further afield in their lust for power and riches.

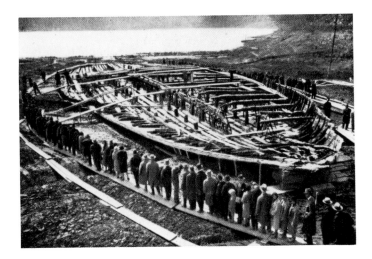

2. **Nemi Ship**

This shows one of the two massive ships from the first century AD that were uncovered by the draining of Lake Nemi (near Rome) between the two World Wars. Both vessels had the flush-laid, tenon-fastened planking common in the ancient Mediterranean, but their great size made them otherwise untypical of shipping of the period. Both Nemi ships were destroyed in the Second World War.

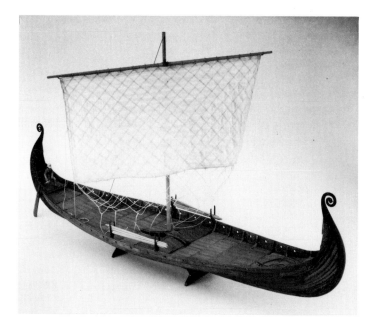

These incursions were all based on the longship [fig. 3] with its mast and square sail, the fighting men becoming rowers, up to thirty-two on each side, when the wind did not serve. The long keel and the upswept bow and stern made the longship a fine seaboat in northern waters, well able to ride out the roughest seas, and the invention of the *beitass*, a pole secured near the foot of the mast and used to stretch out the weather leech of the sail to windward, enabled it to sail closer to the wind and to progress through the sea to windward without having to use rowers to do so. The *beitass* extended the range of the longships and enabled them to ravage the coasts of France and England. Even Spain and the Mediterranean were within their reach, adding to their appetite for plunder.

Perhaps of even greater significance, the *beitass* made possible the northern voyages of which the Norse sagas sing. These voyages began in 984, when Eric the Red fled from Norway to Iceland to escape a charge of murder. There he heard from a Norwegian trader of a new land to the west, and in 985 he decided to investigate. He gave it the name of Greenland.

In the year 1001 Eric the Red's son, Leif Ericsson, met Biarni Heriulfsson, a trading captain, who told him that when he was blown far off course he had sighted land down to the south-west. Leif Ericsson subsequently confirmed the sighting and landed at three places, which he named Helluland, Markland and Vinland. We think that these were what are today known as Baffin Island, Labrador and Newfoundland, as the descriptions he gave roughly match the characteristics of these places. Given the proven capabilities of the longship there is no reason to doubt the authenticity of this voyage to the American continent, pre-dating Columbus by nearly 500 years.

While these northern waters were so often torn by war and piracy, a more peaceful trade was developing. It was originally centred on the Wendish towns of Lübeck, Hamburg, Lüneburg, Wismar, Rostock and Stralsund, where the huge shoals of herring in the Baltic Sea provided a ready source of wealth. As money poured into the pockets of merchants, trade expanded to include Norwegian iron, copper, and timber, French and Italian wine, and English wool and tin. To protect their growing trade the Wendish ports formed a protective association, known as the Hanseatic League, to channel as much of the trade as they could through their exclusive hands. They did this by setting up *Hansas* (trading centres) in the countries with whom they traded, to demand preferential treatment and monopolies. By 1226 the League had set up its first *Hansa* in London, which was quickly followed by others in Holland, Denmark, and Norway.

This burgeoning of international trade was the direct cause of the development of a new type of all-purpose ship in northern waters. Something larger than the longship, and protected with an upper deck, was required to satisfy the needs of the merchants. This new ship was the Hansa cog, with an average over-all length of around 100 feet, a beam of about 25 feet and a draught of 10 feet, which, using modern measurements, gave a capacity of about 280 tons. The cog was built with a long keel, a straight stem at an angle of about 60 degrees and a straight stern at about 75 degrees. It was fully decked and was fitted with a single central mast carrying one square sail, with braces and bowlines to trim the sail to the wind.

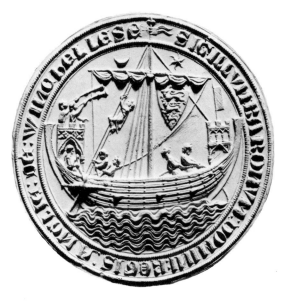

3. The Oseberg Ship

The Oseberg ship dates from about 800 AD, and was discovered in the last century in the burial mound of a royal Viking lady. It had the double-ended, clinker-built hull typical of Viking craft, a side rudder and a single square sail. The complex network of ropes hanging from the lower edge of the sail is a reconstruction (as is much of the ship's rig) based on iconographic evidence.

4. The Winchelsea Seal. *c.*1300–30

This illustrates a type of double-ended ship which was to become obsolete by the fifteenth century. It is equipped with fore- and aftercastles standing on stilts within the hull. The seal shows the ship about to set sail: two of the crew are hauling in the anchor cable, assisted by two more at the windlass. One mariner is shinning up the backstays to unfurl the sail; in the aftercastle two trumpeters blow a call and the steersman stands ready.

All the northern maritime nations seem to have adopted the cog, though with local differences in design and construction. They were built in their hundreds, mainly for trading purposes but for use also as warships when the need arose. A fairly early development was the addition of castles at bow and stern, no doubt to provide accommodation in trading vessels for passengers of importance and, in warships, a means of enabling archers to fire their arrows downwards into an enemy boarding the ship across the low waist [fig. 4].

An even more important development in design than the cog herself was the addition of a hanging rudder on the ship's sternpost. This was substituted for the steering oar over the starboard quarter, which, from the earliest days, had been the sole means of directing a ship. There is still some doubt about the date of this development: a relief carving, of about 1180, of a ship on the font of Winchester Cathedral shows something that looks very like a hanging rudder [fig. 5]; a carving in the plaster wall of Fide Church in Gotland, dated about 1220, shows an undoubted one. Almost certainly it originated in the Baltic. But whatever the date, it is certain that it was in use at the time the Hansa cog was born.

The steady increase in trade around the known world brought with it a growing awareness of the way the ship was developing in other waters, as cargoes between northern Europe and the Mediterranean countries introduced merchants to the sort of ships their competitors were using. At first the Mediterranean merchants learned more quickly than those of north Europe,

adopting both the hanging rudder and the more robust construction of the northern ship. From the Arabian countries they adopted the lateen sail, at first on all masts, but later only on the mizen, and as their ships grew in size, they added a third mast which was eventually to become the standard rig for all large ships for the next 500 years.

The larger Mediterranean ship was the carrack, a vessel of around 1,000 tons. She was built with a high forecastle and a two-decked aftercastle (the equivalent of the later quarterdeck and poop deck), and, even with a lateen mizen, must have been sluggish and unhandy to sail. The standard smaller ship of the Mediterranean was the caravel of from 80 to 120 tons, at first lateen-rigged on all three masts but later given square rig on fore and main. She was developed from the early Breton and Portuguese fishing boats, which used to venture into the Atlantic as far as the Newfoundland Banks to fish for cod. With a bow uncluttered by a castle and a modest quarterdeck aft, they proved excellent seaboats and easily handled with a small crew.

In the north, there was no generic name coined to describe the standard ship. She was smaller than the carrack, usually around 700 tons, but similarly rigged. She, too, had fore- and aftercastles, though not built as high as in the carrack. Because of the generally stormier waters of the Atlantic and North Sea, she had heavier scantlings than her Mediterranean counterpart, which made her sluggish in the water. Her chief merit lay in the strength of her construction and her ability to sail and steer in waters in which the carrack would have been unmanageable.

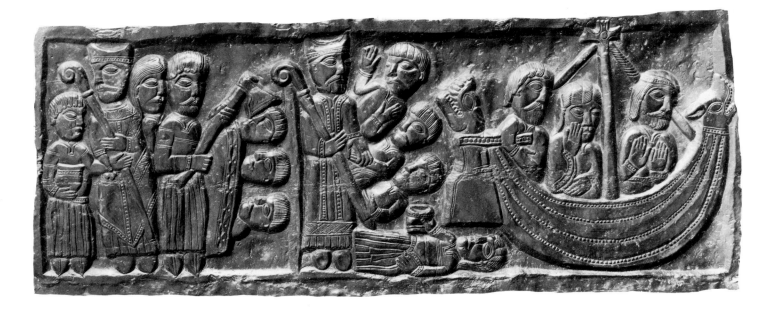

5. The Winchester Font. *c.*1180
The vessel depicted on this fine example of Flemish workmanship is a hulk, whose chief interest to maritime historians lies in the fact that she is shown to be steered by a stern rudder rather than by the previously conventional steering oar.

2. THE EXPANDING WORLD

An event of outstanding importance to the whole future of the world's shipping was the discovery in Constantinople in 1400 of the eight books of Ptolemy's *Geographia*, which had been lost from Alexandria since the fall of the Roman Empire. Ptolemy was a mathematician and astronomer, and, using the earlier work of Marinus of Tyre, had constructed a projection of the then known world using curved meridians and parallels. Its rediscovery opened the eyes of contemporary geographers to the probability of the earth being a sphere instead of a vast flat surface.

Almost simultaneously, the domination of the Mediterranean by the Mussulman advance along the north coast of Africa created the need to discover new trading routes to the east. By the fourteenth century control of the Mediterranean had been taken over by the Ottoman Turks, who split it up into independent caliphates whose leaders thrived on piracy and the sale of slaves. They turned the Mediterranean into a nightmare sea in which no merchant ship was safe from capture. The scale of this piracy cut off from Europe the highly desirable trade from Asia, trade which had until then been brought overland to the Levant ports and shipped across the Mediterranean to eager and impatient markets in the west.

It was this cutting of the Mediterranean trade route that forced Europe into its heroic age of navigation and exploration. Geographers and navigators, accepting that the earth was a sphere, argued that a ship must eventually reach the east if she sailed west. They also argued that there could be another way to the east if the Indian and Atlantic oceans were joined south of the great continent of Africa. This was the belief of Prince Henry of Portugal, better known as 'the Navigator', and in 1420 he set up an 'arsenal' at Sagres, near Cape St. Vincent, where he gathered the best of the European geographers and mathematicians to draw the most accurate sea charts, to prepare astronomical tables, and to construct instruments with which the altitude of heavenly bodies, and thus a ship's position, could be measured. At the same time he sent out expeditions to probe down the west coast of Africa in the hope that they would find an open stretch of ocean beyond its furthest tip.

He did not himself live long enough to see this dream realized

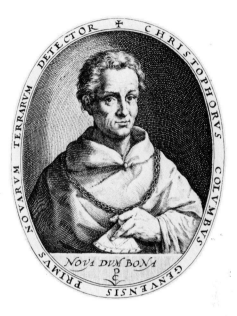

and it was his great-nephew, John II of Portugal, who was present in Lisbon in December 1488 when Bartholomiu Diaz sailed triumphantly up the Tagus having rounded the southern tip of Africa. They had been driven south by a great storm, further south than any man had ever been before, and thirteen days later, when they clawed their way back, they found themselves on the eastern side of Africa. Diaz had named the southernmost point of Africa Cabo Tormentosa, Cape of Storms, but John II changed it to Cabo de Bona Speranza, Cape of Good Hope, because he knew that the great prize of India was there for the taking. And so it was, for the next expedition, led by Vasco da Gama, rounded the Cape in May 1498 and anchored in Calicut on the mainland of India, where da Gama set up the first European trading station.

At about the same time, in 1492, an expedition left Palos in Spain also bound for the east, on the geographers' theory that it could be reached by sailing west. It was led by Christopher Columbus [fig. 6] who had, after long arguments, finally persuaded King Ferdinand and Queen Isabella of Spain that his voyage to the west would finish in 'Cipangu', now Japan, and that China and India lay only a few miles further on. He took a southerly route across the Atlantic and thirty-six days later sighted a white cliff in the morning moonlight. Later that day

6. Christopher Columbus. C. de Passe
Columbus, born in 1451 in Genoa, promoted his 'Enterprise of the Indies' (his plan to sail west to the Orient) for many years before he found support from Ferdinand and Isabella of Spain. He sailed from Palos on 3 August 1492, and reached the West Indies. Three later voyages followed, but, outraged at the crown's ingratitude for his achievements, he eventually died a rejected and disappointed man in 1506.

he and his crews went ashore, discovered that the land was an island, and gave it the name San Salvador [fig. 7]. He knew it was too far to the south to be Cipangu and took it to be an island lying off the coast of India. Discovering more islands as he sailed westward he gave them the collective name of Las Indias, today's West Indies, confident that India itself lay just over the western horizon.

It was not until his third voyage to the west in 1498 that Columbus was finally convinced that what he had discovered was not the outlying islands of China or India but a huge continent blocking the way to the trading riches of the east. A new map

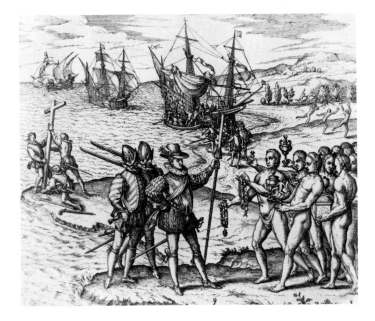

of the world had to be drawn to take account of this continent and the still unknown region that lay beyond it. Yet, if the earth was truly a globe as now all geographers and navigators believed, the still unknown must be India and China. The successful discoveries of da Gama and Columbus were followed by other voyages designed to open up and extend these new sea routes and the names of their leaders ring gloriously like a peal of bells in the history of navigation and exploration. To Bartholomiu Diaz and Vasco da Gama are added Pedro Cabral, Ugolino and Sorleone Vivaldo, Antoniotto Uso di Mare, and Alfonso d'Albuquerque; to Columbus the names of Hernando de Alarçon, Vasco Nuñez de Balboa, Alvaro Nuñez, and Giovanni Verrazano. These were the men who first established that it was possible for ships to sail regularly and safely along the new sea routes and indeed to build a lucrative trade with the new lands. The pattern of world trade was being revolutionized, presenting a challenge to the designers and builders of ships

throughout the nations of Europe, each claiming their share of the new wealth.

In an age when the discovery of new lands automatically conferred exclusive rights of possession and trade, Spain and Portugal took steps to safeguard the potential wealth of their newfound trade routes. Pope Alexander VI issued a papal bull awarding to Spain possession of all land to the west, and to Portugal all land to the east, of a line drawn north and south 370 leagues west of the Azores. The problem presented by this bull to the other maritime nations of Europe, mainly France, England, Holland, and Denmark, was twofold: they either had to discover new sea routes to the riches of the east and west or ignore the bull and uphold the right to trade, by force of arms if necessary. In any case England and Holland, both of which were Protestant, were in no way bound by a papal edict, and France considered that her national interest in increasing her trade weighed more in the balance than her allegiance to the doctrines of Rome.

There were, after all, reasonable grounds for supposing that alternative sea routes to the east were still to be discovered. If there was open water to the south of Africa, as Diaz had proved beyond all doubt, might there not also be open water to the south of America, which would carry a ship to India and China? And if to the south, why not equally to the north? This reasoning gave rise to another series of heroic voyages in search of a northwest and a north-east passage to China and a passage round the south of America to India. Again the names ring out in the history of discovery: Jacques Cartier and Samuel de Champlain of France; John Cabot, Humphrey Gilbert, Henry Hudson,

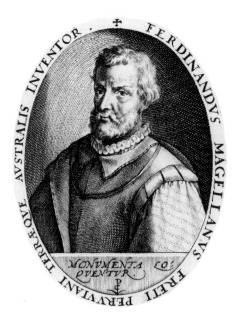

7. Columbus landing at the Bahamas in 1492. Unidentified artist
The expedition had its first landfall on the island of San Salvador on 12 October 1492, where Columbus and his men were greeted with awe by the Arawak natives. The present print is an imaginary reconstruction of the scene, entirely late-sixteenth-century in character.

8. Ferdinand Magellan. C. de Passe
Magellan (1470–1521) persuaded the Spanish Emperor Charles V in 1519 to back his expedition to reach the Spice Islands by sailing westward. He reached the Pacific, by way of the straits which bear his name, in November 1520. Though he was killed on the journey home by natives on the island of Mactan, one of his ships completed the first circumnavigation of the globe, arriving at Seville in July 1522.

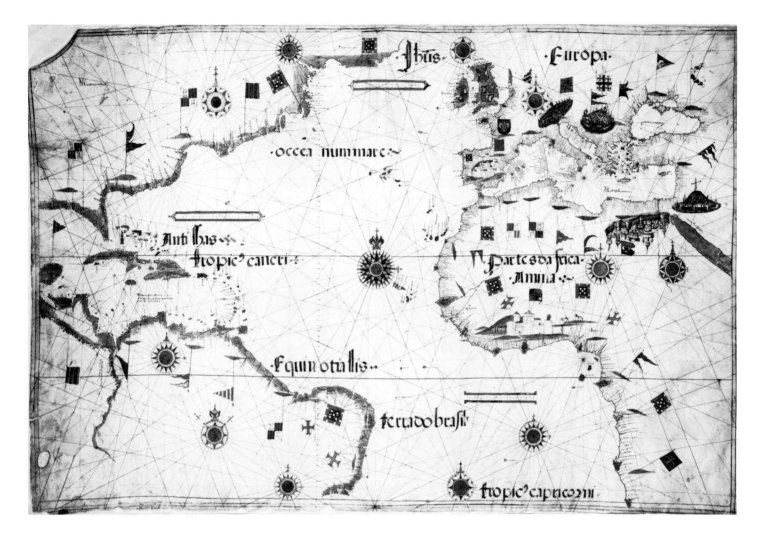

John Davis and Martin Frobisher of England; Willem Barents, Jacob le Maire and Willem Schouten of Holland; and Jens Erikson Munk of Denmark. And in 1520 the greatest navigator of them all, Ferdinand Magellan [fig. 8], discovered a seaway south of America which linked the Atlantic to the Pacific.

Although the explorers in the northern hemisphere found their passage east and west blocked by ice, at least they added to man's knowledge of the new world. As the knowledge spread, world maps, sea charts [fig. 9], and globes reflected ever more accurately the emerging shape of the new world and the sea routes to the areas where lay the promise of a richer trade.

This virtual doubling of the known world, all within the span of some twenty to thirty years, was followed by a doubling or even trebling of the trading fleets of the European merchants. While the small ships of the caravel type had been ideal for the voyages of exploration, they were much too small to bring back worthwhile cargoes from the new lands to European markets,

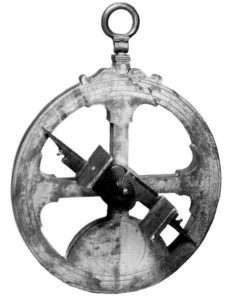

9. Chart of the North Atlantic. Pedro Reinel, c.1535
This chart has been tentatively attributed to the elder half of the Portuguese father and son team of Pedro and Jorge Reinel, 'masters of charts and navigation compasses'. As well as showing coastlines, place-names, flags, and a wealth of other remarkable detail, there are small views of cities such as Cairo, Constantinople, Jerusalem, Venice and Lisbon.

10. Mariner's Astrolabe. c.1588
The mariner's astrolabe was developed from the planispheric astrolabe as an instrument for measuring altitudes at sea. The present example, a cartwheel type, was found in County Kerry, Ireland, near the site of two Spanish Armada wrecks.

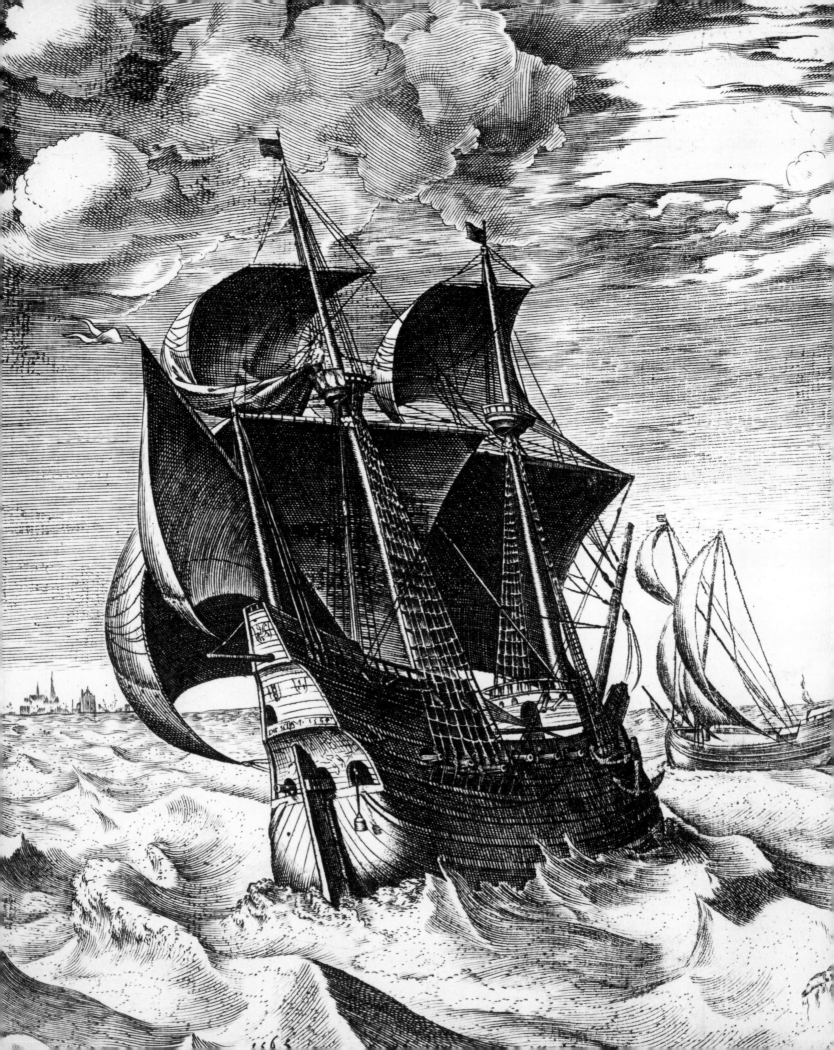

and the only answer lay in larger ships. Though the actual design of the hull changed little, the average tonnage of the merchant ship rose by approximately a half again in all the European countries and the problem arose of providing a big enough sail area to work the ship in all conditions of wind and sea. The three-masted rig had already proved its efficiency and one way of increasing the sail area was by extending the masts with topmasts and topgallant masts and setting more sails [fig. 11].

One other problem remained. With the refusal to accept the papal bull giving the exclusive right to trade in the new lands to Spain and Portugal, merchant ships of other nations needed to go armed and prepared to fight to establish their claims. New and permanent national navies would be required both to fight for a trading foothold and to defend it when won and established.

3. THE TUDOR NAVY AND THE SPANISH ARMADA

During the fifty or so years which followed the Spanish and Portuguese voyages of exploration, England had come badly out of the scramble for new lands with which to open a trade. Spain dominated the West Indies and the Caribbean mainland, and claimed exclusive navigation rights in the Pacific following Magellan's discovery of a way into that great ocean. The new discoveries demanded a big programme of warship construction to protect Spanish interests in these distant waters. In the same way, Portugal expanded her navy to guard her trading empire in India and to build up the territories she had acquired along the western coast of Africa. The Dutch, who had followed the Portuguese eastward, had established an empire in the East Indies (known then as the Spice Islands), and they built a new navy to uphold their claims to the rich trade. France, after Cartier's discovery of the St. Lawrence River, had claimed the whole of Canada for her own and she too joined the warship building race.

The English voyages had borne little fruit. Newfoundland was unpromising in terms of trade and the icy borders of Hudson's Bay were a poor reward for the perils and difficulties of the search for a north-west passage. One opportunity presented itself in the wide gap of possibly rich American land between the French in Canada to the north and the Spanish penetration of the continent in the south, and England planted a few small colonies of settlers along the coastal strip with varying success. Yet England, too, required an expanded navy because, disappointed in the fruits of her own exploration, she needed the means to fight for a fair share of the new wealth.

The English navy of Queen Elizabeth's reign (1558–1603) was the first to adopt the strategic concept that more advantage lay in carrying the fight to an enemy at sea than to wait and fight him defensively when he attacked. It was also the first to recognize that, in fighting for a share of the trade, a new design of warship was necessary, something faster and more weatherly and, above all, much quicker in stays than the traditional high-charged ship which was still the backbone of all European navies.

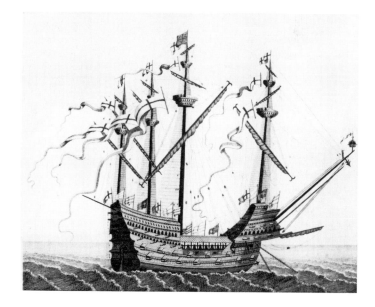

The queen's father and grandfather had both built ships for their navies, following the universal pattern of a high castle forward and aft. Henry VIII's main contribution to his navy was the *Henry Grace à Dieu* [fig. 12], better known as the *Great Harry*. Her armament was 231 small guns, all of them anti-personnel, and 21 bronze cannon mounted in the two castles. Another of Henry VIII's ships was the first to have gunports cut in her sides, which enabled a battery of heavier guns to be

11. A Hulk and a Boeier on the Zuider Zee off Enkhuizen. Frans Huys after Pieter Brueghel the Elder
A large ship of the period, portrayed close-hauled under full sail. The boeier on the right of the engraving is running before the wind under spritsail, fore-staysail and a square topsail. Brueghel's series of marine prints constitutes one of the best extant records of sixteenth-century shipping.

12. The 'Henri Grace à Dieu'. Robert Newton
This nineteenth-century print is after a contemporary illustration in the Anthony Rolls, a list of the King's ships published in 1546. The *Great Harry*, built in 1512, was the largest ship in the English navy at the time. The Rolls include a full inventory of her armaments.

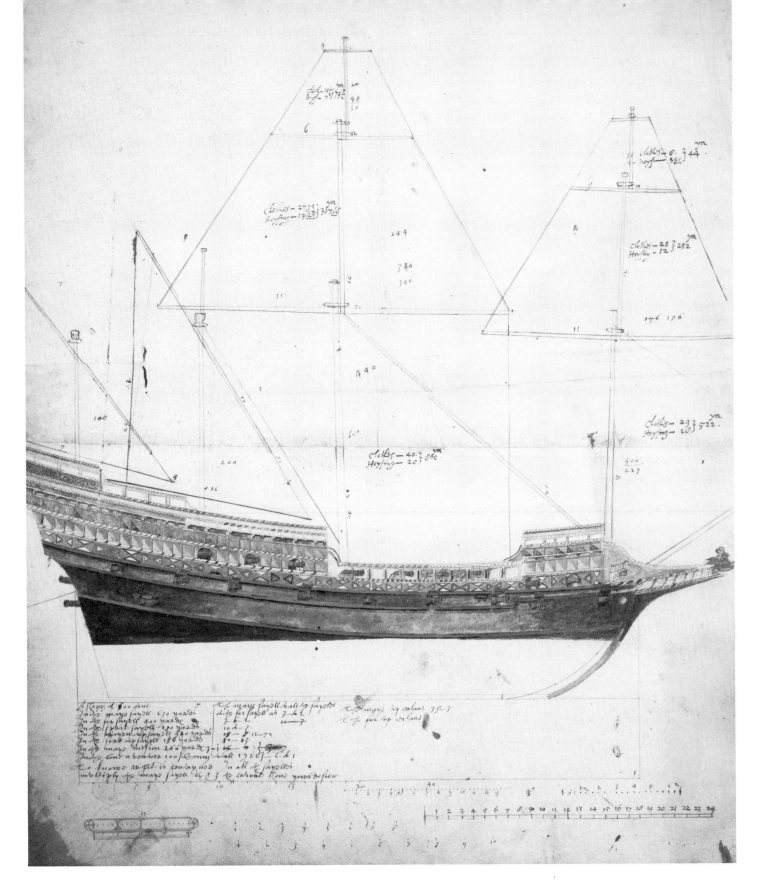

13. Design for an English Warship. Mathew Baker, c.1585

Baker's manuscript *Elements of Shipwrightery* is the earliest work on shipbuilding
to survive, and includes many designs for ships. None can be identified with
any ships as built, but they illustrate the type of race-built warship developed
by Hawkins. The sail-plan in this design appears to be a later addition.

mounted lower down without making her top-heavy. She was the *Mary Rose*, and a sadder claim to fame is that she was the first ship to capsize at sea by flooding through her open gunports.

The initial English naval involvement in the fight for lucrative trade was to include a king's ship on a profit sharing basis in the small squadrons assembled by merchant adventurers. This royal ship provided the squadron with the force it needed to persuade reluctant foreigners to trade, and provided the king with a share of any success and, nominally, no responsibility nationally if the venture attracted the wrath of the occupying power.

Elizabeth increased the scale of this policy when she came to the throne, contributing her ships one by one to many of these ventures. When John Hawkins asked for a royal ship for his third 'triangular' voyage the queen contributed her *Jesus of Lübeck* of 700 tons, high-charged as were all such ships. In 1568, while lying at San Juan de Ulloa with Spanish permission to replenish with food and water, the squadron was attacked without warning. The two smaller ships of the expedition, *Judith* and *Minion*, escaped without much difficulty but the *Jesus of Lübeck*, slow and difficult to steer, was unable to work her way out of the harbour and was captured.

It was, in a way, an unfortunate attack for the Spaniards. The captain of the *Judith* was Francis Drake [fig. 15], a man of strong Protestant convictions, and the combination of his faith and a passionate desire for revenge was to make him an active thorn in the Spanish flesh for the rest of his life. Hawkins also escaped and, being an experienced seaman, realized why the *Jesus of Lübeck* was unable to follow the smaller ships out of the harbour. The reason lay in the size of the forecastle, presenting a large area to the wind, which pushed the bows down to leeward and made her slow in stays.

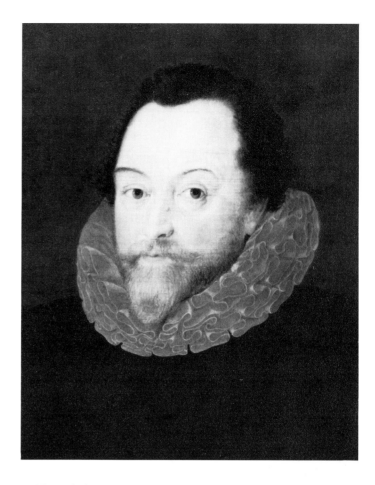

The solution Hawkins proposed was to cut down the ship's high sides so that she lay more snugly in the water, remove the high forecastle and replace it further aft with a lower structure, reduce the height of the aftercastle, substitute a square stern for the normal rounded one, and increase the length-to-beam ratio from about $2\frac{1}{2}$ to 1 to 3 to 1. The new design, known as the low-charged ship, proved faster, easier for a helmsman to handle, able to sail nearer the wind, and quicker in stays. It was rapidly adopted in all English shipbuilding [fig. 13], spread to Holland during the 1590s, and by the middle of the seventeenth century had been adopted by all the seafaring nations of Europe.

In the meantime Drake had been busy. After a successful raid on the Spanish Main in 1572 he followed in the steps of Magellan with a circumnavigation of the world in 1577–80, returning home to be knighted by the queen. Although the treasure he brought home with him was enormous, of more importance was his demonstration that English ship captains had nothing to fear from Spain's edict that the Pacific was closed to every ship except those of Spain.

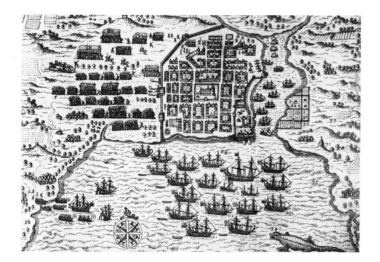

14. Drake's Attack on San Domingo, 1586. Unidentified artist
Drake's expedition to the West Indies, 1585–6, was intended to demonstrate English seapower, and to earn profits for its promoters, who included the Queen. The sack of San Domingo on the mainland of America was one of Drake's successes, though it yielded much less treasure than expected. Drake's ships are shown here in the harbour, with troops disembarking on the left.

15. Sir Francis Drake. Unidentified artist
A detail from a painting on panel, probably by a Netherlandish artist working in England and certainly by a follower of Marcus Gheeraerts. Drake (1540–96) was the first Englishman to circumnavigate the world and was an audacious privateer and a brilliant military tactician. Through the nature of his exploits he is, for some, the founder of British naval tradition.

It was inevitable after Drake's adventures in the Pacific that a state of war between England and Spain should exist, though it was a limited war and never directly prosecuted. Elizabeth offered active support to Philip's rebellious Dutch provinces, but it was only following the trial and execution of Mary Queen of Scots in 1587 that the war flared into activity. It had now become clear to the Pope and to Philip II of Spain that the return of England to the faith of Rome by natural succession was no longer possible. Philip announced the building of a great fleet which, together with the Spanish Duke of Parma's army in the Netherlands, would ensure the defeat of England and bring her back to Catholicism. It was to be ready in 1587.

Philip was supremely confident of success. In 1571 a combined fleet of the Christian nations bordering the Mediterranean had defeated a Turkish fleet in the last great battle fought between galleys manned by oarsmen. The Christian fleet had been commanded by Don John of Austria, Philip's natural brother, and his victory broke for ever the Turkish command of the eastern Mediterranean. The battle was fought off Lepanto [plate 2], near the Gulf of Patras, with 200 Christian galleys facing 273 Turkish galleys. By removing the real and increasing threat of Turkish domination of the Mediterranean, Philip was now able to concentrate his whole force against England and Holland.

In their resolve to carry the fight to the enemy, the English naval leaders persuaded Elizabeth to authorize in 1587 an amphibious expedition against Cadiz, Spain's naval base on the Atlantic coast. Drake was in command and he destroyed around thirty warships and an unknown number of merchant ships bringing stores for Philip's 'Enterprise of England'. He also captured the Portuguese carrack *San Felipe*, returning from the Far East with a cargo valued at £114,000. Much more important than the cargo were the charts and papers captured with her, indicating to British merchants the vast profits of a trade which they had so far not attempted.

In the following year, Philip launched his fleet against England, with the blessing of the Pope. Comprising 130 ships, 8,000 sailors and 19,000 soldiers, it must have seemed a formidable force. It was, in essence, a huge armed convoy, with some thirty-five heavily armed warships escorting large, more lightly armed merchantmen, crowded with men and supplies. The plan was for the Spanish commander, the Duke of Medina Sidonia, to sail up the Channel, defeating the English fleet if possible. He was then to rendezvous with Parma's army off the coast of Flanders, and to guard the transport barges on their passage to England. The plan had two fundamental flaws. First, there was no safe, deep-water port where the Spanish fleet could anchor while awaiting Parma's barges. Secondly, Parma could only hazard

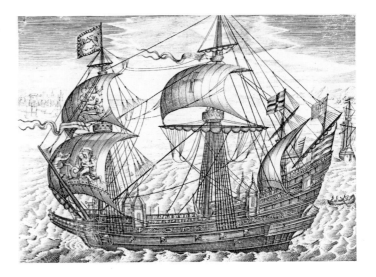

his barges if the weather were calm and the English and Dutch fleets had been neutralized.

The English fleet, divided into two squadrons under Lord Howard of Effingham, had a similar number of capital warships to the Spanish, which were of comparable fighting power. The rest of the fleet comprised much smaller merchantmen from London and the coastal ports. Most of the English ships, royal as well as private, had been built or rebuilt to Hawkins's new design [fig. 16]. They lay lower in the water, presenting a smaller target, were about one knot faster and could sail about one point closer to the wind. Their armament of lighter, long-barrelled guns was designed for hitting ships at a range of up to half a mile. The Spanish tactic was to use their heavier short-range cannon as a prelude to boarding. The English, closing the range to just beyond reach of the guns of the slower-moving Spanish ships, never gave them the opportunity. At the same time, actual damage inflicted by the English guns, in spite of a huge expenditure of powder and shot, was much less than anticipated. No ship was directly sunk by gunfire, though the damage to men and rigging took its toll.

After a long, running fight up the English Channel [plate 3; fig. 17], the Duke of Medina Sidonia reached Calais, where he was to embark the Duke of Parma's army and land it in England. Two of his large ships had fallen into the hands of the English fleet, a third was reduced almost to a wreck by English gunfire. Nevertheless, the Armada was in relatively good order, though beginning to run short of powder and shot. However, Parma's army was not ready and during the delay the English fleet, reinforced by a squadron from the Downs, anchored about a mile upwind of the Armada. The wind was fresh from the south-west and three nights later eight fireships in a compact line were

16. English Warship. C. J. Visscher, *c*.1600

One of a set of ten Armada prints by the well-known Dutch engraver, Visscher, five of them battle scenes and five ship views. Though tentatively identified as the *Ark Royal*, it is unlikely that this print represents a specific ship; it is rather crude and generalized in treatment.

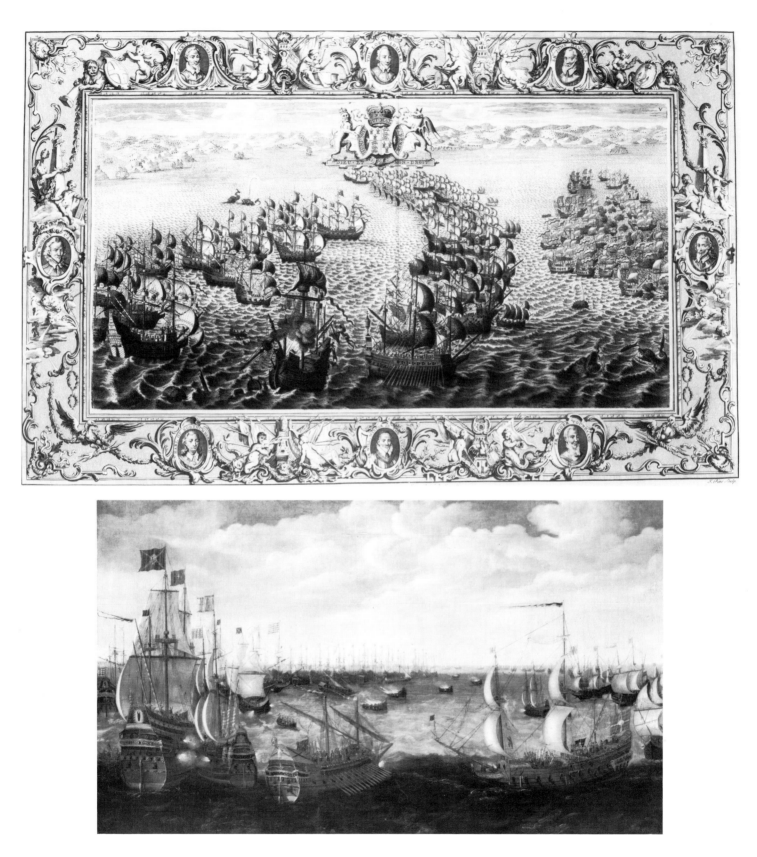

17. The Spanish Armada: Capture of the 'San Salvador', 22 July 1588. John Pine

One of ten engravings after Hendrik Vroom's 'Armada' tapestries. This example features the unexplained explosion at 4 p.m. of the *San Salvador* (foreground, left of centre), a Spanish urca which was the flagship of the Guipúzcoa squadron. The print's decorative borders include portraits of commanders of the English fleet; Lord Howard's likeness is in the upper centre.

18. Launch of the Fireships, 1588. Unidentified artist

On the night of 7 August 1588 eight English fireships were sent amongst the Spanish fleet anchored at Calais. This picture, in which the principal action is an engagement between two rival flagships and a galleasse in the foreground, is a loose, symbolic interpretation of that event by a contemporary Flemish artist.

towed towards the Spanish fleet, fired, and set adrift [fig. 18]. The Spanish ships slipped their anchors in the darkness. Daylight revealed a sorry scene. The largest Spanish galleasse, the *San Lorenzo*, was ashore and being attacked by boats of the English ships; some of the Spanish warships, drifting in the strong east-going tide, were widely separated from the main body of the Armada, and the English fleet, under sail and led by Drake in his flagship, the *Revenge*, was already in pursuit. Sending pinnaces to round up the straying ships, Medina Sidonia, with his stoutest ships, stood to meet the English attack. In the ensuing battle two Spanish ships were sunk and two more were so badly damaged that they had to be abandoned in a sinking condition. The damage in others, including the flagship *San Martin*, was so severe that they could no longer be counted as fighting ships.

Medina Sidonia, however, found himself facing a new danger even more menacing than the English fleet. Wind and tide were forcing his ships down towards the shallow banks of the Dutch coast, threatening wholesale shipwreck. At the last moment the wind backed and brought relief from the danger, but even as it did so, it added a new problem to Medina Sidonia's worries. After the failure to embark Parma's army he knew he would

have to return to Spain with Philip's great 'Enterprise of England' in ruins. Blocking his way home down the English Channel lay the English fleet, still undefeated and still full of fight. He had no choice but to lead his Armada up to the north and find his way home round Scotland and Ireland. A storm was blowing up, to make even more precarious the long voyage home. In the final accounting only sixty-seven of the 130 ships returned to Spain.

The Spanish Armada was the first 'modern' battle fought between fleets at sea, and was one of the most decisive in the world's history. European eyes were looking at something of a miracle, greater indeed than that of a relatively new and untried navy overcoming the greatest fleet the world had yet seen. What they were seeing was the start of the decline of Spain as the world's greatest maritime power and the beginning of the rise of English sea power. It was a political and economic turning point that was to affect every nation in Europe in the years to come. Its more immediate effect was to stamp the low-charged ship design as the model of all new ship construction. Another improvement which sprang from the battle was the gradual abandonment of a fourth mast in large ships and the return to three masts as providing a better, aerodynamically balanced rig.

4. EARLY DUTCH MARINE ARTISTS

The origins of Dutch marine art go back to the late sixteenth century, and are closely linked to the development of landscape painting. From that period Dutch artists began to paint independent landscapes in a style increasingly atmospheric and naturalistic. A passion for descriptive information coincided with a remarkable artistic resurgence, based on the new wealth generated by trade and empire. The houses of the wealthy burgher class were filled with pictures, predominantly secular in subject, portraits, genre scenes, still lifes, and, above all, landscapes.

Of landscapes, a significant proportion were of marine subjects. The reason for this is obvious. The Dutch provinces have long coastlines; naval power had played a vital part in enabling them to resist Spain during the long and bitter conflict for independence; much of their wealth came from trade and fishing. It was natural for artists to record the familiar scenes of the coast, the picturesque inshore craft, as well as the big ocean-

going ships, subjects for which there was always a ready market. The power of the sea has long been a source of terror and fascination to mankind. Early marine paintings draw on a rich vocabulary of allegorical allusion and superstition, once commonplace, but obscured by the rationalism of later periods. Rocks and sea monsters represent the dangers of the deep; ships departing may stand for the journey of the soul, the voyage of love, the ship of state or the ship of fools; shipwreck [fig. 19] may imply damnation as well as natural disaster.

The hero of early marine art is Hendrik Vroom (1566–1640) [plate 5; fig. 20]. He established many of the subject categories that remained popular throughout the century; shipwrecks, coastal shipping, beach and port scenes, ship portraits, gala events, battle pictures. His ships are carefully painted and finely detailed; he understood the movement of waves, and the effect of weather; sea, ships and coast are drawn in correct spatial proportion. Through his eyes we can see what ships of the time really

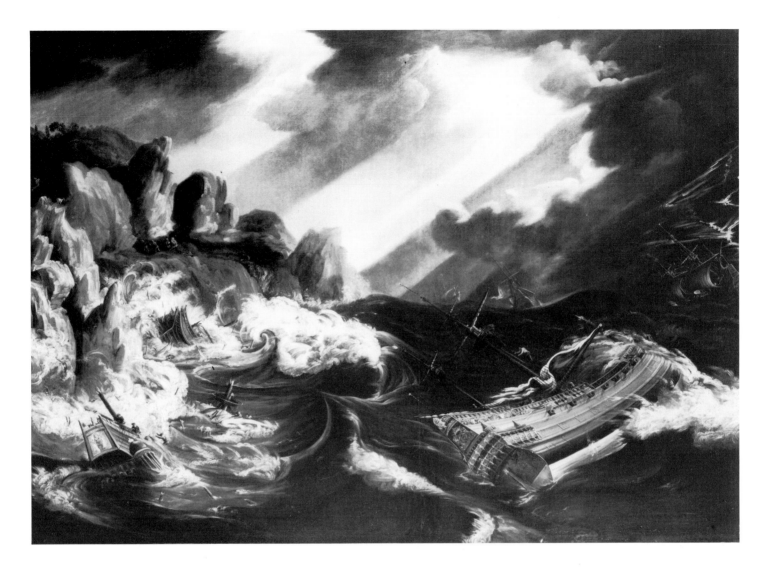

looked like. Clearly this accuracy of detail was a requirement for his patrons, some of whom had strong maritime links. His huge painting of the return of the first Dutch East Indies fleet to Amsterdam in 1599 was almost certainly commissioned by or for the Dutch East India Company, founded in 1602. The four ships, whose return aroused such resounding acclaim in Holland, are shown at anchor, dwarfing the swarm of little boats bringing VIPs and spectators to greet them. In this picture, Vroom established the type of pageant-full commemorative marine subject which would remain popular for another two and a half centuries. At the same period, he painted his panoramic bird's-eye view of the fireship attack on the Spanish Armada, and designed the cartoons for the famous set of Armada tapestries (now destroyed), which were commissioned by the English Commander, Lord Howard of Effingham. Later com-

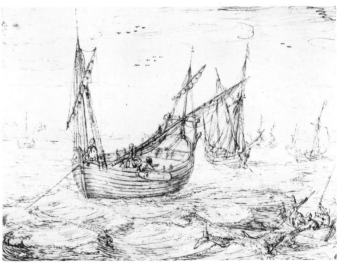

19. The Wreck of the 'Amsterdam'. Unidentified artist

This painting's melodramatic treatment throws doubt on its former attribution to Cornelis Claesz. Van Wieringen. Though close in feel to the Netherlandish genre of allegorical shipwrecks, the principal subject (a three-decker, port quarter view) is identified as an actual ship: the arms on her stern are those of the City of Amsterdam.

20. Fishing off the Shore. Hendrik Cornelisz. Vroom

In contrast to later depictions of herring or whale fishing far out at sea, this drawing shows fishing boats operating in the shallow waters off the coast of Holland, a subject to be exploited by artists of following generations throughout much of the seventeenth century.

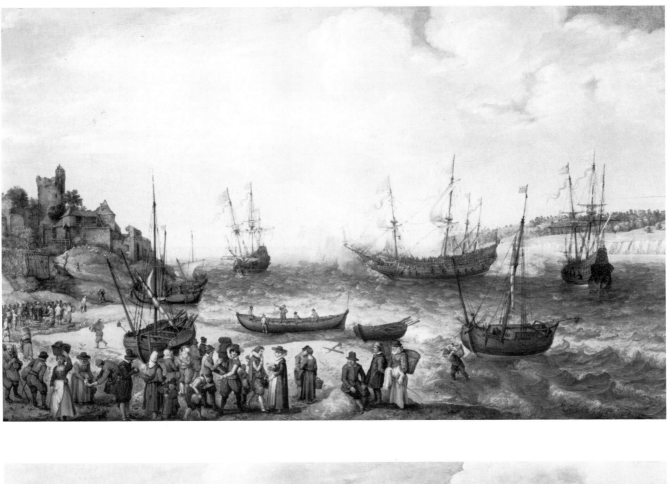

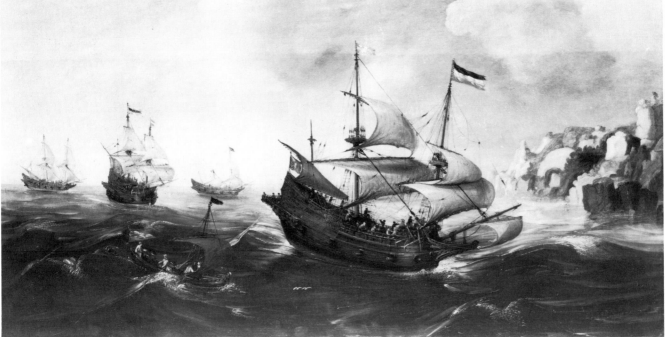

21. Departure of an English East Indiaman. Adam Willaerts, 1640

With their stock of imaginary settings and their standard formulae for portside bustle, Willaerts' 'arrivals' and 'departures' are often difficult to distinguish from one another. But in this fine picture, formerly thought to portray the return of Sir Edward Michelbourne from the East in 1606, the principal ship, just right of centre, is evidently weighing anchor and preparing to get under way.

22. Dutch Ships running down onto a Rocky Shore. Andries van Eertvelt

The smooth, almost metallic, painting of the sea is typical of the early work of Eertvelt. The subject, with symbolic meaning suggested by the rocky coast and the large fish or whale, is a common one in the early seventeenth century and derives from the work of Hendrik Vroom.

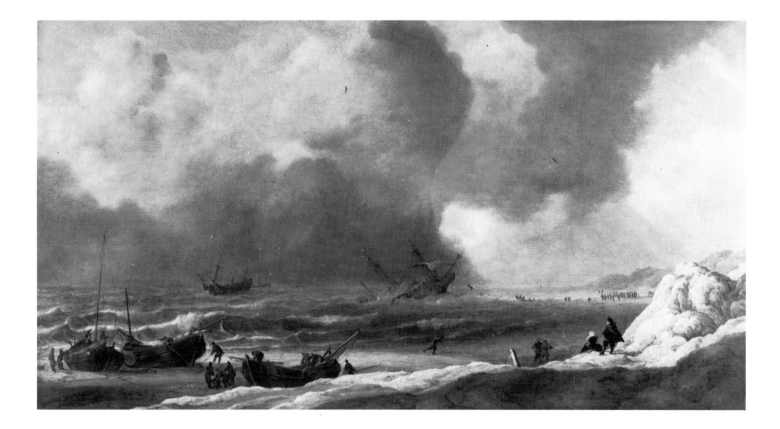

missions at the English Court included a painting of the return of Prince Charles to England in 1624 after his abortive attempt to marry the Spanish Infanta. Led by the *Prince Royal*, pride of the English navy, a squadron of warships parades across the canvas, follow-my-leader style.

Vroom was an international figure, and a major force in the artistic community of Haarlem where he settled. His success encouraged rivals, including his son, Cornelis, with whom he quarrelled, and his pupil, Cornelis Claesz. van Wieringen (1580–1635). The latter won the commission for the *Battle of Gibraltar* (Scheepvaart Museum, Amsterdam), 1607, because, it is said, he quoted a lower price than Vroom. The quirky and idiosyncratic Andries van Eertvelt (1590–1652) of Antwerp painted another version of the East Indies fleet returning in 1599 [fig. 29]; and Adam Willaerts of Utrecht (1577–1664) painted the arrival at Flushing of the Elector Palatine and his young bride, Princess Elizabeth, in 1613 [plate 4], a subject also depicted by Vroom. Willaerts' rendering of the English flagship, the *Prince Royal*, recurs in scenes of departure and arrival, of which he made a speciality, placing them against imaginary rocky coastlines [fig. 21]. The little figures who people his beaches have an individual character, and his palette with its typical fresh greens and blues, and vivid accents in red, is seductive and unmistakable.

The early marine painters concentrated on ship portraits and maritime events, crowding their pictures with closely observed detail. The transition to the atmospheric seascape, in which individual ships or boats are subservient to an overall effect of space and light, wind and weather, is a development of the late 1620s, usually associated with Jan Porcellis (1584–1632). His beach and fishing scenes [fig. 23] suggest a direct response to the realities of nature quite outside the terms of reference established by Vroom and Willaerts. The movement towards realism was not confined to maritime painting, but should be seen as part of the new spirit of Dutch landscape art. Some of the greatest seventeenth-century marines were painted by artists better known as landscapists, Jan van Goyen (1596–1656), Albert Cuyp (1620–91), and Jacob van Ruisdael (1628–82), to name only the most obvious. Their achievements have tended to overshadow those artists whose work was more naturally maritime in subject-matter. Ruisdael shows us the sea under conditions of haunting beauty. A burst of light catches the white sails of a small and solitary fishing boat, the only object in a scene of boisterous waves and threatening clouds.

23. A Fishing Boat in Rough Seas. Jan Porcellis
The varied reactions of men and vessels to a developing storm, on shore and at sea, form the theme of this most direct, foreboding and atmospheric seascape. The boat in the centre riding rough breakers, shown before the wind on the starboard tack, is a hoeker.

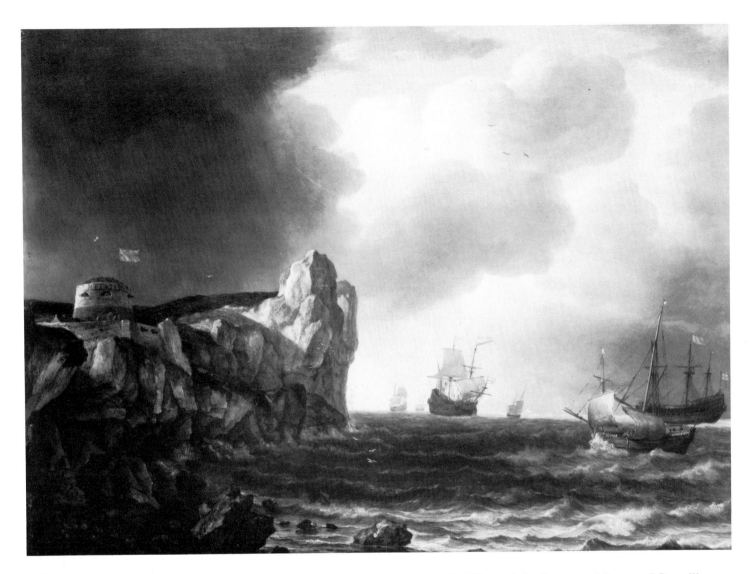

Simon de Vlieger (1600?–53), a follower of Porcellis, was thoroughly versed in maritime affairs, but he had little to learn from his better-known contemporaries when it came to harmonies of space and light. His delicately adjusted compositions of ships off rocky shores [plate 6; fig. 25], painted in a range of muted greys, are as original and imaginative as anything in marine art. De Vlieger could produce accurate portraits of ships and boats [plate 8], or spacious and delicately painted beach scenes [plate 7], as well as dramatic images of storm and shipwreck. Peter Mulier the Elder (c.1615–70) and the Younger (c.1637–1701), and the Antwerp artist, Bonaventura Peeters (1614–52) [plate 11], all painted powerful seascapes in this tradition, and their works stand out from the many productions of more prosaic marine artists. Regnier Nooms (c.1623–67), often called Zeeman (or sailor) because of his working knowledge

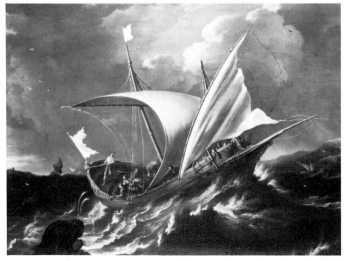

24. Jonah and the Whale. Attributed to Carlo Antonia Tavella
In this powerful interpretation of the well-know biblical story, possibly by Tavella, a follower of Peter Mulier the Elder, Jonah is shown being thrown over the side of a two-masted lateen-rigged vessel of the Mediterranean settee type. In the left foreground a fantastic sea monster awaits the prophet, open-mouthed.

25. Shipping off the English Coast. Simon de Vlieger
The setting of this exhilarating yet most delicately painted subject is probably Flamborough Head. Overlooked symbolically by a group of soldiers and a fort flying the Cross of St. George, a Dutch vessel is intercepted as it sails incautiously through English shipping lanes.

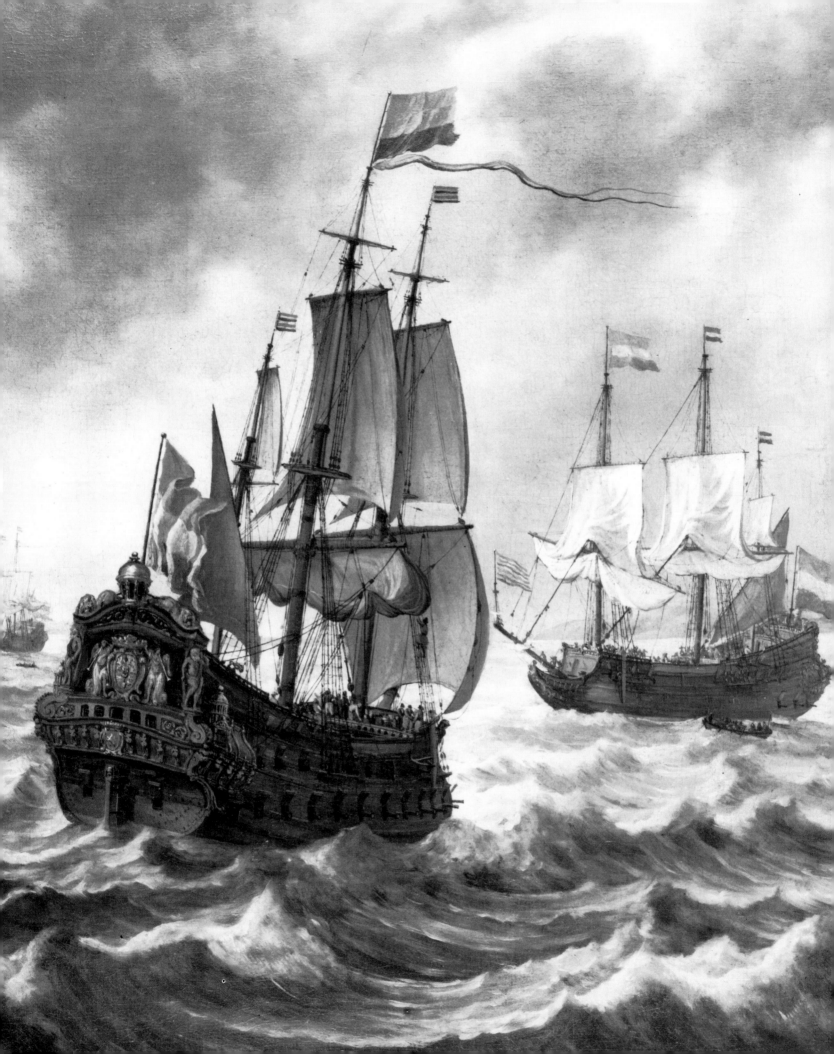

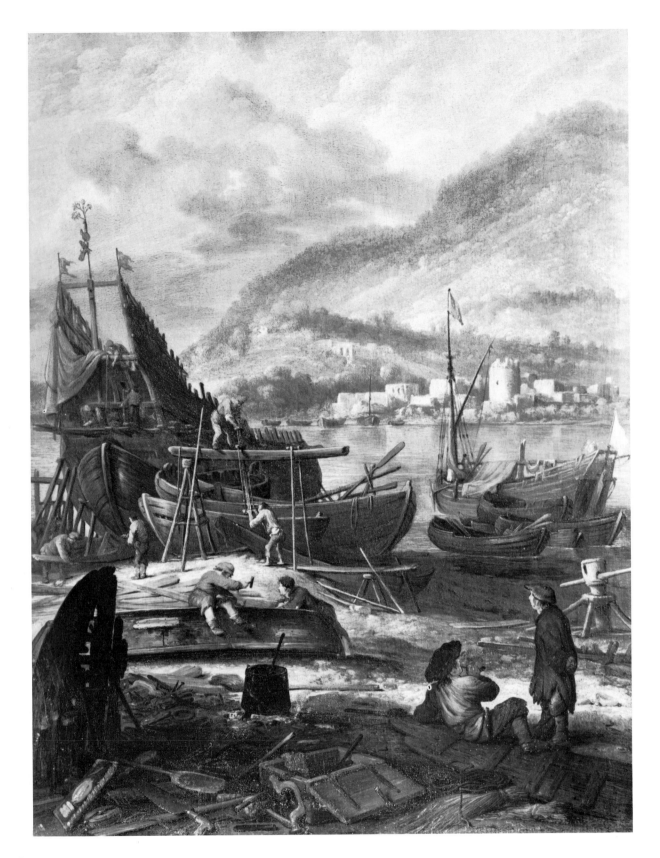

26 (previous page). 'Amelia' in the Straits of Dover. Regnier Nooms, called Zeeman

The *Amelia*, a 57-gun man-of-war launched in 1632, is portrayed undramatically in choppy seas off the English coast with other vessels of the Dutch fleet. The decoration of the tafferel is recorded by Nooms with characteristic attention to detail; the carved coat of arms is that of Prince Frederick Hendrick.

27. Shipbuilding at Porto San Stefano. Regnier Nooms, called Zeeman

In this meticulous and highly detailed composition the well-documented description of shipbuilding forms the main narrative. To the right a dismasted settee comes into the yard for repair; to the left a ship under construction is on the stocks. A plant is placed at the stem of the latter in continuance of an ancient and superstitious shipbuilding tradition.

of ships, is one of the attractive figures of marine art, though little detail is known of his life or career. His large-scale compositions, of battles and fleets at sea [fig. 26], lack the sophistication of de Vlieger, but he has an unerring eye for the lines of a ship and the minutiae of rigging and tackle. He painted several scenes

of shipbuilding [fig. 27], careening and views of ports, especially in the Mediterranean, which he must have visited by ship. Like Porcellis, he produced prints of local fishing and coastal craft, and helped to popularize the accurate documentation of Dutch shipping.

5. THE EAST INDIA COMPANIES

A notable success of Drake's raid on Cadiz in 1587 was the capture in the *San Felipe* of the charts and accounts of Portuguese trade in India and the east. Several English merchants perceived the substantial profits to be made from voyages to India around the Cape of Good Hope and they formed themselves into a group of merchant adventurers to exploit the knowledge gained from the *San Felipe*. At first they traded individually to the east, their ships armed with guns as were all merchantmen in those days, and if one or two occasionally fell victim to piracy or attack by foreign ships attempting to preserve their 'prior' rights, enough of them prospered to attract yet more adventurers. In 1600, 125 such merchants formed a company with a capital of £72,000 and were incorporated by a royal charter as the Honourable East India Company, with the exclusive rights to trade in far-eastern waters, including China and Japan. As before, each shareholder traded individually, carrying all the cost and risk

of each voyage and taking all the profit, but in 1612 a new system was adopted under which the Company owned and operated the ships, organized the voyages, appointed captains and crews, collected and sold the cargoes, and shared the profits among the shareholders. It had already set up two trading stations in India at Masulipatam and Pettapoli, and in this year of 1612 its ships had reached Japan and established a trade there.

Following the example of England, seven other European nations set up East India companies, Holland, France, Denmark, Austria, Spain, Sweden, and Scotland. Of the eight, only those companies of Holland, England and France were really significant, the others in many ways lacking the drive and ambition to defend to the hilt the enterprise of their merchants. The Dutch merchants had already established themselves with monopoly powers in the East Indies and trading stations on the mainland of India and in Ceylon [figs. 28, 29]. The formation

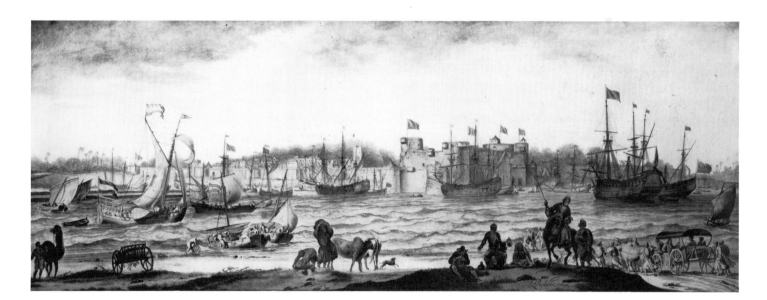

28. Surat from the Sea. Ludolf Bakhuizen
This monochrome painting, which is one of a pair depicting views of Surat, ably suggests the healthy maritime trade of a Dutch East Indies factory port in the mid-seventeenth century. The admixture of familiar ships (though drawn with only sketchy attention to detail) in exotic surroundings is particularly evocative.

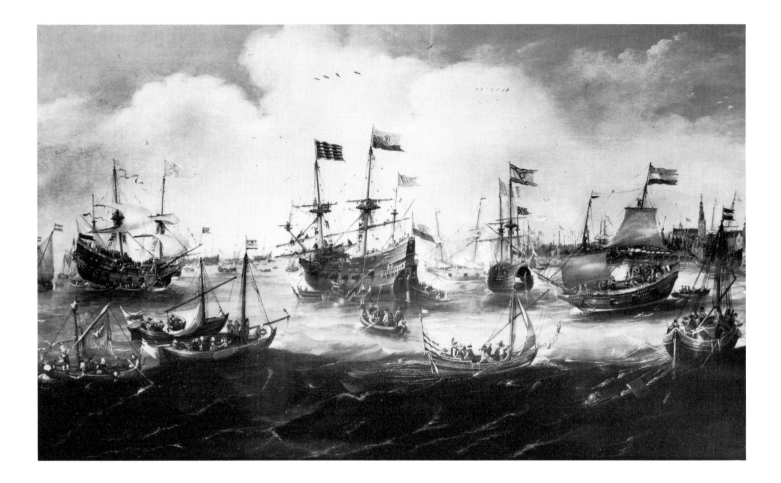

of a Dutch East India Company in 1602 was designed to provide legal powers, backed by the home government, to enforce the trading monopoly against all comers. At the height of its power in the mid-seventeenth century it had a fleet of more than 150 armed merchantmen and 40 warships, and an army of 10,000 soldiers. From the first there was bitter hostility between the Dutch and English companies, reaching a peak in 1623 when the English merchants at Amboyna, talking under a flag of truce, were tortured and massacred by order of the Dutch Governor. The continuing war between the two companies swung gradually in favour of the English. By the end of the seventeenth century the Dutch company had been driven from mainland India and from Ceylon, leaving only the East Indian islands as its trading base. Even there it was facing difficulty, for the financial burden of maintaining enough force to police its declared monopoly of trade was crippling. It fell into bankruptcy and before the end of the eighteenth century was officially wound up.

Yet in spite of all the bitterness and fighting it would be diffi-

cult to exaggerate the influence of all the active East India companies on the development of the sailing ship, both in design and in numbers. Within a very few years of their incorporation the major companies had developed their own private dockyards where they designed and built their own ships [plate 11], always with an eye to improved performance during their long voyages out and home. Without exception they followed the basic design of the low-charged warship, though with the increase in size which they needed for economic trading they added an additional poop deck aft to accommodate the company officials and their ladies, and important passengers. The resulting small increase in height above the waterline aft in fact improved the ship's sailing qualities by helping to hold the bows up towards the wind. Most of their ships had two gundecks for self-defence, giving a broadside of up to 24 guns, and were built with a full underbody to provide the necessary carrying capacity as merchant ships. They had a better length-to-beam ratio than the pure warship, around 4 or 4½ to 1, enough to give them a good turn of speed and the ability to hold a slightly better course

29. Return of the Dutch East India Fleet, 1599. Andries van Eertvelt

This shows the return to Amsterdam of the first trading expedition to the Far East, led by Houtman. Only four of the original eight ships arrived home: they are grouped here in the middle distance with the *Hollandia* at their centre. Eertvelt's painting was based on a composition by his master, Hendrik Vroom.

nearer the wind than the average merchant ship of the time. The vast increase in value and bulk of the trade called for a continual acceleration in building, and great numbers of these magnificent ships, larger and finer than any others in the world, were launched down the building slips of the European companies. It is no wonder that East India ships were widely regarded as the aristocrats of the oceans.

Although this eastern trade was expanding at a great rate, it was by no means the only source of wealth open to ships. Western Europe was an avid market for the produce of the east, particularly its spices, needed to disguise the taste of basic foods which, without means of preservation, deteriorated rapidly. Its silks, its tapestries and carpets, its teas and above all its jewels, never lacked buyers. Yet western Europe was at the same time wide open for trade in its own products, timber and furs from Russia, mast timber and tar from the Baltic, wool and tin from England, wine from France and Spain, the multifarious manu-

factures from every country, and above all for fish. Meat was scarce and expensive and most European countries decreed one or two meatless days each week when fish was the natural substitute. Moreover fish could be preserved by drying and, unlike meat, became a long-lasting food.

During the fourteenth century the herring had migrated from the Baltic to the North Sea, had proliferated there at a great pace, and spread round the north of Scotland into the coastal waters of the eastern Atlantic. The two great cod fisheries south of Iceland and on the Newfoundland banks were proving a plentiful and self-renewing supply of prime food. Most of the European fishing craft were small, tubby ships known as busses [fig. 30] and they were to be counted in thousands. For the more distant fishing grounds, three-masted ships of from 50 to 75 tons were the main vessels used. There was also a flourishing whale fishery in the Arctic Ocean [fig. 31].

The great majority of this European seaborne trade, and par-

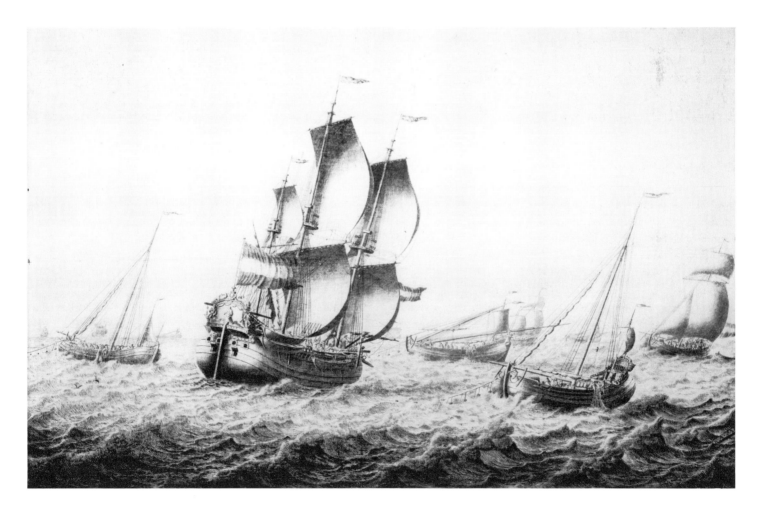

30. Herring Fishery. Adriaan van Salm
This is a subject typical of van Salm, showing Dutch herring busses with their nets out and a whaler, the *Maria*, running between them.

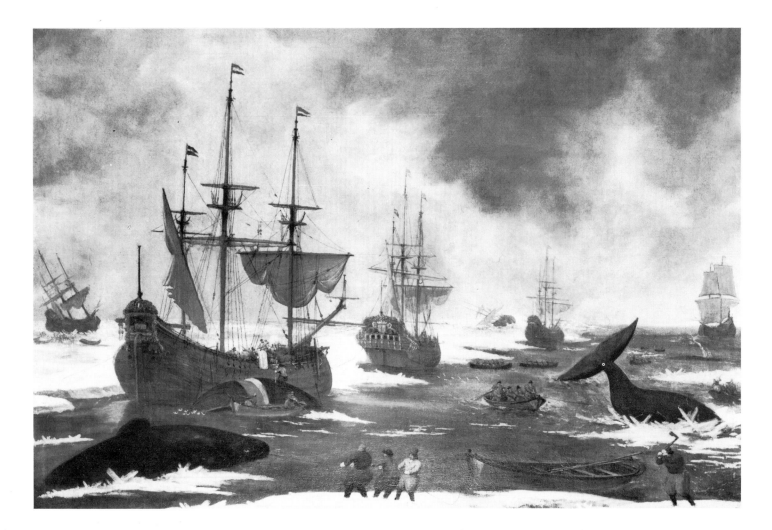

ticularly the trade in fish, was in the hands of Dutch merchants, backed by the native skill of their ship designers and builders. No place was too distant for their ships if it gave promise of worthwhile trade, and they were to be seen as far north as Archangel [fig. 32] for the fur and timber trade, throughout the Baltic [fig. 33] as the main carriers of essential shipbuilding material such as masts, tar, and flax for sailmaking, around Europe and down the west coast of Africa where they were setting up trading stations and repair and replenishment ports for their East Indiamen, across the Atlantic to break into the growing West Indian market, and in huge numbers in the North Sea for the herring. Holland was reputed to make the longest drift nets in the world to harvest its herring catch.

The nearest rival in this race for seaborne trade was England, but the lack of interest in the sea and shipping of the first Stuart successors of Elizabeth allowed a vigorous English response to the Dutch growth in trade to go by default. James I, even allow-

ing for the building of the *Prince Royal*, at the time a much praised vessel, had little interest in the navy and many of its once-proud ships which had defeated the great Armada of Spain were neglected and left to rot. The *Prince Royal* [plate 4], launched in 1610, was in a state of decay eleven years later and had to be virtually rebuilt. Forgotten were the words of Raleigh in the days of Elizabeth: 'Whosoever commands the sea commands the trade; whosoever commands the trade of the world commands the riches of the world, and consequently the world itself.'

James's son Charles, realizing the necessity of a strong fleet if England were to prosper in the race for trade, set about the creation of a new English navy. To him we owe the magnificent *Sovereign of the Seas* [figs. 34, 35], the first English three-decker, which had a capacity of 1,522 tons and was launched in 1637. It was Charles's misfortune that he pursued the dream of the divine right of kings in opposition to a recalcitrant Parliament, who would not vote him the money for his navy. During the

31. Whalers in the Ice. Abraham Matthys

The Antwerp painter Matthys concentrated on painting whaling subjects, which must have derived from firsthand experience, as he is known to have gone to sea for a period in his father's whaling ships. He painted some portraits, including one of the marine painter Bonaventura Peeters, and he was also a collector.

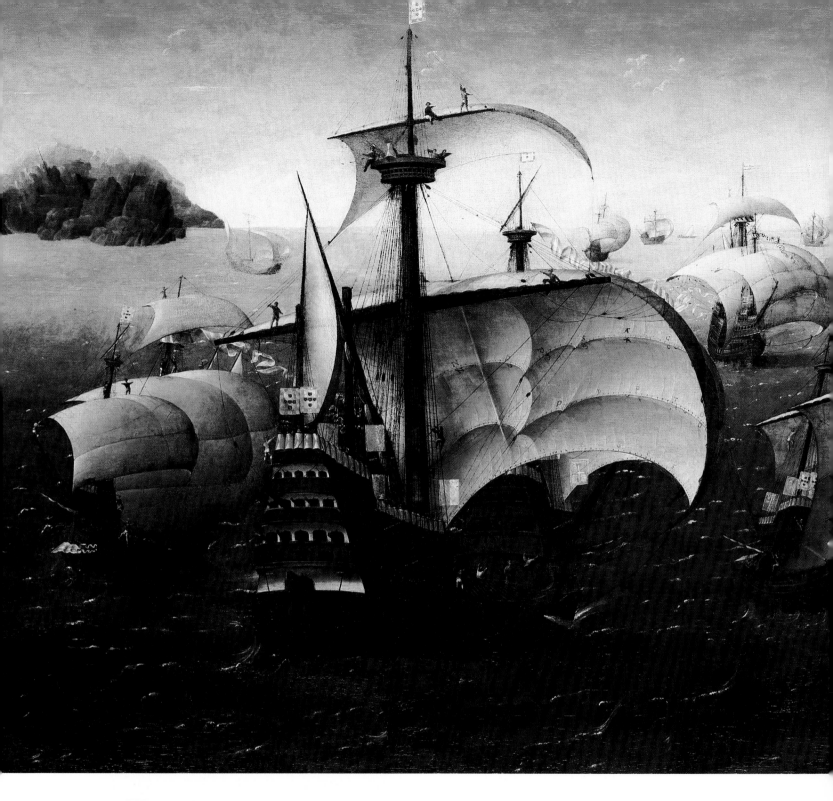

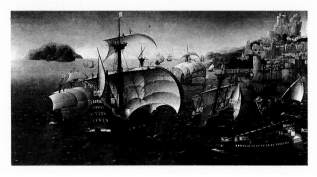

Plate 1. Portuguese Carracks off a Rocky Coast. Unidentified artist, c.1540

This unique and highly important marine painting is the earliest and most accurate representation of the great three- or four-masted ships which made the first oceanic voyages of trade and discovery. A squadron of ships bearing the Portuguese flag is shown approaching a walled Mediterranean city rising to a castle perched on a rocky pinnacle. The occasion has tentatively been identified as the arrival of the Portuguese Infanta Beatriz, daughter of King Manuel, who came from Lisbon to Villefranche, by way of Marseilles, to marry Charles III of Savoy in 1521. The galley coming out to meet the ships flies pennants with the arms of Savoy. The three ships in the foreground probably represent three views of the same vessel. Noteworthy are the high fore and stern castles, the heavy, built-up mainmast, the immense length of the main yard-arm and the size of the billowing main course.

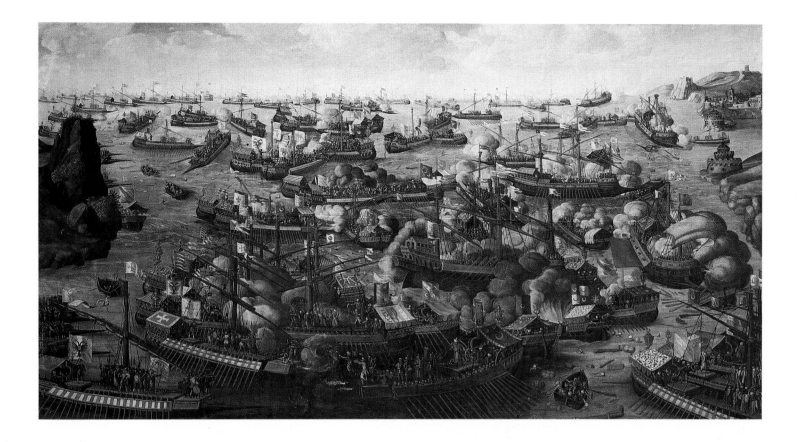

Plate 2. Battle of Lepanto, 7 October 1571. Unidentified artist

This victory by the combined fleets of Spain, the Papal States and Venice over
the Turks proved to be a decisive turning point in European history. It took
place in the gulf of Lepanto, off the Greek coast, and involved several hundred
ships. The battle was fierce and bloody. Greater fire power and more
disciplined troops swung the issue in favour of the Christian forces. The picture
shows a confused mêlée of galleys and galleasses, only a token representation
of those present. On the left, the flagship *Andrea Doria*, commanding the
Christian right, is locked in battle with her opposite number, *Uluch Ali*. The
galley of Don John of Austria, the commander-in-chief, is in the middle
distance supporting a Venetian ship against the Turkish admiral Ali Pasha,
who was killed. The picture is similar in composition to the many prints of the
battle broadcast across Europe, and reflects the cartographic viewpoint
adopted for such scenes in the sixteenth century.

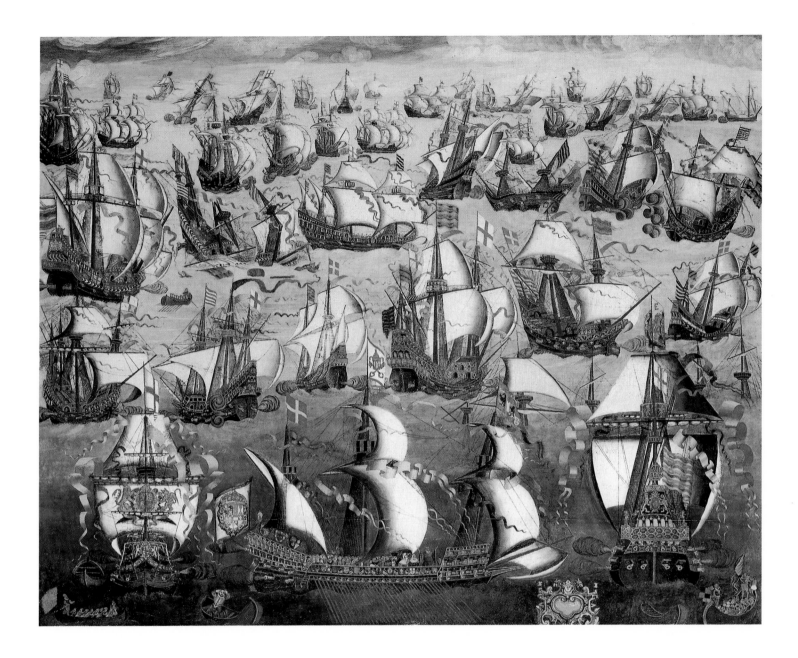

Plate 3. An Engagement between the English Fleet and the Spanish Armada, 1588. Unidentified artist

In the foreground, two English warships flank a Spanish galleasse. That on the right, stern view, must be Lord Howard of Effingham's flagship, *Ark Royal*, for she wears the royal standard at the main. The ship on the left, bow view, is probably Sir Francis Drake's *Revenge*. The galleasse in the foreground bears the standard of the Spanish commander-in-chief, the Duke of Medina Sidonia, though his flagship, the *San Martin*, was a galleon. The four Spanish galleasses did not play a significant role in the campaign, but they captured the imagination of the English, and they appear prominently in all representations of the battle. Beyond the foreground ships, the composition divides into a succession of bands with alternating warships of either nation firing broadsides. Though heraldic in treatment, the picture gives a good idea of the form of warships at the period, the stormy weather encountered by both fleets, and the skirmishes that characterized the conflict.

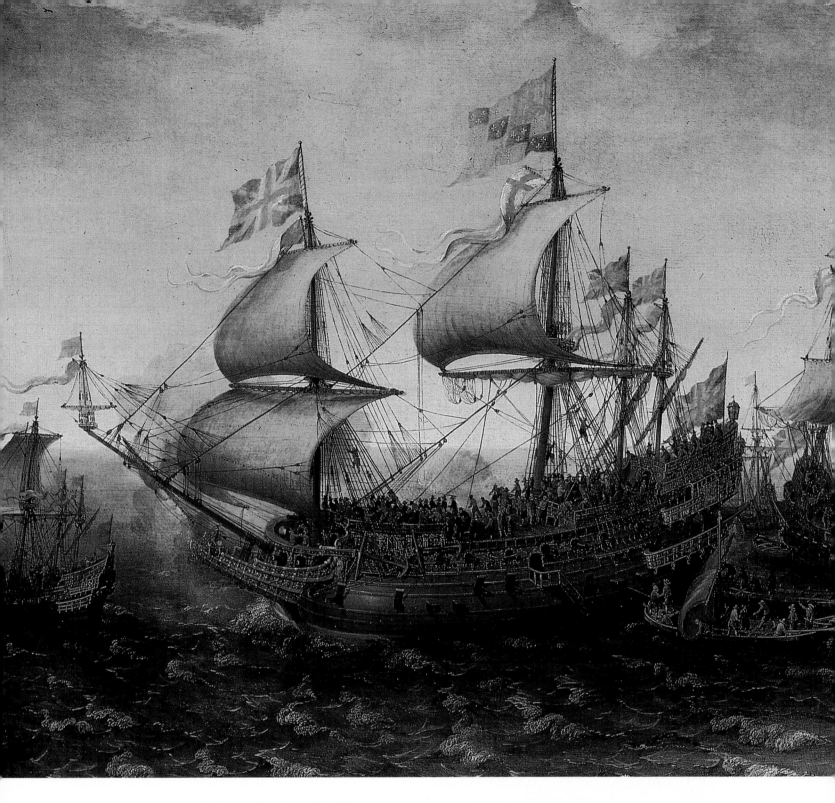

Plate 4. The Embarkation of the Elector Palatine and his Wife at Margate, 23 April 1613. Adam Willaerts, 1623

Frederic, Elector Palatine, married Princess Elizabeth, daughter of James I, in a much publicized match in 1613. Regarded as one of the champions of Protestantism in Germany, Frederic lost both Bohemia (where he was king for less than a year) and the Palatine at the start of the Thirty Years War. His beautiful wife became the ill-fated Winter Queen. Willaerts' picture shows the departure of the royal couple from Margate aboard the English flagship, the *Prince Royal*. Launched in 1611, and named for Henry, Prince of Wales, who had died shortly before his sister's wedding, it was the pride of the fleet. Liberally decorated with the feathers of the Prince of Wales, and with the figurehead of St. George, the *Prince Royal* is seen firing a salute on the point of departure. The bay behind is crowded with warships and a variety of small craft, including barges and fishing vessels. The departure is watched by a crowd of figures on the beach.

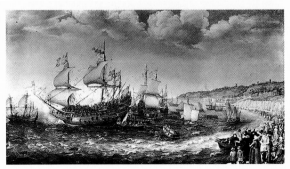

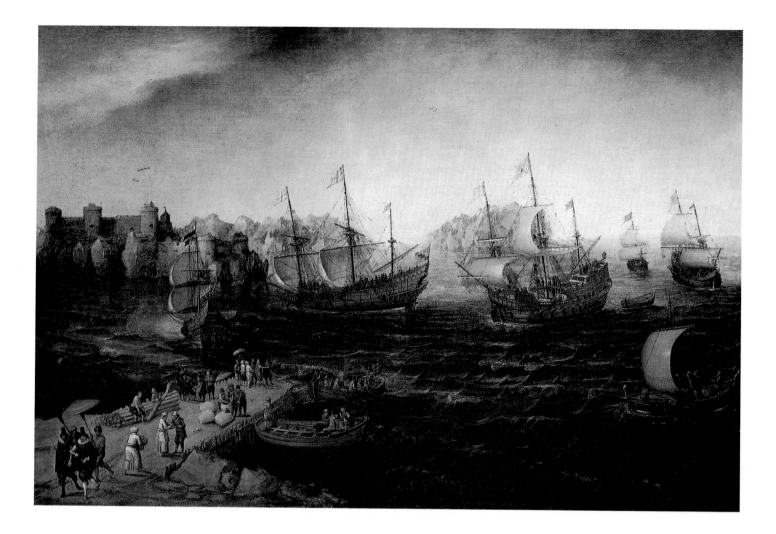

Plate 5. Ships trading in the East. Hendrik Cornelisz. Vroom, 1614

This picture of a mixed squadron of European ships arriving at a port in the
East can only be regarded as highly Utopian. Commercial, as well as political,
rivalry precluded such scenes of peaceful co-operation. The ship on the left,
flying the Dutch flag at the main, is coming to anchor, lowering the yard of
her mainsail and firing a salute. The English warship left of centre is sailing
into the bay under courses. To the right is a Spanish warship, under forecourse
and maintopsail, flying a flag with the arms of Spain at the main. Another
Dutch vessel is seen on the far right, with a French vessel beyond her flying
a flag bearing three fleurs-de-lys. The boat in the foreground on the right is
a fanciful Oriental version of a Dutch ferry boat. In the foreground are small
boats and a quayside with European and Oriental merchants engaged in the
business of bartering.

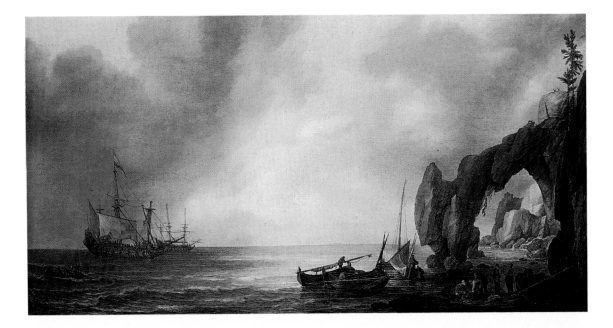

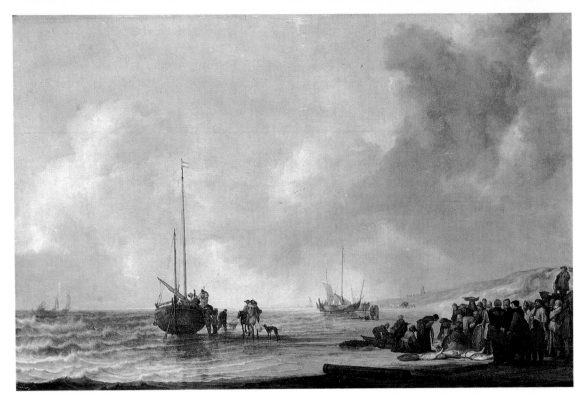

Plate 6. A Craggy Coast with Dutch Men-of-War Becalmed. Simon de Vlieger

Two ships lie at anchor on the left. The nearer ship is flying the Dutch flag at the main and her crew are evidently striking down or stepping up the foretopmast. On the right, three fishing vessels lie close to the shore, with a group of figures passing the time of day on the beach. The rock arch and coastline beyond lend an air of exotic enchantment. This is reinforced by the still and dreamy atmosphere of the scene, the pearly translucence of the light, which is disturbed only by the gentle lapping of the waves. The subtle balance of ships and shore, and the intervals between them, reveal de Vlieger as a virtuoso composer. He painted many such panoramic marines in which he explored variations on a theme. It has been suggested that this picture was painted at Rotterdam, where de Vlieger was resident until *c*.1633, and where his style most closely reflects that of his master, Jan Porcellis.

Plate 7. The Beach at Scheveningen. Simon de Vlieger, 1633

Scheveningen is a village beside a famous stretch of sand close to the Hague, and a favourite place for artists to sketch. The day's catch is being unloaded from a beached fishing pink left of centre. On the right an impromptu fish market takes place on the sand; while further down the beach there is a coach with four white horses. Beach scenes are among the most familiar motifs in Dutch landscape art. De Vlieger's picture is an astonishingly early example of the type of sweeping atmospheric scene later associated with Jacob van Ruisdael. The picture opens out to include us as spectators, and to make us experience its exhilarating sense of space and charged effects of weather. From the transparent fringe of water over sand, and de Vlieger painted few things more beautiful, the eye is led along the dramatic curve of the beach to the grey infinity of the horizon.

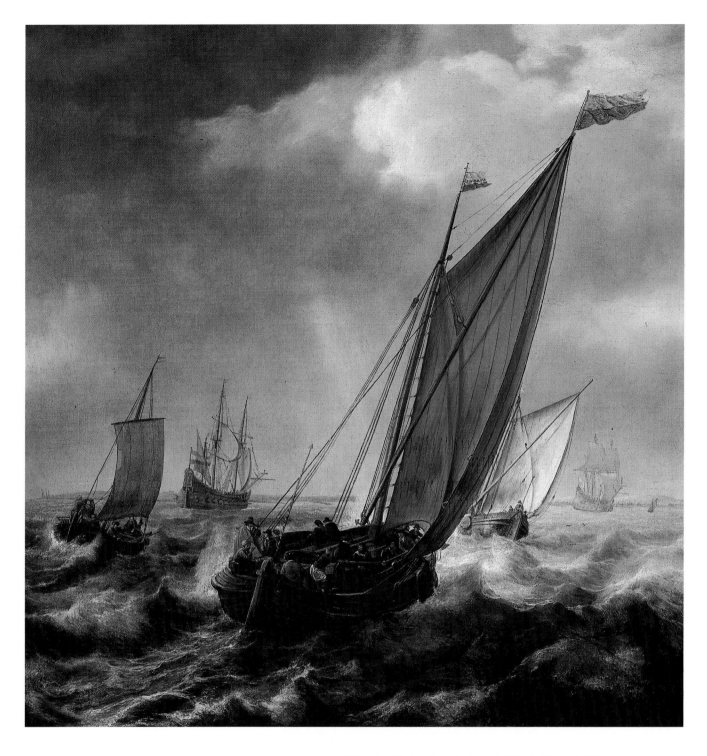

Plate 8. A Dutch Ferry before the Wind. Simon de Vlieger

This depiction of a breezy day off the Dutch coast is unusual in the prominence
given to the boat in the foreground and the almost square proportions of the
picture. The boat is a kaag, a common type of ferry boat. She has a sprit-rigged
mainsail, and flags at the masthead and the peak. A sailor, poised on the edge
of the gunwale, hauls in the sail, while the passengers are scattered on benches
down the centre of the boat or round the sides. Apart from highlights, the boat
and foreground waves are in shadow, while the middle ground is hit by a
dramatic sunburst. On the left is a fishing pink, with a fluyt in the distance
beyond. On the right, half hidden by the sails of the kaag, is a smalschip or
wijdschip heeling in the fresh breeze.

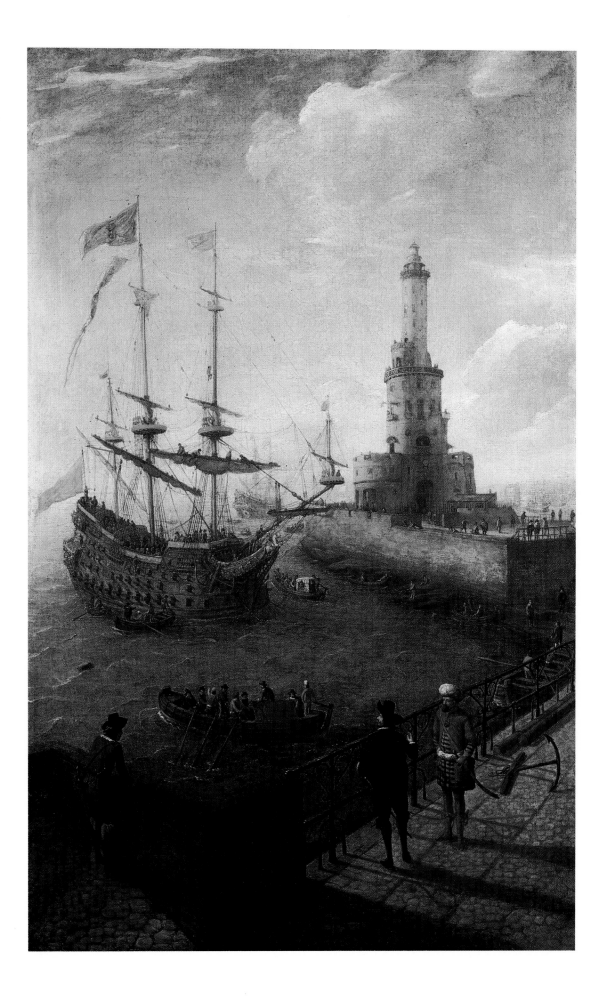

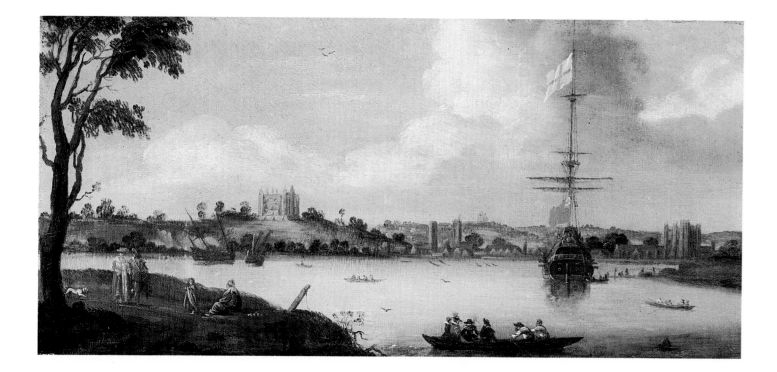

**Plate 9. A Spanish Three-Decker lying at Naples.
Abraham Willaerts, 1665**

Abraham Willaerts continued to paint port scenes in the old-fashioned
tradition of his father. This picture is unusual in its upright format, and the
dramatic perspective of the foreground terrace, and it may be only a fragment
of a once much wider painting.

The kingdom of Naples was under Spanish rule throughout the seventeenth
century and the three-decker lying at anchor in the harbour flies a Spanish flag
at the main. Of the three figures in the foreground, casting long shadows, two
are Europeans, one a turbanned Turk or Moor. A ship's boat draws out into
the harbour, other figures line the Molo by the lighthouse. The lanterna or
lighthouse at Naples was a much simpler structure than the tower depicted
here, and the identification of the location as Naples is not necessarily correct.

**Plate 10. Greenwich Palace with a Man-of-War at Anchor.
Unidentified Flemish artist, c.1630**

The picture is a rare topographical record of the old Tudor palace of Placentia
at Greenwich, and a masterpiece of early English landscape art. Its sweeping
panoramic view and feeling of space belies its modest size, that of a cabinet
picture. The view is from the north bank of the Thames at Blackwall. Visible
in the centre background are the two towers of Henry VIII's armoury of
1516–18, which dominated the tiltyard. To the left is the chapel, and to the
right a range of gabled buildings ending in a massive gateway tower. The
square keep-like building on the hill to the left has not been certainly identified.
Greenwich was a favourite residence of Tudor and Stuart monarchs; foreign
dignitaries were received there, elaborate ceremonials and entertainments were
staged and hunting took place in the park. The warship on the right has
tentatively been identified as the *Mary Rose*, a later namesake of Henry VIII's
ill-fated vessel.

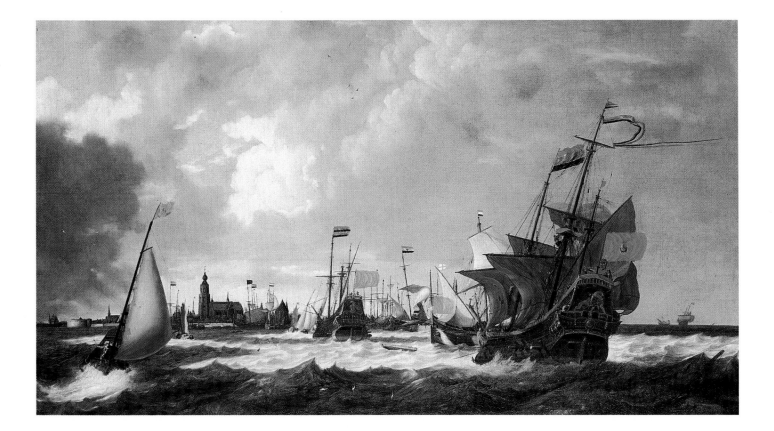

**Plate 11. A View of Hoorn with the Ships 'Hercules' and 'Eenhorn'.
Bonaventura Peeters the Elder, 1634**

Peeters is best known for dramatic shipwreck and storm pictures. Here, he
works in a naturalistic idiom, evoking a breezy day in the roads off Hoorn, one
of the most prosperous ports of the Zuider Zee, prominent in the East Indies
trade and the fishing industry. The Dutch warship on the right of the picture,
the *Hercules*, has just come to anchor, and is lowering the sails on her fore and
mainmasts. She flies the Dutch flag at the fore. Immediately ahead of her, the
stern of a small merchantman is visible. Beyond lies a second warship, the
Eenhorn, with sails furled. On the left is a single-masted speeljacht, a type of
Dutch pleasure yacht common in the seventeenth century. The identity of the
Hercules is not certain. Two ships called *Eenhorn* are recorded: a warship of
34 guns built in 1623, and one of 30 guns built in 1625.

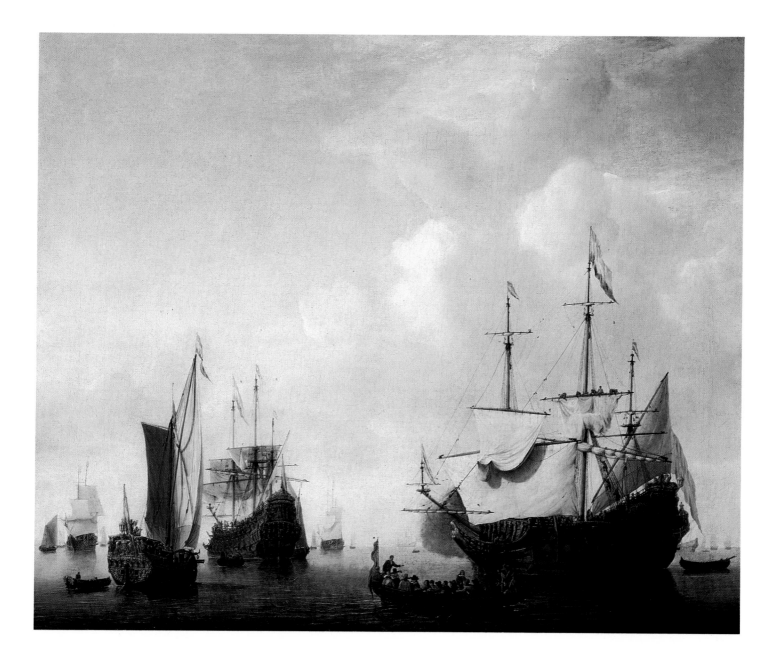

Plate 12. Calm: A Dutch Flagship coming to Anchor with a States Yacht before a Light Air. Willem Van de Velde the Younger

One of the younger Van de Velde's early calms. The eye is led into the luminous space of the picture along a central vista defined by a receding row of ships. The ship on the right, shown on the starboard tack with only the lateen mizen sail drawing, with forecourse and the fore and main topsails loosed, and with men on the main topsail yard beginning to furl the sails, has been tentatively identified by Michael Robinson as the *Eendracht*, built in 1653. She is firing a salute to starboard. The states yacht on the left, with the arms of Orange and twin supports on the tafferel, is the yacht laid down for Prince Frederik Henrik in 1647. Beyond is a second warship, the *Huis te Zwieten*, at one time the flagship of Admiral de Ruyter, built at Amsterdam in 1653 and captured by the English in 1665.

Plate 13 (overleaf). The Four Days Battle, 11–14 June 1666. Abraham Storck

This long-running and bloody engagement in the Channel, during the second Anglo-Dutch War, resulted in no decisive outcome. The English fleet under Albemarle was outnumbered and severely mauled by the Dutch, but escaped through the timely reappearance of Prince Rupert's squadron; he had been despatched to counter a threat from the hostile French fleet. Storck's picture is an amalgam of incidents from the battle, and does not represent a particular moment in time. The two fleets, Dutch on the left, English on the right, are seen close-hauled on the starboard tack, mostly quarter stern view. The ship on the right is the *Prince Royal*, flagship of Admiral Berkeley of the white squadron, which grounded on the Galloper sands and surrendered to Tromp on the third day of the battle. On the left is de Ruyter's *Zeven Provincien*, probably a rather more accurate ship portrait than those of the English fleet. Ahead of the *Prince Royal* is Albemarle in the *Royal Charles*. The English ship in the distance which is being boarded is apparently Berkeley's *Swiftsure*, captured on the first day.

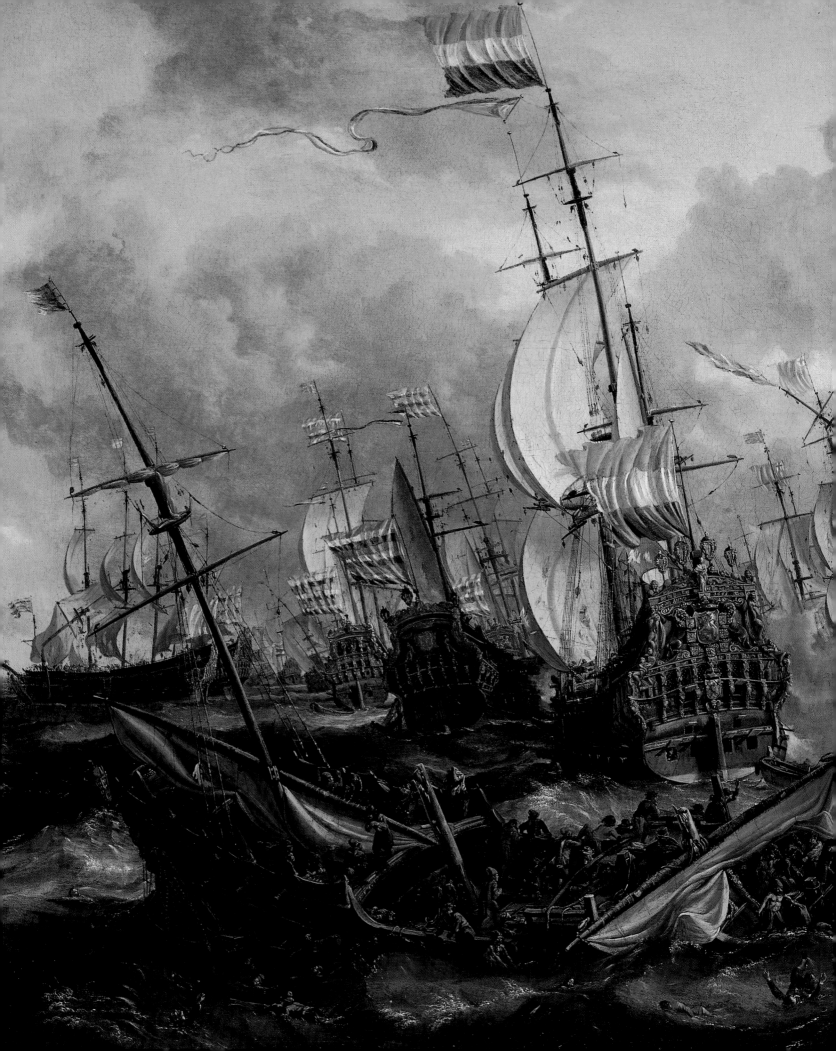

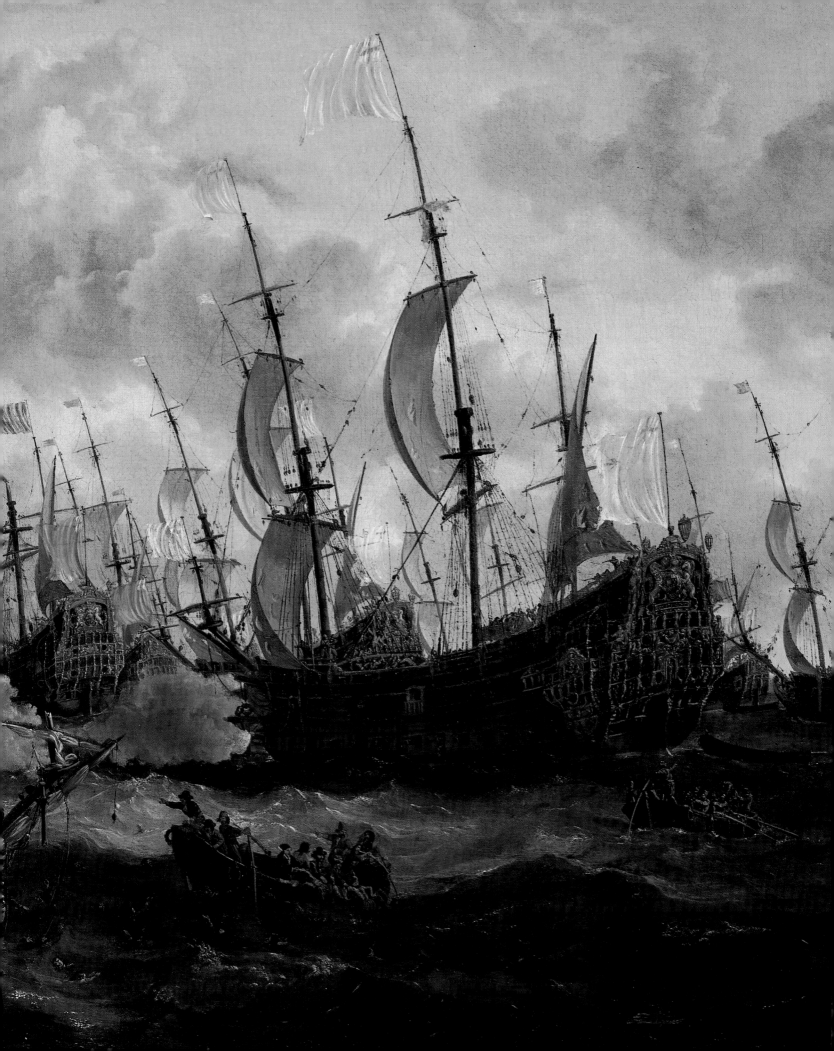

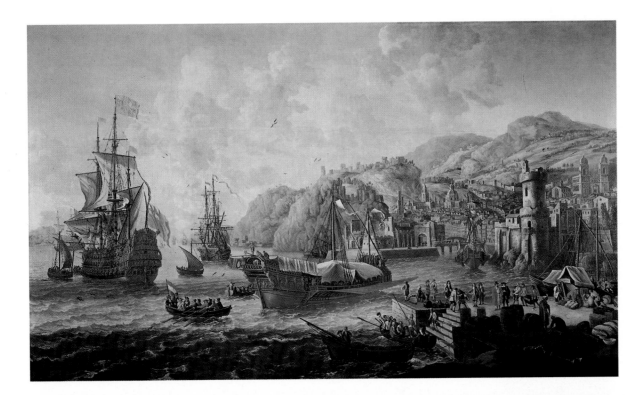

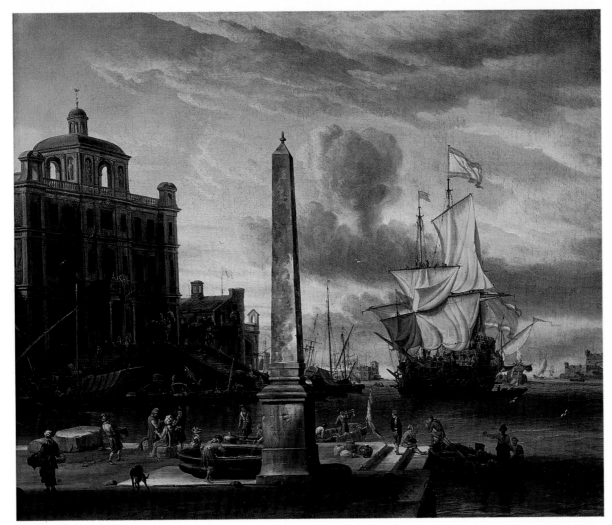

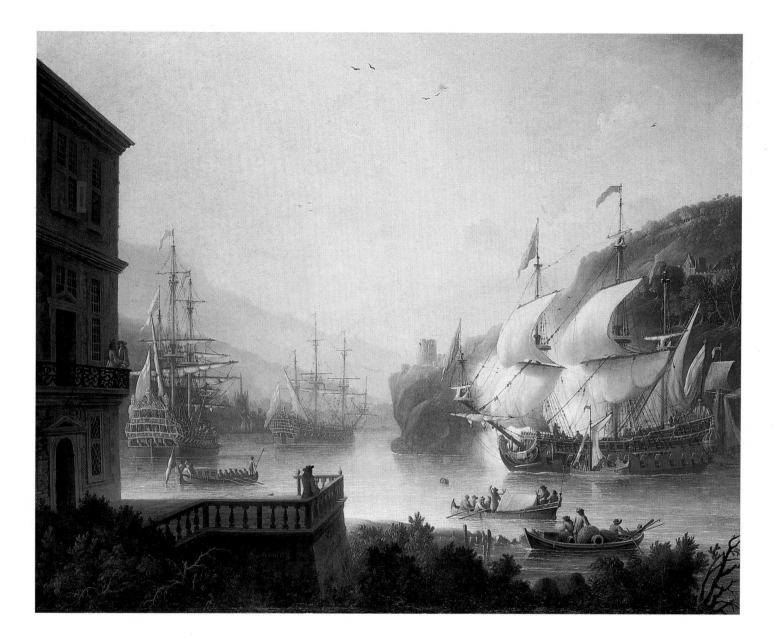

**Plate 14. Ships and Galleys in an Italian Port.
Unidentified artist, *c.*1680**

The enormous size of the picture, and the presence of the royal standard on
the English warship to the left, have led to suggestions that it might be
associated with a royal event, for example the departure of Charles II's bride,
Catherine of Braganza, from Lisbon in April 1662. However, the imposing
English three-decker, seen from the stern quarter and as yet unidentified, is
certainly of a later date, and the town bears no resemblance to Lisbon. The
scene as a whole is probably imaginary, combining a picturesque walled city
of Italian character, with ships of different nations. The centre of the picture
is dominated by a large galley, her deck covered by an awning, oars raised
coming to anchor. A second galley lies nearby. To the left, a Dutch rowing boat
carries officers to land, presumably from one of the warships in the distance.
Two figures take leave of one another on the crowded quayside.

**Plate 15. A Venetian Pilgrim Ship in a Mediterranean Port.
Abraham Storck, 1697**

A typical example of the capriccio port scene in which Storck excelled. An
obelisk dominates the foreground and divides the composition of the present
picture in two. A stately two-decker warship fills the right-hand side of the
picture. She lies at anchor, sails hanging slackly to dry, flying the flag of
Jerusalem at the main to indicate her status as a pilgrim ship.

Plate 16. Shipping in an Estuary. Jan van Beecq, 1701

Previously identified as a view of the Bristol Avon, the topographical features
of the scene preclude such a possibility. Two English two-deckers lie at anchor
in the river. A third is slowly approaching the anchorage in the evening sun,
and firing a salute as she does so. Van Beecq is known chiefly as a ship
portraitist in the tradition of the Van de Veldes; he rarely produced
compositions of such charm and accomplishment as this one.

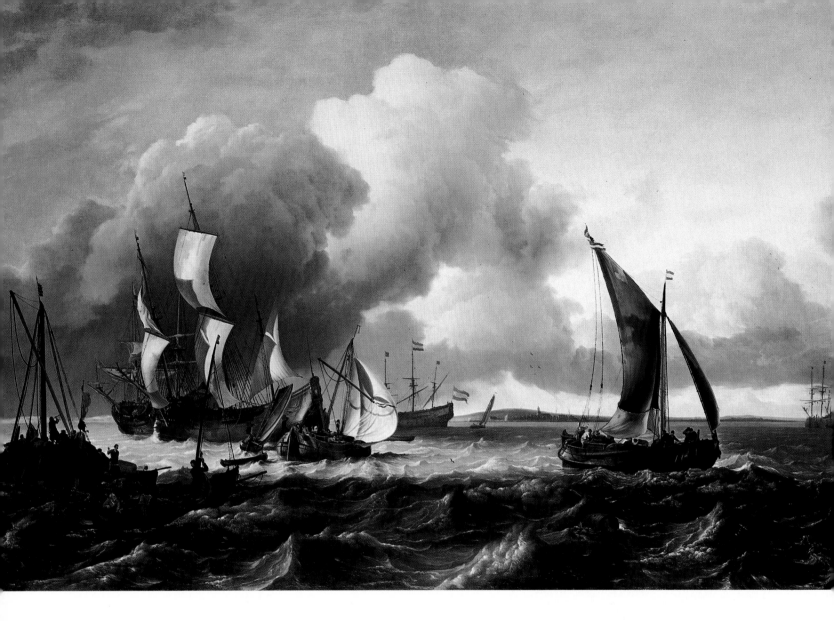

Plate 17. Dutch Shipping off the Coast in a Fresh Breeze.
Ludolf Bakhuizen, 1665

The setting for the picture is the merchant shipping roadstead off the eastern
coast of Texel, one of the group of northern islands guarding the entrance to
the Zuider Zee. A group of three larger ships is shown in the middle distance
on the left: a fluyt under sail with a larger ship partly hidden beyond, and to
the right and further back a Dutch warship at anchor. Another fluyt lies at
anchor on the far right. In the foreground a group of small craft, so typical
of Dutch inland waterways, is tossed about by the boisterous weather. On the
left is a wijdschip, with a weyschuit or punter lowering sail in the immediate
foreground. Another wijdschip is seen from the stern under billowing canvas,
close under the stern of the fluyt. On the right is a kaag, a common type of
ferryboat, running before the wind with sprit-rigged mainsail and a foresail.
Bakhuizen combines this anthology of beautifully observed craft with a
composition of majestic proportions.

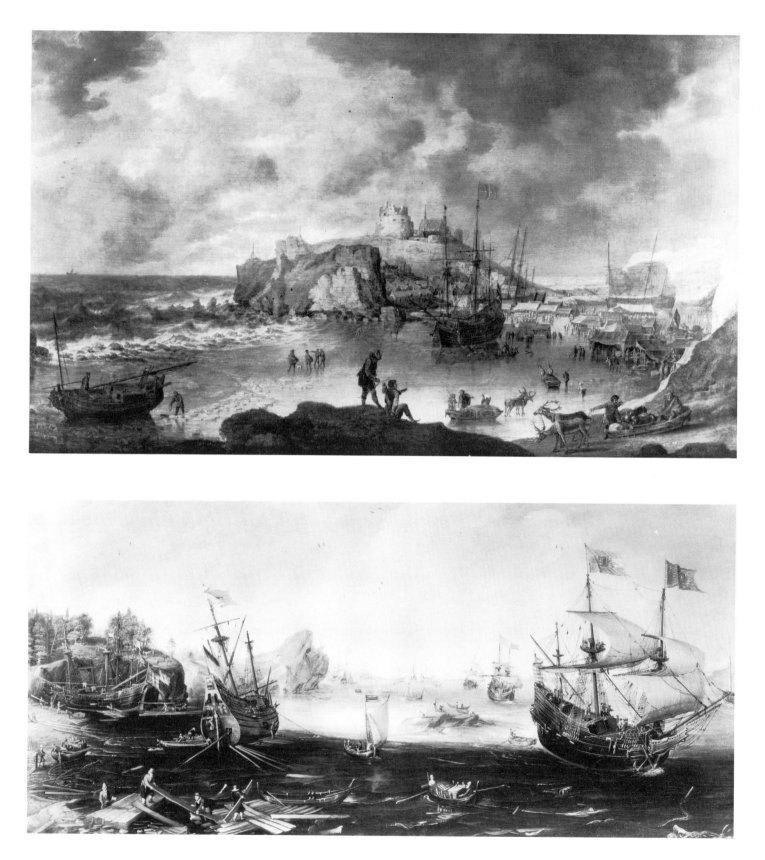

32. The Port of Archangel. Bonaventura Peeters the Elder, 1644

Archangel was an Arctic port much used by English and Dutch ships trading
with Russia. Peeters, setting his scene in winter, convincingly conveys a feeling
of the port's intense cold, which, in view of his extensive travels, he may well
have experienced at first hand.

33. Loading Timber at a Northern Port. Andries van Eertvelt

On the right is a Dutch ship from Amsterdam, before the wind, presumably
laden with timber despite her curiously precarious stance. To the left, ships
inshore load timber through stern ports. The setting of this industrious scene,
painted with all of Eertvelt's appealing eccentricity, is probably imaginary,
though it is evidently designed to evoke the atmosphere of a northern port.

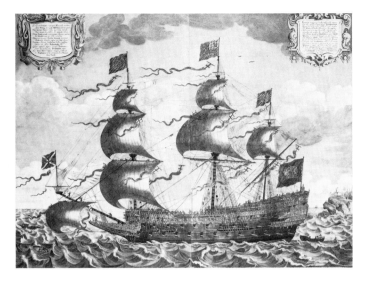

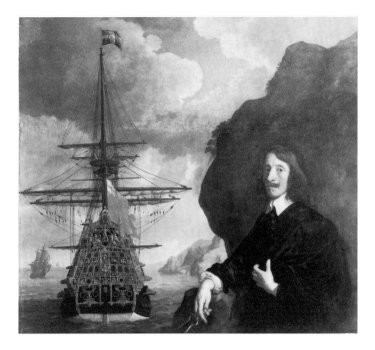

years of personal rule (1629–40), Charles revived the tax known as Ship Money, but provoked opposition by imposing it upon all areas of the country rather than on the seaports which had traditionally found it. In spite of opposition by John Hampden in a famous case of 1637, the tax brought in some £190,000 a year and the navy prospered. But it was not to last. No matter how worthy the result in terms of naval regeneration, the imposi-

tion of Ship Money was one of many arbitrary acts which alienated Charles from his countrymen, and led to the outbreak of civil war.

6. THE ANGLO-DUTCH WARS

The execution of Charles I was followed by the foundation of a Commonwealth, later to be transformed into a Protectorate. One of its early moves to stimulate the revival of English seaborne trade was to pass a Navigation Act in 1651. Under this all trade entering or leaving England had to be carried in English ships or in ships of the exporting country. It also laid down that all ships of foreign nations, including warships, must salute English warships when met in English waters. In anticipation of this Act, Cromwell had continued Charles's rebuilding of the English fleet, and concentrated mainly on ships of up to about 1,000 tons, with two gundecks, mounting between 60 and 80 guns. In the first five years of Parliamentary rule, no fewer than eighty-six new ships of the line, almost all of them of this size, had been added to the English fleet.

The Navigation Act and the rapid rebuilding of the fleet was of course aimed directly against Dutch shipping, the great car-

riers of world trade, and the Dutch were not slow to respond. In 1652 an English squadron under the command of Robert Blake encountered in English waters a Dutch fleet commanded by Marten Tromp and demanded the salute as laid down in the Act. Tromp was slow in responding and Blake fired guns to remind him of his obligation, only to be answered with a broadside from Tromp's flagship. A scrappy engagement followed in which the Dutch lost two ships. Two months later, the official declaration of war followed.

With the English Channel as the main highway of Dutch overseas trade, particularly to the East Indies, the only way of getting Dutch merchant ships safely past the English fleet was to sail them in convoy. These were large and unwieldy operations, outward bound ships from Holland being escorted as far as La Rochelle and homeward bound ships being collected there and escorted home. An English fleet was always there to dispute the

34. 'Sovereign of the Seas'. John Payne, c.1637
The magnificence of the *Sovereign of the Seas* made her of considerable interest to painters, engravers, and their public alike.

35. Peter Pett and the 'Sovereign of the Seas'. Sir Peter Lely
Peter Pett was a member of a famous family of shipwrights, and is here shown holding a pair of calipers to symbolize his craft. He supervised the building of the *Sovereign of the Seas* between 1635 and 1637, to the designs of his father Phineas (see also fig. 56). Lely painted only the portrait section of this picture: the ship is by another contemporary hand (conceivably Isaac Sailmaker).

passage. Of the six major battles of this two-year war [fig. 36], two were direct convoy battles. The fortunes of battle, if counted in ships lost and seamen killed, lay with the English, mainly because their warships were larger and armed with a greater number of guns than those of the Dutch, who had to be able to sail in shallower waters. In terms of merchant ships captured or lost, the English advantage was considerable. English privateers operating in the Channel and southern North Sea reaped a rich harvest, bringing in 1,700 merchant ships to be set against a loss of 440 to the Dutch. These prizes formed the basis of a hugely expanded English merchant fleet, which, from very modest beginnings, gradually came to challenge the Dutch monopoly.

A second war with Holland was fought between 1665 and 1667, again basically to resolve the trade rivalry between the two nations. England was once again a monarchy and the king's brother, the Duke of York, was appointed Lord High Admiral. One of his first acts was to draw up instructions for the better management of the fleet, a long-needed reorganization setting out in detail the duties and responsibilities not only of the serving officers but also of all officials in the administration and the dock-yards. He also commanded the fleet in the first battle of the new war fought off Lowestoft. It was a considerable victory with the Dutch fleet driven off with heavy losses.

The decision of France to enter the war on the side of Holland, though in fact she took no active part in it, was, however, the cause of a severe English defeat in the Four Days Battle. Part of the English fleet was sent westward down Channel in the mistaken belief that a French squadron was about to sail from Brest to reinforce the Dutch. For three days the remainder of the English ships fought against considerable odds and though it was a distinct Dutch victory [plate 13], the English fleet was far from destroyed. Less than two months later it was at sea again and had slightly the better of an engagement with the Dutch off the North Foreland. The war ended with a painful and humiliating rebuff to the English fleet. Upon expectations of peace and to relieve the hard-pressed Treasury, the warships were not recommissioned in 1667 but continued at their winter moorings in the Medway river. In June the Dutch Admiral de Ruyter arrived in the Thames with a fleet, captured the town of Sheerness, and sailed up the Medway [fig. 38]. Eight of the laid-up warships were burnt at their moorings, a ninth, the

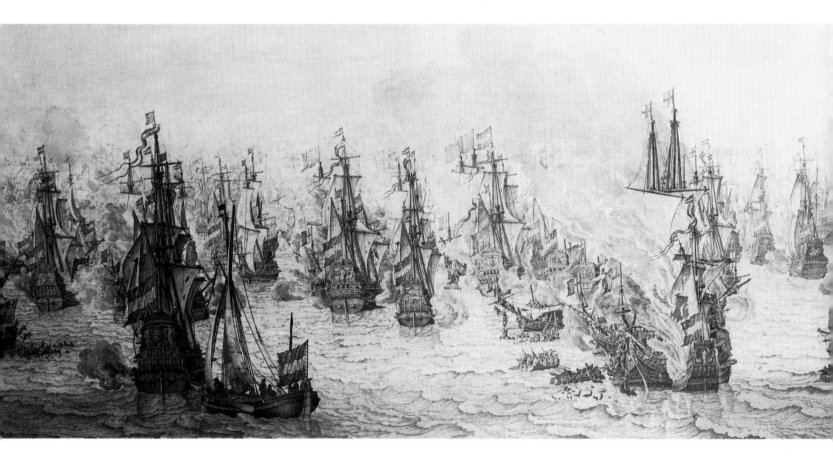

36. The Battle of Scheveningen, 31 July 1653. Willem Van de Velde the Elder, 1655

The battle portrayed was the final engagement of the first Anglo-Dutch war. On the right of Van de Velde's crowded composition, the burning *Andrew* is grappled by the Dutch fireship *Fortuin*; in the middle distance the *Brederode*, flagship of the Dutch Commander-in-Chief Marten Tromp (who was to die in this conflict), is engaged with the *Resolution*. (See also fig. 43.)

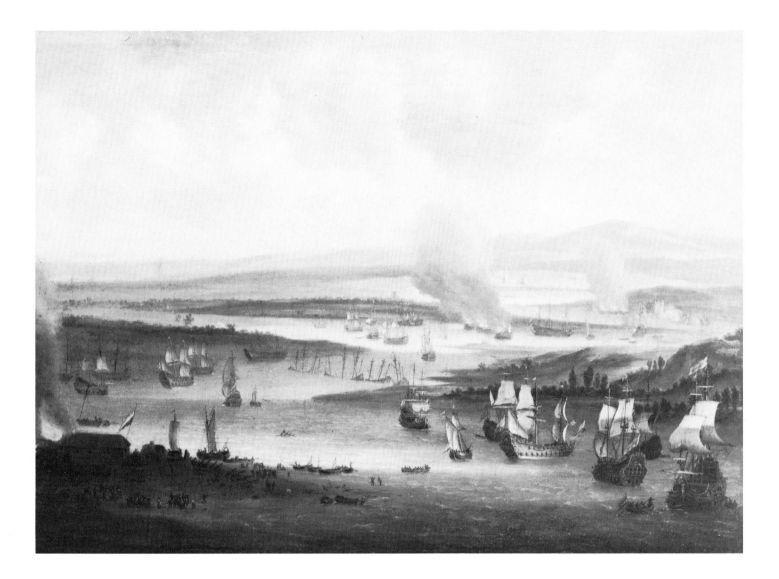

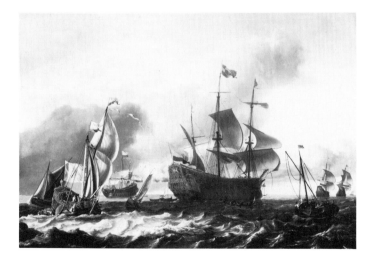

English flagship *Royal Charles* [fig. 37], was towed home to Holland as a prize. Nevertheless, in the peace which followed, Holland was forced to give up her colony in North America, to leave England in sole possession of that rich and prospering land.

Five years later a third war against the Dutch was fought, this time with France on the English side. The Dutch situation was perilous; with a French land invasion in the south the fleet had inevitably to be concentrated in Dutch waters to guard against an allied invasion from the sea in the north. The war was fought by the Dutch navy with consummate skill and three attempts to land an army in Holland under cover of the Anglo-French fleet, two off Schoonevveldt and one off the Texel [plate 18], were frustrated. The allied lack of success in each of the sea battles was due mainly to the reluctance of the French

37. 'Royal Charles' brought into Dutch Waters.
Ludolf Bakhuizen, 1667
De Ruyter's most valuable prize from the Medway invasion was the *Royal Charles*. To judge by the number and type of smaller craft in attendance and by the symbolic contrast between dark skies behind and light ahead, her subsequent journey from England to the Netherlands is here almost complete.

38. The Dutch in the Medway, 9–14 June 1667. Willem Schellinks
Admiral de Ruyter's audacious foray into English waters is here viewed from above captured Sheerness. In the middle distance lie the ships sunk at Mussell Bank; beyond, the *Unity* is captured by *Vrede*, and fireships wreak further havoc just to the left of the fated English flagship *Royal Charles*, soon to be taken.

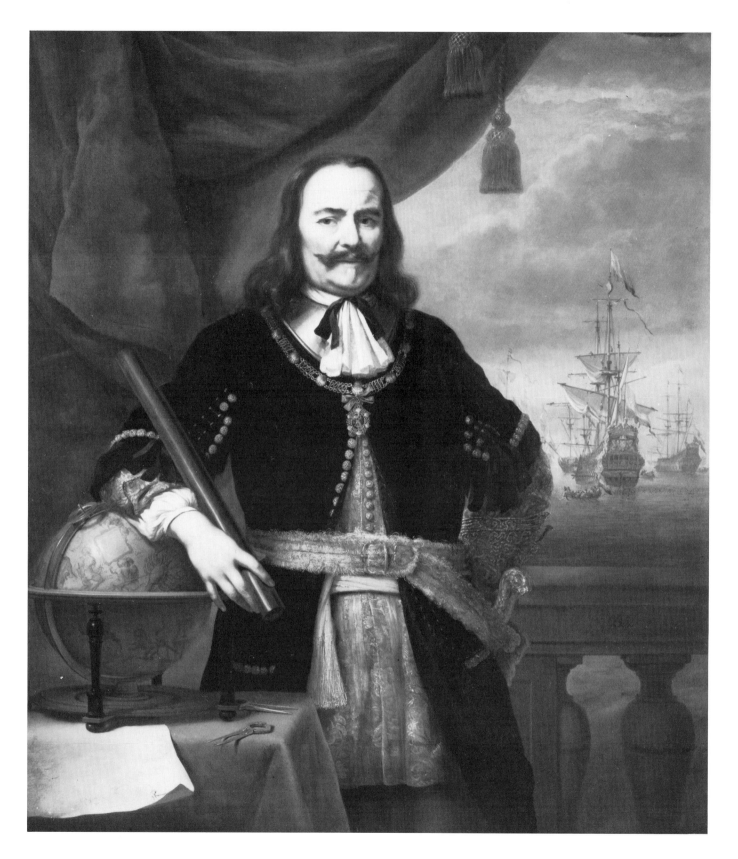

39. Portrait of Michiel Andrienszoon de Ruyter. Ferdinand Bol, 1667

Commissioned shortly after he had masterminded victory over England in the Four Days Battle of 1666, this likeness of the imperious and brilliant Admiral Michiel de Ruyter (1607–76) was painted by a pupil of Rembrandt. In the right background de Ruyter's flagship, the *Zeven Provincien*, appears together with other ships of the Dutch fleet.

squadron to engage at anything but long range. The war was brought to an indecisive end with no concessions on either side beyond a slight easing of the terms of the English Navigation Act in favour of the Dutch.

The three Anglo-Dutch wars threw up some remarkable men as sea commanders. Three soldiers, translated to the sea, became the principal fighting admirals of the English fleet, Robert Blake [fig. 40], George Monck, Duke of Albemarle, and Prince Rupert, cousin of Charles I. Blake was the most brilliant of the three, handling his fleet with commendable skill even when the odds were heavily against him, but the other two were not far behind. Between them, they developed the tactical control of fleets in battle in place of the indiscriminate chaos of previous fights. The start was made by Blake when he issued a disciplinary code, the *Articles of War*, and a tactical code, the *Fighting Instructions*, in 1653, which were expanded and refined later by the Duke of York, Monck, and Prince Rupert.

On the Dutch side, the great names were Marten and Cornelis Tromp, father and son, and the family of Evertsen, of whom the four most famous were all admirals who commanded fleets and squadrons during the three wars. But the most famous of all, standing head and shoulders above every other admiral, English or Dutch, was Michiel de Ruyter [fig. 39], a born leader, a fine seaman, and a man of exemplary character. He fought in all three wars as admiral, in the second and third as commander-in-chief. He was a skilled tactician and, like Blake, worked ceaselessly to introduce the ordered handling of a fleet in battle. He is credited with the introduction of the controlled line of battle in place of the previous indiscriminate charge, but though this may well have been his philosophy of battle, the impatience of the Tromps and the Evertsens to get to grips with

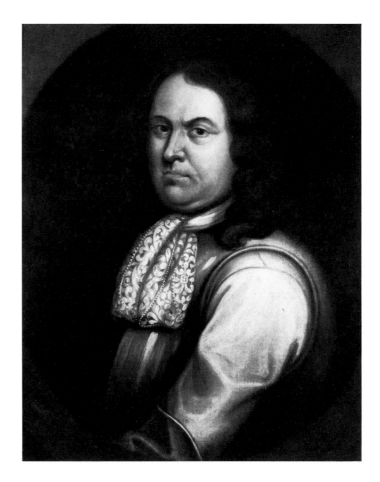

their enemies brought it all to nought. In his lifetime his name was one to conjure with; today he is recognized as Holland's greatest admiral, indeed as one of the great admirals of all time and all navies.

7. THE ART OF THE VAN DE VELDES

The great maritime events of the seventeenth century would be poorly represented if it were not for the achievements of the Dutch painters. Of the land battles of the English Civil War, we have only crude illustrations in the form of woodcuts. For the Anglo-Dutch conflict, on the other hand, there exist numerous paintings of great sophistication, which vividly convey the realities of the war at sea. Marine painters found lucrative employment in recording the achievements of the Dutch

navy. Two of the most famous, Willem Van de Velde the Elder (1611–93) and his son Willem the Younger (1633–1707), changed sides halfway through, coming to England to record events, primarily for Charles II, in the early 1670s.

Painters can only afford to be patriotic if they can find patrons to buy or commission their work. It would be too easy to interpret the move of the Van de Veldes simply as a reflection of the changing balance of power and wealth between Holland and

40. Portrait of Robert Blake. Unidentified artist
This modest and rather unattractive portrait of Robert Blake (1599–1657) was probably painted *c.*1640 before he achieved fame, initially as a commander in the Civil War (on the side of Parliament), later as a general-at-sea in the first Anglo-Dutch war, and finally for his action against the Spanish fleet at Santa Cruz in 1656. After his death his body lay in state in the hall of the Queen's House, Greenwich.

England. The disastrous conditions in Holland following a land invasion by the French made it impossible for artists like the Van de Veldes to continue their work. Family problems, too, hastened their departure: Willem the Elder's affair with another woman had led to a breakdown of relations with his wife. Finally, there was the tempting prospect of employment at the court of an English king noted for his generosity and love of the sea.

Born in Leiden in 1611, the son of a seaman, Willem Van de Velde the Elder emerged as an artist in the 1640s, with drawings of local craft and his characteristic grisailles. Drawn in pen and ink on painted grounds, they combine the precision of engraving with the delicacy and luminosity of painting. Van de Velde's portraits of individual ships [fig. 41] are breathtaking in the complexity of form and detail which they reveal. What was formalized in the grisailles was a profound knowledge of ships observed and sketched with obsessive passion in hundreds of fresh and vivid drawings. Van de Velde could not only draw a stern with an unerring eye for its architectural proportions, its wealth of decoration and sculptural detail, he knew how to draw the ship herself in correct perspective, what effect the wind has on the set of the sails, how one part of the rigging relates to the next, the whole way in which a ship moves and sits in the water. He often combined two or three views of ships from different angles in the same composition, with perhaps a jetty or beach scene in the foreground, or a distant port scene behind.

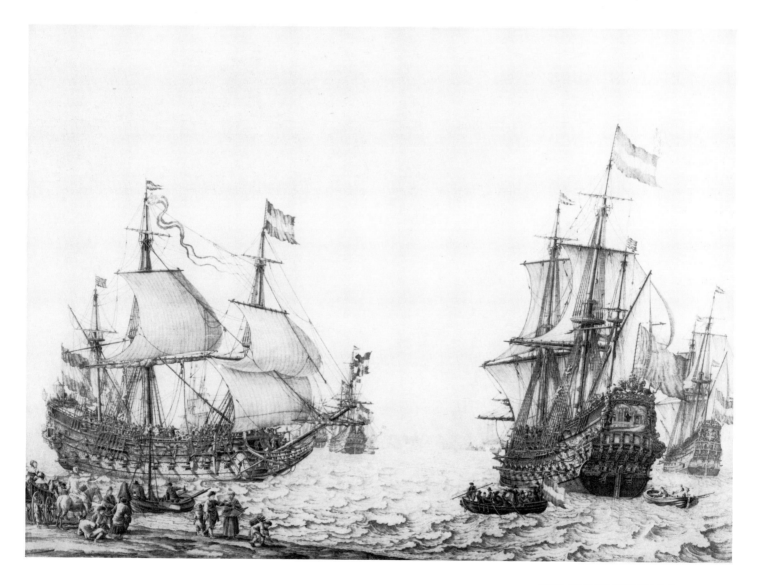

41. Two Views of a Dutch Flagship. Willem Van de Velde the Elder, 1654

The flagship shown under sail in two positions is almost certainly the *Huis te Oosterwyk*, built in 1653 and named after the Lord of the Manor of Oosterwyk. The picture demonstrates amply the artistic possibilities of grisaille painting: here Van de Velde has successfully fused extraordinary attention to detail with a notable compositional grandeur.

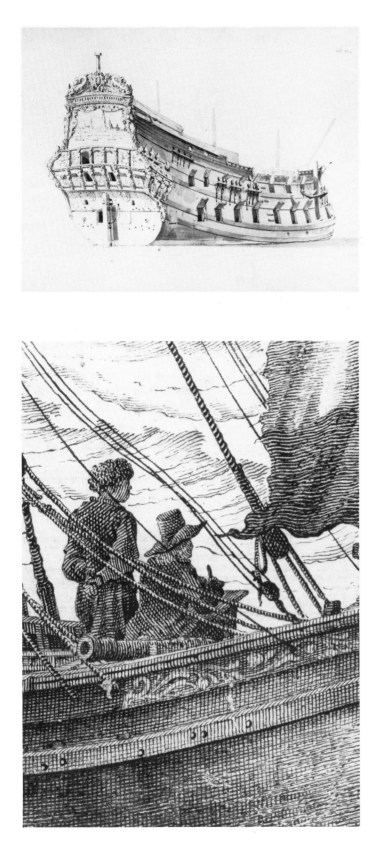

His figures were no less beautifully drawn than his ships, and he employed a wide range of character types.

Willem Van de Velde the Elder emerged on the public stage as a battle painter. He was uniquely equipped to record the conflicts of the first Anglo-Dutch war and later conflicts with the Swedes in the Baltic. He seems to have occupied a semi-official position with the Dutch navy, and many of his commissions must have emanated from official sources. A drawing of Dutch ships in the foreground, with the distant English fleet cruising off the Dutch coast, is inscribed, 'View of the fleet, ready to sail, before the harbour, when I put to sea in a galliot with letters for Admiral Tromp on Friday afternoon at 2 o'clock, 8 August 1653'. The big grisaille of the ensuing Battle of Scheveningen [fig. 36], shows a galliot in the left foreground, with the artist at work sketching [fig. 43].

In September 1658 Van de Velde sailed with the Dutch fleet to the Baltic on board the *Stavoren*, and witnessed the Battle of the Sound at first hand [plate 19]. Direct observation of a sea battle was something few marine artists had experienced and it gives Van de Velde's work an uncompromising veracity. He had to cope with far greater numbers of ships than in his ship portrait grisailles, and to interpret them in violent action, but his talent for ordered and rhythmic composition never deserted him. He sometimes raised his viewpoint, closer to the bird's-eye view of earlier and simpler battle painters, for the sake of clarity, but the detail expended on individual ships is as precise as ever, and so is the enveloping sense of drama and danger.

It was left to Willem Van de Velde the Younger to interpret his father's lessons in oils. They worked side by side for forty years, developing the most famous partnership in the history of marine painting. While Charles II paid a salary of £100 to the elder for 'taking and making draughts of sea fights', he paid £100 to the younger 'for putting the said draughts into colours'. The thousands of their drawings which survive, 1,200 at the National Maritime Museum at Greenwich alone, constitute the single most comprehensive record of seventeenth-century shipping, from fleets and battles [fig. 44], to stately warships [fig. 42] and the smallest of inshore craft. To his father's clarity of observation and profound nautical experience, Van de Velde the Younger brought the ideas of the new school of realist landscape painters. He had studied for a time during the late 1640s at Weesp with Simon de Vlieger, and imbibed the principles of atmospheric seascape painting from that notable master.

To de Vlieger's chamber music, Van de Velde the Younger brings the full orchestra. There is an opulence of form in his treatment of ships, a complexity of composition and of chiaroscuro, and a sumptuous palette that can only be described

42. Portrait of the 'Gouda'. Willem Van de Velde the Younger, *c.*1664

The *Gouda*, carrying 56 guns, was first mentioned in 1656. She was wrecked in 1683. On the tafferel at the stern of the vessel is depicted a view of the town of Gouda, with the River Ijssel in the foreground.

43. Detail of fig. 36

In this detail from *The Battle of Scheveningen* (fig. 36), the elder Van de Velde depicts himself aboard a galliot, observing and sketching the progress of the conflict. Though he witnessed in a similar way at least six battles of the Anglo-Dutch wars he rarely portrayed himself as prominently as this: the aim is to remind us of his presence at this important event and thereby to convince us of the complete accuracy of what is represented.

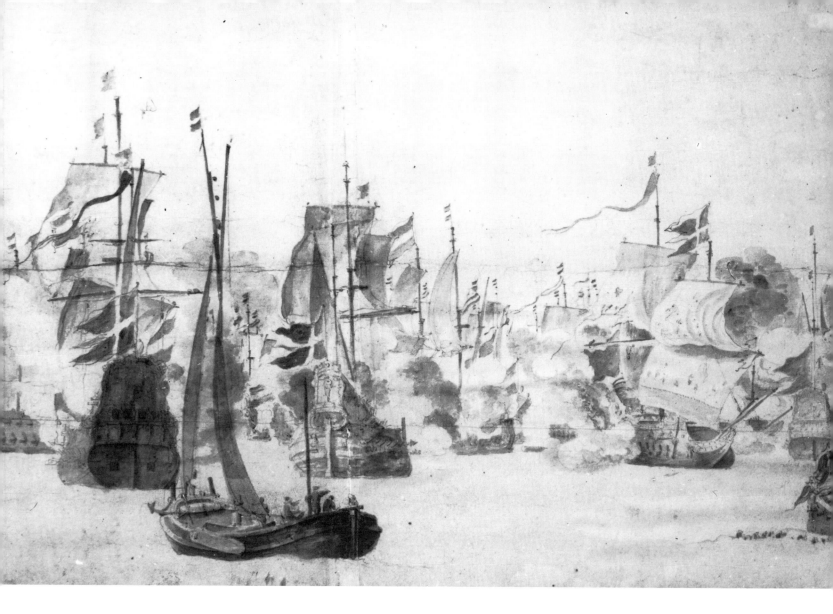

as baroque. A panorama like *The Battle of the Texel* [plate 18] is a virtuoso performance, a spectacle of sea power on the grand scale, superbly organized, intensely dramatic. *The Action with Barbary Pirates* [plate 21] is a piece of high theatre: burning boats against a night sky, falling spars, fluttering flags, torn sails, and an atmosphere of carnage. Van de Velde combines all this with an unerring eye for the thing seen, the ship as it really is, the movement of the waves, the effect of the weather. He and his father never ceased to observe or to experiment, striving always to improve and refine their art. Van de Velde the Younger's great luminous calms, his ceremonial pictures of fleets arriving and departing, his studies of states yachts, his noble ship portraits, storms and shipwrecks, provided a repertoire of motifs and themes that would continue to inspire his successors [plates

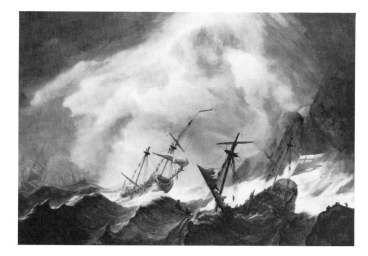

44. The Battle of the Sound, 8 November 1658. Willem Van de Velde the Elder, 1658

A section from a long drawing depicting the battle between the Dutch and Swedish fleets, of which Van de Velde made a finished grisaille (also in the collection of the National Maritime Museum). Prominent in the foreground is the artist's galliot.

45. A Storm: Two English Ships wrecked on a Rocky Coast. Studio of Willem Van de Velde the Younger, *c.*1700

The ship in the right foreground, sinking by the head with heavy seas breaking over her, is the only part of the picture which may be confidently ascribed to Van de Velde himself. The remainder was evidently painted in conjunction with studio assistants. The dramatic power of the composition as a whole is nevertheless considerable.

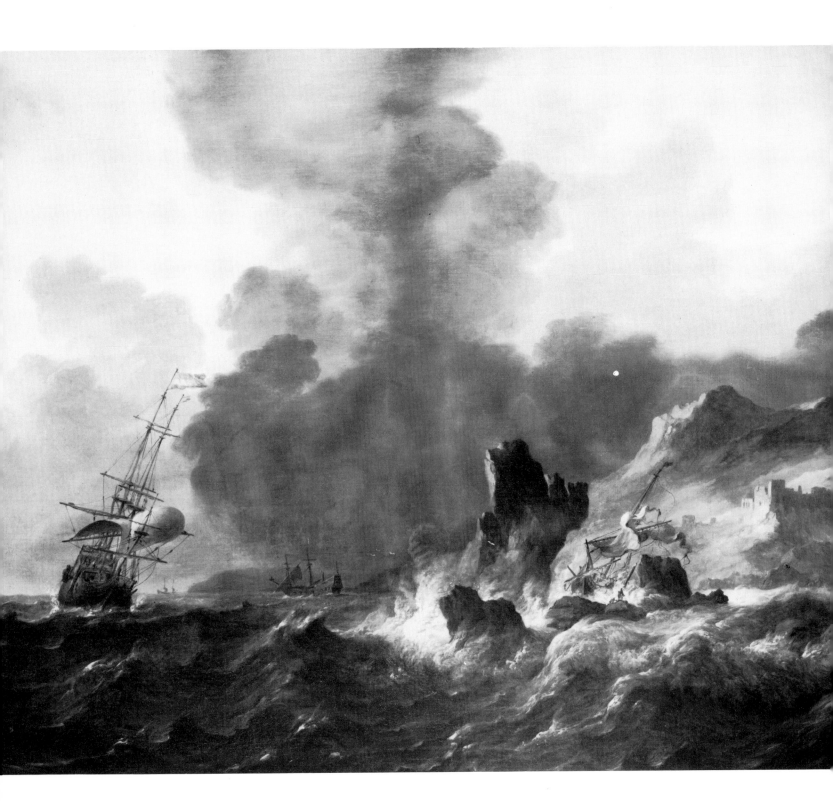

46. A Dutch Ship wrecked on a Rocky Coast. Ludolf Bakhuizen

In this unapologetically dramatic early work by Bakhuizen, three Dutch ships
in a storm are seen at various stages of peril. Its sombre if theatrical tones are
characteristic of his attempts at this period to emulate, and if possible to outdo,
the fashionable wreck scenes of Simon de Vlieger.

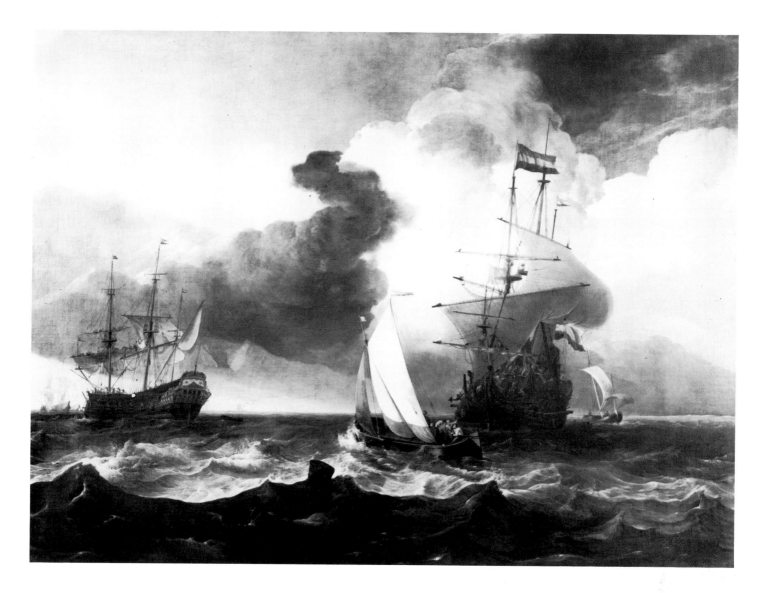

12, 20, 22, 23; fig. 45]. It is difficult to think of any significant marine painter for the next 150 years who remained immune to his influence.

Another marine artist of the time was Jan Van de Capelle (1624–79). He was a wealthy merchant who painted a small group of luminous and mysterious calms, artful and decorative arrangements of boats and sails, apparently for his own pleasure. But his work cannot compare in range with that of the Van de Veldes. The only seascapist of comparable stature to the Van de Veldes was Ludolf Bakhuizen (1631–1708). Bakhuizen had come to art by way of clerking and calligraphy, and he must have benefited professionally when the Van de Veldes left for London. His pictures of shipping have grandeur and depth, clean drawing, clear light and an awesome sense of space [plate

17; fig. 46]. His colours too are much cooler, luminous greens, sleeting greys. He was an accomplished figure painter, as some of his independent subject pictures show. Bakhuizen takes liberties with facts, even when recording specific events, in the interests of imaginative composition. Like the work of the Van de Veldes, his pictures appealed to the grander types of patron, and he was represented in aristocratic collections throughout Europe. He must have had good English connections, because he painted several impressive battle scenes from the Anglo-French wars, including Barfleur and Vigo Bay [plates 25, 26].

Van de Velde the Younger and Bakhuizen represent the tip of an iceberg. The growth of a market in marine paintings in the second half of the seventeenth century coincided with a tremendous upsurge in profits from trade, much of it finding its

47. A Smalschip Close-Hauled, passing under the Bow of a Dutch Flagship. Hendrick Jacobsz. Dubbels

Dubbels was an Amsterdam painter working chiefly within the tradition established by his master, Simon de Vlieger. In this scene, where strong contrasts of light and dark dominate both sea and sky, there is ample evidence of the influence Dubbels exerted on his own pupil, Ludolf Bakhuizen.

way into the pockets of Dutch and English merchants. While a few new subjects made their appearance, like the whaling scenes of Adriaan van Salm and Adam Silo for example, or the capriccio port scenes by Abraham Storck [plate 15], the majority of painters were content to supply a readily identifiable market with saleable work. It is difficult to be certain of the sources of their patronage. Many of the ship pictures and sea battles were evidently specific commissions, but decorative sea pieces, which often feature in pictures of Dutch interiors, must have had a universal appeal.

8. ANGLO-FRENCH WARS 1688–1713

One of the legacies of the three Anglo-Dutch wars was the development of tactics for a fleet in battle. The national fleets had grown so large that, even though they were divided into three squadrons each commanded by an admiral and with its own coloured flag for instant recognition, attempts to develop coherent central control of the fleet as a whole failed. The failure was due in part to the lack of any code of signals, but more to the impetuosity of the junior admirals commanding the squadrons. Almost all the major actions of the wars developed into three minor and separate battles as the squadrons dashed in to engage their opposite numbers at the closest possible range.

One answer to this fragmentary form of attack was to organize the three squadrons in a single line of battle so that the commander-in-chief could enforce his control of the fleet as a whole. Certainly Blake thought of this as the solution; Monck had similar ideas; and de Ruyter recognized that it had to come.

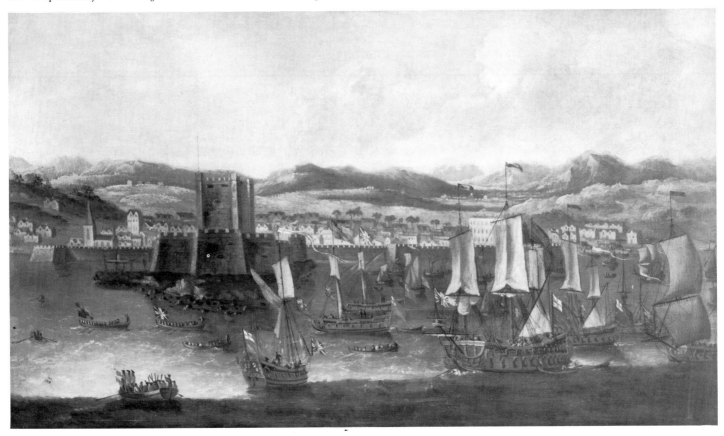

48. Landing of William III at Carrickfergus, 14 June 1690. Unidentified artist
King William is seen in a barge, about to land at Carrickfergus Castle. On his voyage to Ireland he had been escorted by Sir Clowdisley Shovell, whose flag flies from the *Monck* (right foreground).

49. William III. Jan Wyck, 1688
William of Orange (1650–1702) is depicted after landing with the Anglo-Dutch fleet at Torbay in 1688, a critical phase of the Glorious Revolution which would make him King of England. His horse rears into a familiar pose traditionally symbolic of monarchy.

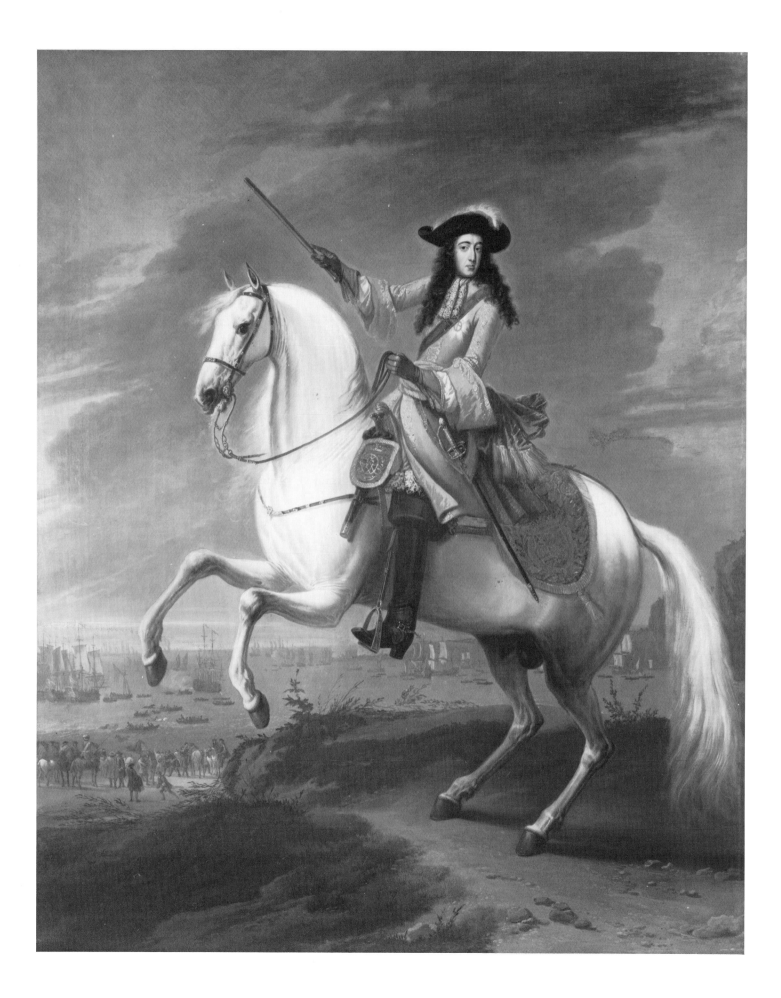

The first evidence of its use can be seen in the Four Days Battle of 1666 [plate 13]. The French historian de Guiche, who witnessed the battle as an observer with the Dutch fleet, wrote: 'Nothing equals the beautiful order of the English at sea. Never was a line drawn straighter than that formed by their ships; thus they bring all their fire to bear upon those who draw near them. . . . They fight like a line of cavalry which is handled according to rule, and applies itself solely to force back those who oppose; whereas the Dutch advance like cavalry whose squadrons leave their ranks and come separately to the charge.' The introduction of the line was the first evolutionary step in the control of a fleet in battle and although it may have introduced a certain rigidity of manoeuvre, it was a great step forward from the disorganized clash of earlier battles.

The 'Glorious Revolution' in England in 1688, in which Parliament invited the Protestant William of Orange [plate 24; fig. 49] to replace the Catholic James II on the throne, provided a new twist to the tangled politics of Europe. Louis XIV was not only moving his armies deep into southern Germany and renewing the threat of invasion of the southern provinces of Holland, but also publicly announced his decision to reinstate James II as king of England. As the first move in this direction he landed James in Ireland with an army of 8,000 men. After some initial success, the attempt failed when the English squadron in the Irish Sea broke James's siege of Londonderry and landed William III and his army near Belfast [fig. 48]. It was enough to bring England and Holland into alliance to hold in check the territorial ambitions of France.

The French navy, under the drive and genius of Jean Colbert, Louis XIV's minister of marine, had by now reached a high level of excellence. The new ships he built were the best designed and best equipped in Europe [fig. 50] and his new system of manning, in which every French seaman served for six months in the navy every three or four years, produced skilled crews without need of compulsory recruitment of mainly unwilling men. If Colbert had been able to train his admirals to the same degree of excellence as he trained their crews, the French fleet would have been formidable indeed.

In the two battles fought at sea during the short war against France, one off Beachy Head, the other off Barfleur, the French had the better of the first, the English and the Dutch the better of the second. In both, the fleets were unevenly matched, the French superiority in numbers being considerable at Beachy Head, the English-Dutch superiority overwhelming at Barfleur [plate 25]. The final episode of Barfleur was a night attack at La Hougue. At the end of the day most of the French fleet had escaped through the perilous passage of the rock-strewn

Alderney Race; the remaining twelve ships had rounded Cap La Hougue and hauled themselves close inshore into the shallows and beyond the range of the English guns. Boats from the English ships went in that night and put them to the torch [fig. 51]. They were all destroyed in full sight of James II and an army of 30,000 men which the French fleet was to have transported to England after it had won the naval battle.

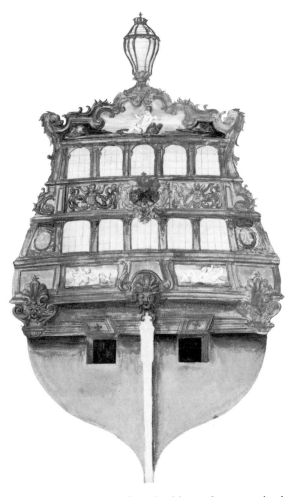

In both these actions the fleets had been drawn up in the new line of battle formation and much of the indecisiveness of the results was due to the rigidity of the formation which inhibited individual squadronal action when an opportunity presented itself. The lack of a strong and steady wind on both occasions also contributed to the failure to achieve a positive result. Nevertheless, the gain of unified control over the movements of a fleet as a whole in battle was certainly a great advance over the undisciplined individual actions which had so characterized the battles of the Anglo-Dutch wars.

Even though, in the end, the defeat at Barfleur broke the

50. Poop of 'Le Volontaire'. Unidentified artist
The details of the decoration distinguish this warship as French. There are *fleurs de lys* on the gunport lids, and the royal monogram is supported by dolphins. *Le Volontaire*, a fourth-rate, was built at Toulon in 1695 and was captured and destroyed by the Anglo-Dutch fleet at the Battle of Vigo Bay on 12 October 1702.

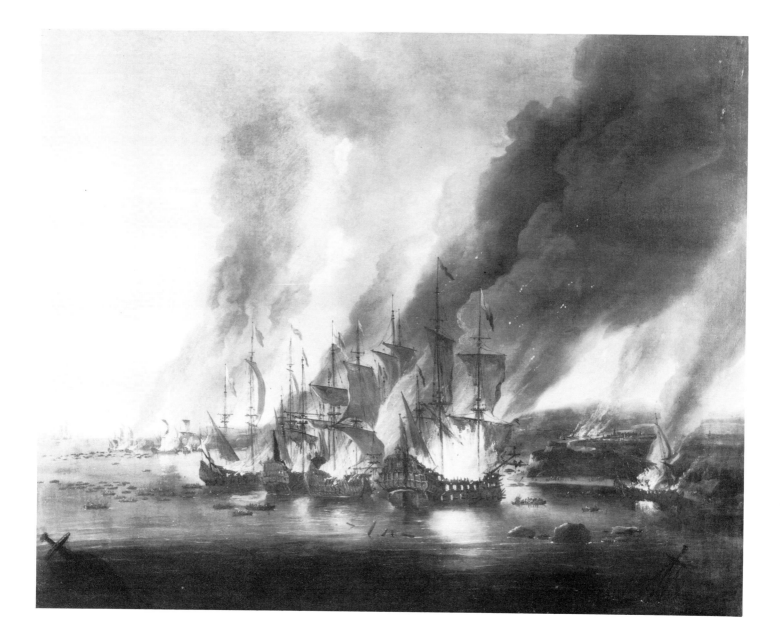

morale of the French fleet, the purely naval side of the war was in fact of less importance to the combatants than the *guerre de course* waged against trade by both sides. It was almost entirely in the hands of privateers, private ships whose owners had received a licence from their government, known as a Letter of Marque, to operate against the merchant ships of the enemy and to keep for themselves a large proportion of the value of every ship captured and brought into port. The average privateer was small, fast, and well armed, relying on her speed and fire power to intimidate and capture the normally slow and unwieldy merchant ship. The North Sea, the English Channel,

and the seas around the west coasts of France and Spain were the hunting grounds of the privateers. The French are credited with capturing 4,000 prizes, the English and Dutch with rather less. Nevertheless, by the end of the war France was exhausted, her trade in ruins, and Colbert's fine fleet no longer able to challenge the still growing sea power of England.

After five years of peace, Europe was again torn by war, the cause being the succession of the French Philip of Anjou to the throne of Spain, left vacant by the death of the Habsburg Charles II. The threat of a Franco-Spanish alliance was not one which the other nations of Europe could contemplate with

51. Battle of La Hougue, 23 May 1692. Adriaen van Diest
This battle, the spectacular follow-up to the Anglo-Dutch success at Barfleur, saw a further decimation of the French fleet. This view, by one of Van de Velde the Younger's most talented followers, looks from the west towards Cherbourg. Six French ships burn in the centre foreground, a seventh burns on the shore, and the allied fleet attacks another group of ships further round the Bay of La Hougue.

any confidence and they formed an alliance to oppose the French succession. England was drawn in, apart from the need to protect her overseas trade interests, mainly because Louis XIV was once again championing James II's claim to the English throne.

The war was fought largely on land, the naval involvement being peripheral to the main conflict. On the English side it was begun in the West Indies with an inglorious little action off Cartagena, in which a French troop convoy with an escort of five ships was attacked by an English squadron of seven ships under the command of Admiral Benbow, whose autocratic methods of command were resented by his captains. Five of them refused to follow him into the attack. Benbow was beaten off by the French and himself mortally wounded. The captains who had deserted Benbow were brought to a court martial for cowardice and two of them were sentenced to death.

The other naval actions of the war were mainly afterthoughts. In 1702 an English-Dutch fleet under Admiral Rooke attacked Cadiz, a somewhat half-hearted affair that ended in failure. Learning on his way home that a Spanish convoy from the West Indies had arrived at Vigo, Rooke decided to use his ships and the troops which were to have captured Cadiz in an attack on the harbour and the convoy [plate 26]. It was a complete success. Six French ships of the line were captured and the rest of the ships in harbour destroyed, with only slight losses of men in the allied fleet.

Two years later another Anglo-Dutch fleet, again with Rooke in command, was in the western Mediterranean seeking to bring to action a French fleet which was reluctant to leave port at Toulon. Almost as a diversion Rooke mounted an attack on Gibraltar and after a brief skirmish the garrison surrendered. This stung France into ordering its recapture, but following an indecisive action off Malaga the French fleet withdrew leaving Rooke in strategic control of the western Mediterranean waters. Later operations of the alliance in these waters, with English

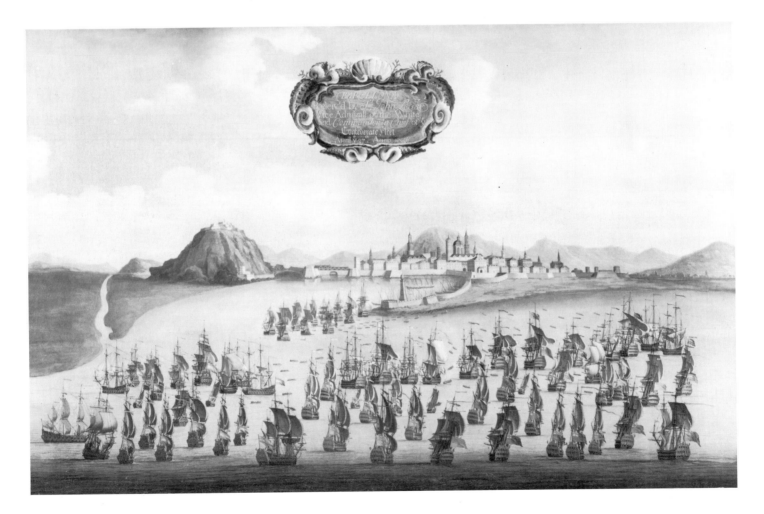

52. The Relief of Barcelona, 27 April 1706. H. Vale
The French forces who supported the Bourbon claimant to the Spanish throne laid siege to Barcelona by land and sea. In March 1706 King Charles sent an urgent plea for help to Admiral Sir John Leake. Hearing of Sir John's approach with a superior fleet, the French Comte de Toulouse escaped with his ships, while the Duke of Anjou was forced to raise the land siege.

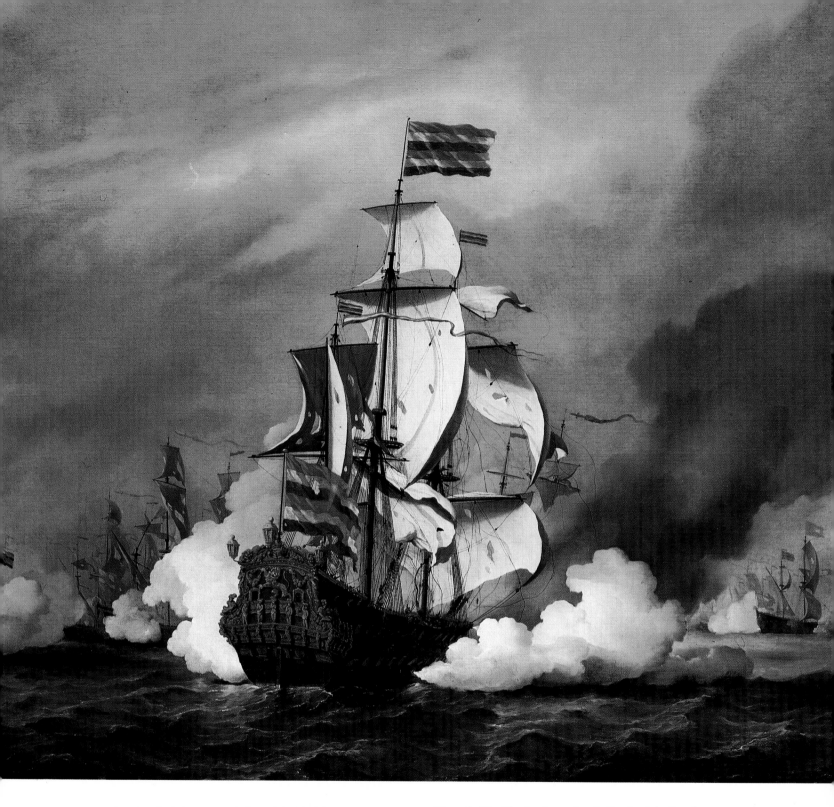

Plate 18. The 'Gouden Leeuw' at the Battle of the Texel, 11 August 1673. Willem Van de Velde the Younger, 1687

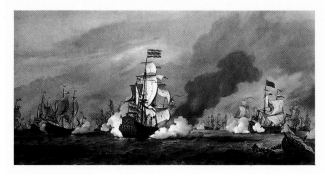

Painted in 1687 some fourteen years after the event, probably to adorn Cornelis Tromp's house in Trompenburg, this large battle-piece is one of the finest by the artist. The picture depicts the opening moments of the last great battle of the Anglo-Dutch wars when, off the coast of Holland, the combined English and French fleets aimed to defeat the Dutch under de Ruyter in preparation for an invasion of the country from the sea. Although no ships were sunk, the Dutch put up a tremendous fight, forcing the allied fleet to retire, and claimed a strategic victory. In the centre of the picture the *Gouden Leeuw* (*Golden Lion*), Tromp's flagship, fires guns to port and starboard. To the left is the *Charles* with Chicheley's red flag at the mizen falling, and to the right the *Prince*, flagship of Sir Edward Spragge, with her mizen topmast falling. The *Royal Sovereign*, flagship of Prince Rupert, Commander-in-Chief of the allied fleet, may be seen in the distance to the right of the *Gouden Leeuw*.

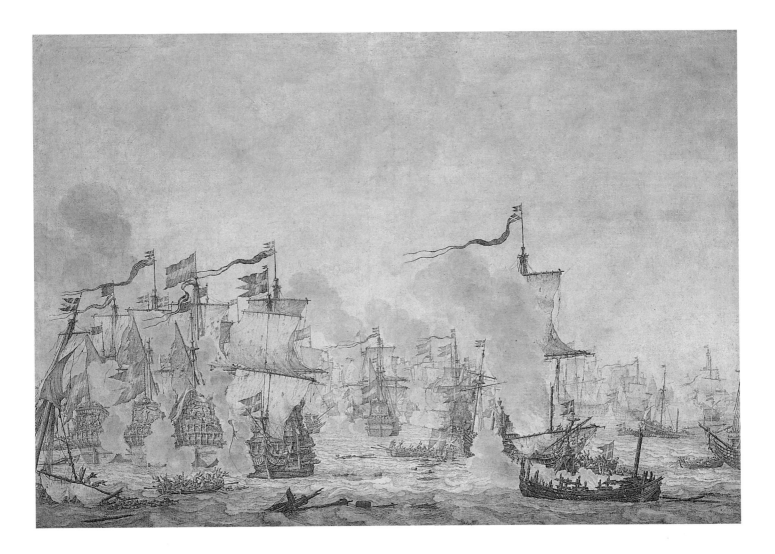

Plate 19. The Battle of the Sound, 8 November 1658.
Willem Van de Velde the Elder

Van de Velde the Elder was an eye witness to this battle, which was fought
off Copenhagen; the towers of Kronborg Castle can be seen on the right. By
successfully attacking Copenhagen, Sweden occupied the Sound, the stretch of
water between Sweden and Denmark, thus blocking important trade routes to
the Baltic. The Dutch therefore sent a fleet under Admiral Van Wassenaer
which completely defeated the Swedes, forcing them to withdraw.

In the left foreground four Swedish ships are in close action with Van
Wassenaer in the *Eendracht*; on the right a Swedish private ship is on fire.
Another, the *Morgenstjernan*, already captured, is sinking. In the right
background the Swedish commander Admiral Wrangel in the *Viktoria* is
heading for the shelter of Kronborg.

This is a fine example of the grisaille or *penschilderij* (a form of pen painting
on a prepared surface such as canvas or wood) of which the elder Van de
Velde was a great exponent.

Plate 20. The English Ship 'Resolution' in a Gale.
Willem Van de Velde the Younger, *c*.1690

Even before they came to live in England in 1672/3, the Van de Veldes were
making detailed and accurate ship portrait drawings which could be used in
the composition of paintings. Amongst the many such drawings in the
collections at Greenwich there are two of the *Resolution* dated 1676.

It seems likely that this portrait was painted as a commission for Sir Thomas
Allin, who went in the *Resolution* to the Mediterranean as Commander-in-Chief
in 1669. Quite possibly the picture refers to a specific event, such as the gale
experienced by Allin off the coast of Spain in December that year.

The *Resolution*, one of the first 70-gun two-deckers, was built at Harwich in
1667. She was rebuilt at Chatham in 1698 but foundered on the Sussex coast
in November 1703.

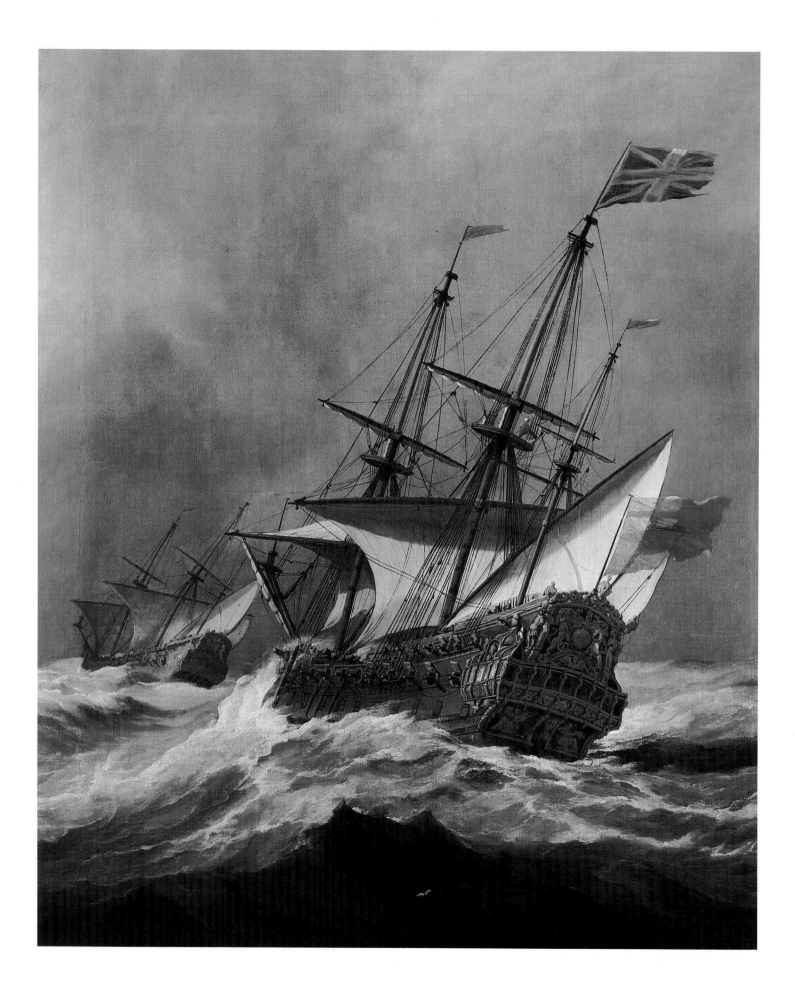

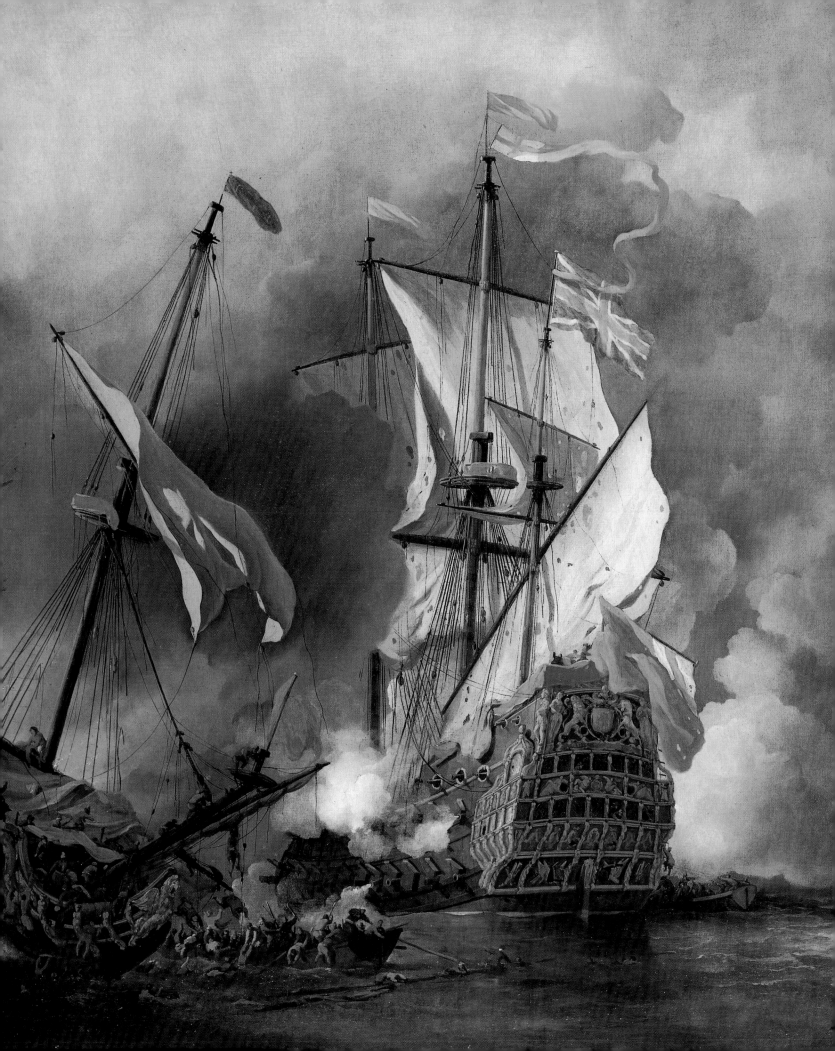

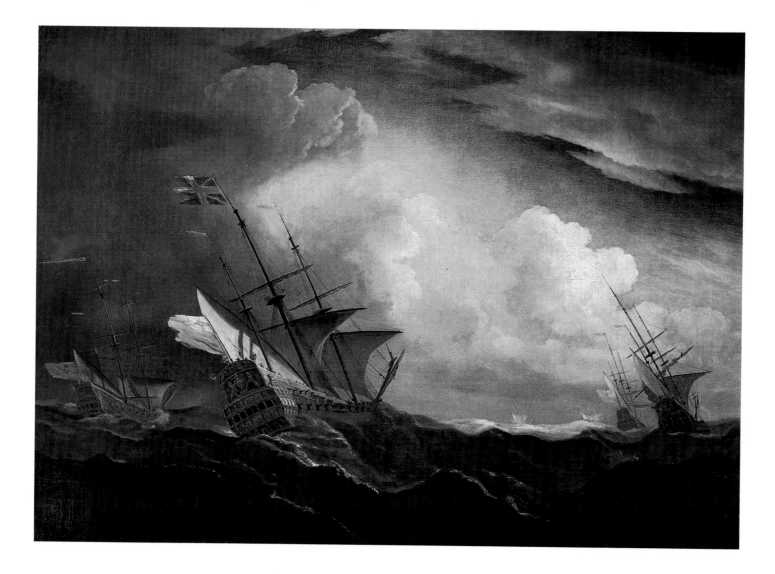

Plate 21. The Action with Barbary Pirates. Willem Van de Velde the Younger, c.1678

This detail of the picture depicts one of the many actions fought against Barbary corsairs in the 1670s and 1680s, some of which are not recorded. It is not clear which particular action this is intended to be, and attempts to identify the English ships have failed. The Barbary pirates, or corsairs, from the military republics of the North African coast were a persistent danger to merchant shipping not only in the Mediterranean but also in the Atlantic, their activities extending north as far as Ireland and Iceland. They operated from Tripoli, Tunis, Algiers, Bône and Salli, engaging not only in plunder but also in Christian slavery. Their activities reached a peak in the seventeenth century.

It seems probable that Van de Velde painted this colourful and flamboyant picture in 1678. A large English two-decker engages with Barbary ships to port and starboard. In the left foreground is a damaged Barbary ship.

Plate 22. A Squadron going to Windward in a Gale. Willem Van de Velde the Younger, c.1690

Probably painted as a commission for one of the flag officers who were allowed to fly the Union flag when in command of a detached squadron outside home waters, this picture clearly demonstrates the younger Van de Velde's ability to portray accurately weather conditions and their effect upon handling of ships at sea. On the left are dark storm clouds while on the right the sun breaks through, illuminating the sea in the distance. The squadron is close-hauled on the starboard tack. The English marine painters of the eighteenth century sometimes adapted the composition of pictures by Van de Velde the Younger to their own uses. Charles Brooking based at least one work on this painting, replacing the seventeenth-century ships with those of his own period.

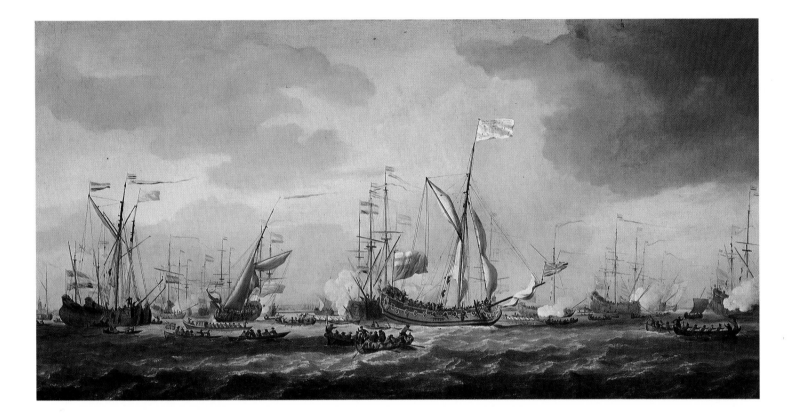

Plate 23. The Arrival of Princess Mary at Gravesend.
Willem Van de Velde the Younger

Although William III landed at Torbay on 5 November 1688, it was three
months before his wife Princess Mary travelled from Holland to join him.
Arriving at Gravesend on board the *Mary* yacht on 12 February 1689, she then
travelled by coach to Greenwich where she was met by both her sister Anne
and Prince George of Denmark, her brother-in-law.

The *Mary*, flying the special white standard of the Revolution with the legend
'For the Protestant Religion and the Liberties of England', is taking in her sails
and is probably about to anchor off Gravesend, the church tower of which can
be seen on the extreme left. The scene is viewed from the middle of Gravesend
Reach, looking upstream to the west. Princess Mary is standing in the stern
of the yacht, which is shown starboard broadside view. She is surrounded by
barges and wherries rowing upstream after her. To her left another royal yacht
is luffing up into the wind, and beyond her another is firing a salute.

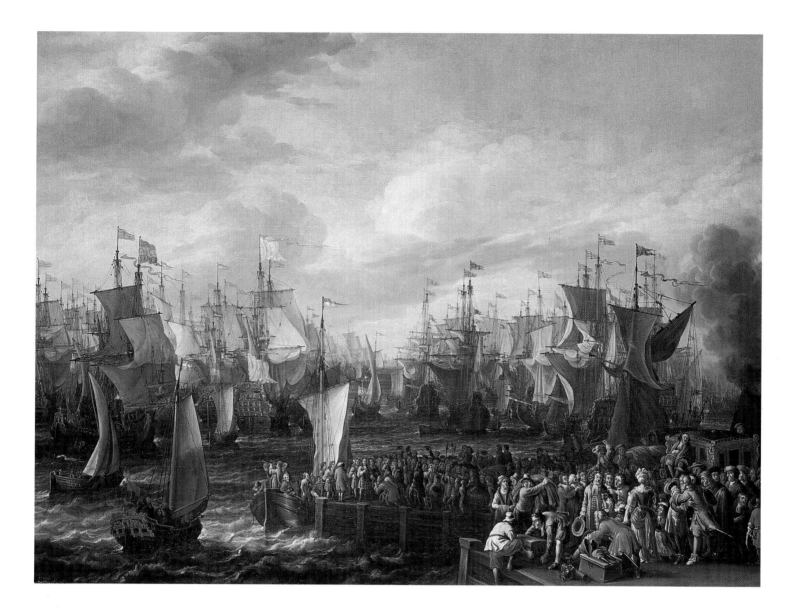

Plate 24. Departure of William III from Hellevoetsluis, 19 October 1688. Unidentified artist

William of Orange embarked at Hellevoetsluis on the coast of Holland on 19 October 1688, prior to his invasion of England and the flight of James II. William's Dutch fleet, assembled at the mouth of the Maas, consisted of 50 ships of the line, 50 smaller warships and frigates and about 400 transports. The English Admiral Arthur Herbert was given overall control and hoisted his flag in the *Leiden* on 17 October. William himself went on board the *Briel* on the 19th, but owing to bad weather the fleet did not leave the coast of Holland until 1 November, eventually landing at Torbay on 5 November.

The foreground of the picture depicts the jetty at Hellevoetsluis, with William, Admiral Herbert and Bentinck taking leave of the dignitaries of the town, who are kneeling. Behind William is the pink which will take him to the *Briel*, and the background is crowded with the fleet; Herbert's flagship is prominent (left of centre).

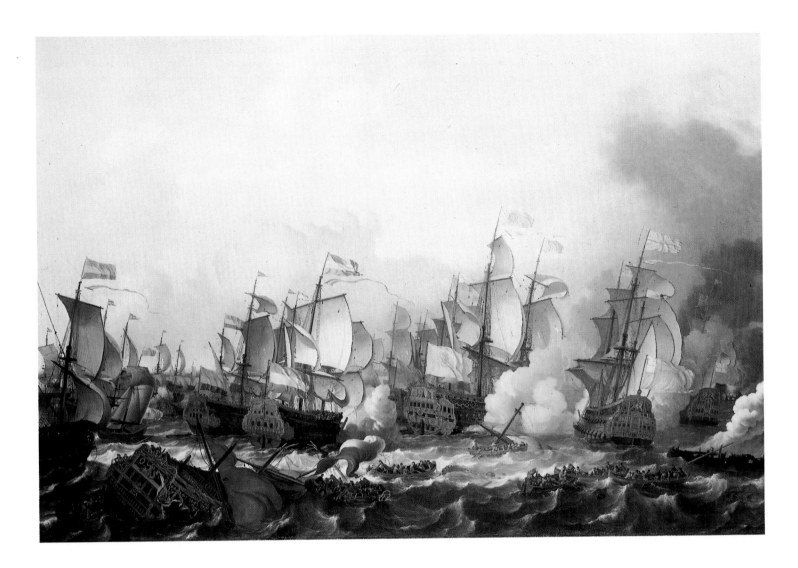

Plate 25. The Battle of Barfleur, 19–24 May 1692. Ludolf Bakhuizen

While the deposed King James waited at La Hougue on the coast of Normandy with a large mixed force ready to embark for the invasion of England, the Comte de Tourville rashly engaged the superior Anglo-Dutch fleet off nearby Barfleur. He had impatiently left the anchorage in Bertheaume Bay before the arrival of d'Estrées's squadron from Toulon; in addition, two despatches from the French Court, ordering him to avoid action, had failed to reach him. Nevertheless, with a force half the size of the Anglo-Dutch and with the action hampered by fog, de Tourville put up a brave fight. It was, however, the prelude to a disaster for the French, who were pursued westwards along the coast. The flagship, the *Soleil Royal*, the *Triomphant* and the *Admirable* were burnt in Cherbourg Bay on 22 May, and on the following two days twelve more French ships sheltering in the Bay of La Hougue were burnt.

    The central vessel in Bakhuizen's somewhat fanciful picture is the French flagship, the *Soleil Royal*. She is shown in close combat with the *Britannia* (flagship of the allied fleet) on her starboard side.

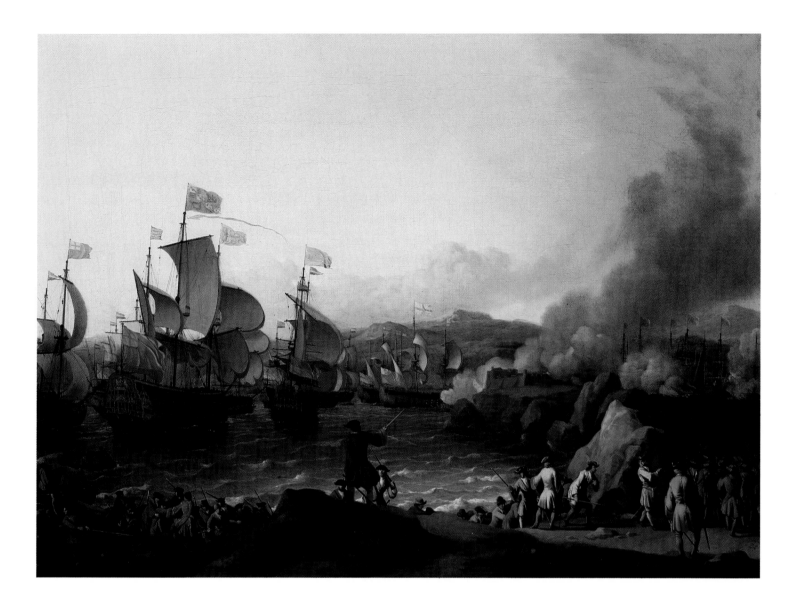

Plate 26. The Battle of Vigo Bay, 12 October 1702. Ludolf Bakhuizen

In the opening year of the War of the Spanish Succession an Anglo-Dutch fleet was assembled under Sir George Rooke to attack Cadiz. It was then learned that a French fleet with Spanish treasure galleons was not far away in Vigo Bay. The allied fleet accordingly changed course, and anchored in Vigo Bay on 11 October. The French and Spanish ships lay in Redondela harbour, where a boom of masts had been laid across the entrance. The *Torbay*, flagship of Sir Thomas Hopsonn, broke the boom and led the allied fleet through. The French commander fired his own ship, ordering the others to do the same, and the entire Franco-Spanish fleet was destroyed, including seventeen treasure galleons. Simultaneously the Duke of Ormonde landed with troops and marched on the harbour.

The battle is viewed from the south shore, where Ormonde's troops are landing. The *Torbay* is about to break the boom, followed by ships of the allied fleet, including the *Zeven Provincien*. The main ship in the picture is probably the *Royal Sovereign*, although she was actually not involved in the action.

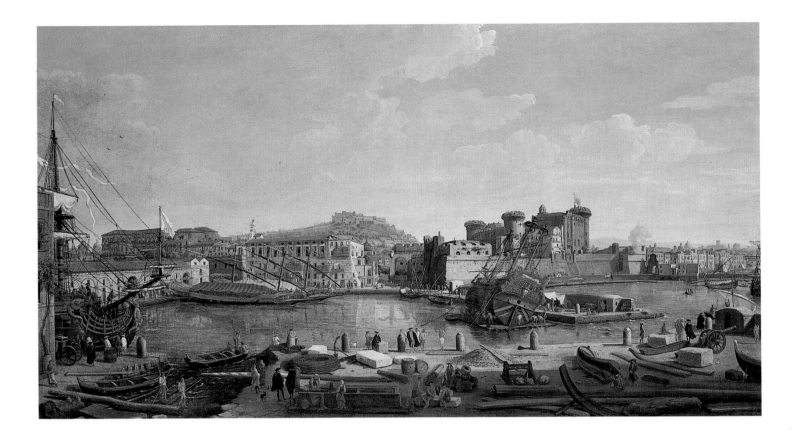

Plate 27. The Harbour of Naples. Gaspar van Wittel, 1703

This Dutch-born artist (also known as Van Vitelli) lived in Italy from the age
of nineteen, in Venice, Rome and Naples, where he produced topographically
exact *vedute*. These usually contain important architecture, in excellent
perspective, and are staffed with small figures. This most colourful view shows
the bustling activity in Naples harbour. In the right foreground in front of the
Castello Nuovo a merchant ship is being careened. The foreground is taken up
with merchants and their wares, and on the left, beyond the bows of a ship,
a galley with a striped awning is moored. In 1703 Sir Clowdisley Shovell sailed
to the Mediterranean, one of his aims being to attempt to restore Sicily and
Naples to the house of Habsburg.

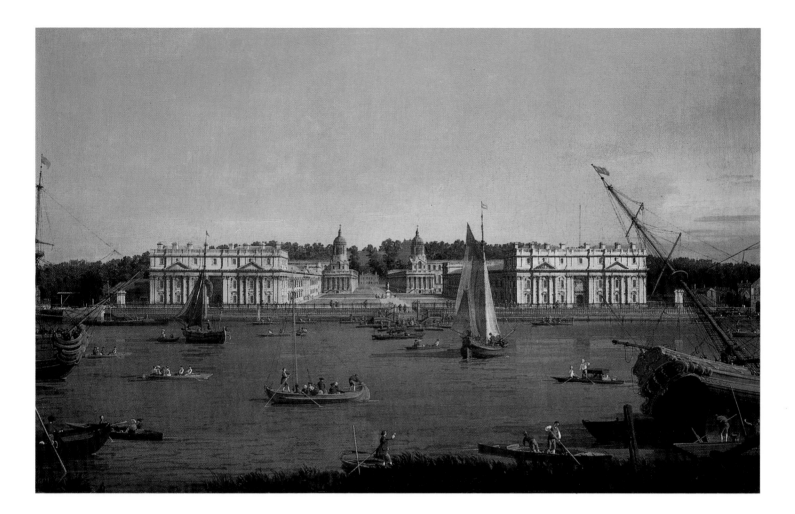

Plate 28. Greenwich Hospital. Giovanni Antonio Canale, called Canaletto

The rebuilding of Greenwich Palace was begun by Charles II in the 1660s on the site of the old Tudor palace. The first block, King Charles, facing the river on the right-hand side, was not completed until the reign of William III. By this time, however, the site had been handed over as the Royal Hospital, to be a home for old and disabled seamen from the Royal Navy. Progress on the building of the four blocks rather depended on the French wars, which themselves provided candidates for admission while the prize money was used to extend the hospital. The Queen Mary block, which contains the chapel, was the last to be completed, just after the end of the War of Jenkins's Ear in 1749, and it is from this period that Canaletto's painting dates.

The view remains today virtually unchanged, with the statue of George II still in the quadrangle, the Queen's House at the end of the vista, and the Old Royal Observatory crowning the hill beyond.

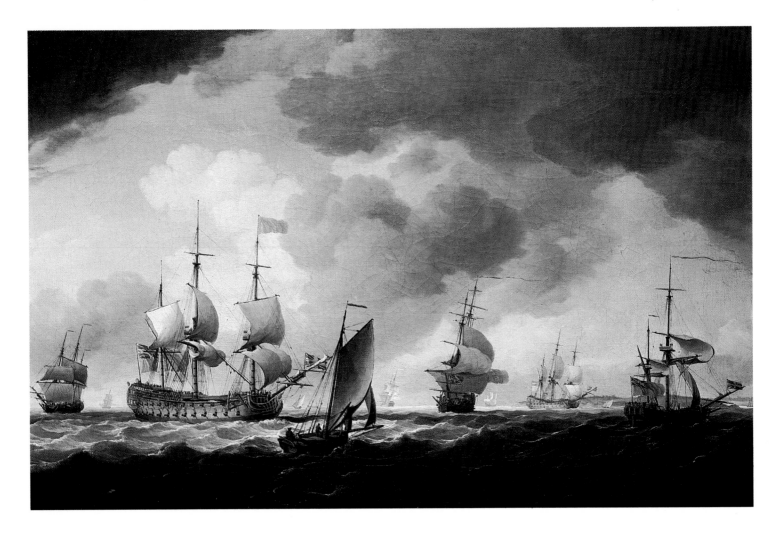

Plate 29. A Vice-Admiral of the Red and a Squadron at Sea.
Charles Brooking

This picture demonstrates the artist's intimate knowledge of ships and shipping
as well as his keen appreciation of the conditions in which they sailed. Like the
Van de Veldes, Brooking was utterly faithful to all aspects of the build and
rigging of ships, and the effects of weather and light upon the sea.

   Although the identity of the flagship is uncertain it is possible that she is the
Boyne, when she was Admiral Byng's flagship on his return to England in 1748.
To the right is a ketch-rigged bomb-vessel, the masts set well back to give a
clearer forward field of fire to the mortars.

   There are versions of this picture in the Tate Gallery, London, and the
Foundling Hospital, London (presented to the latter in 1754).

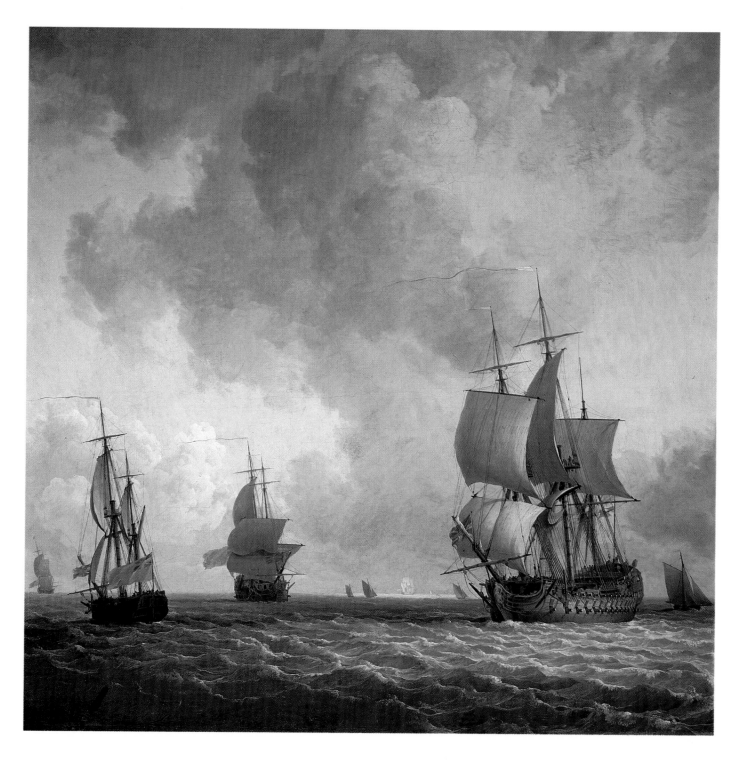

Plate 30. A Ship in a Light Breeze. Charles Brooking

Charles Brooking was perhaps the most original of the native English marine
painters of the first half of the eighteenth century, developing a style quite
independent of the Van de Veldes. However, in his acute awareness of weather
conditions, and in the accurate description of ships, he remained faithful in
spirit to the Dutch masters. Particularly beautiful in this picture is the painting
of the small steep waves which indicate wind against tide. The main vessel is
a two-decker, with a cutter astern of her. On the left is a ketch-rigged sloop
or perhaps a bomb-vessel, and in the middle distance is another two-decker.

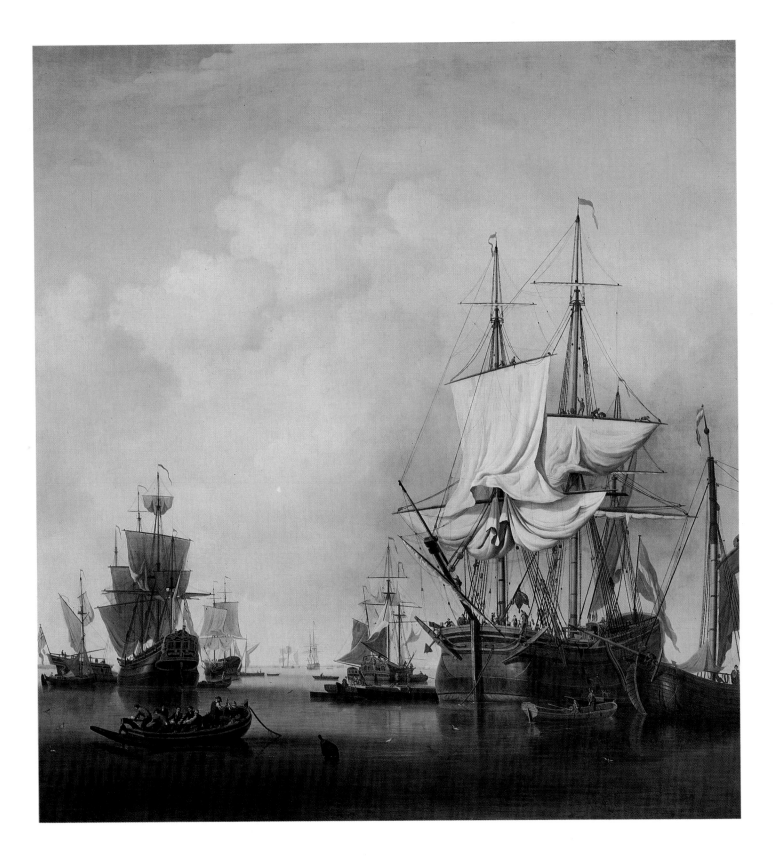

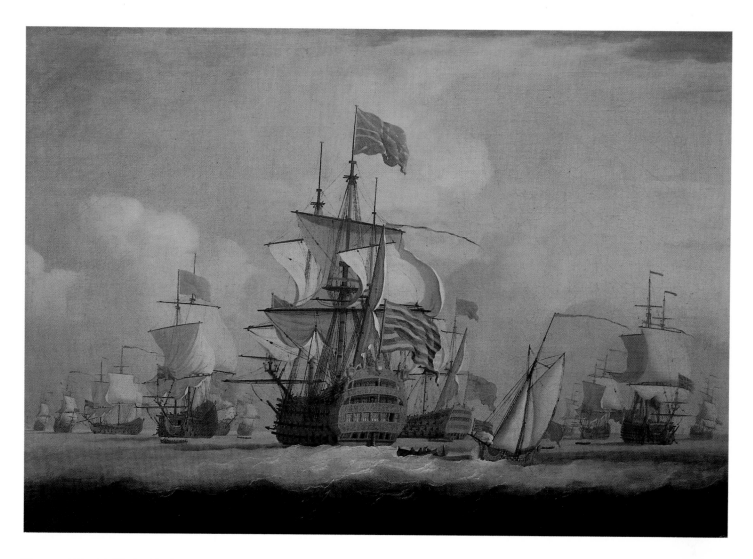

**Plate 31. A Danish Timber Bark getting under Way.
Samuel Scott, 1736**

This large picture, for which there is a drawing in the National Maritime
Museum, shows men in a boat weighing and fetching home the anchor of the
timber bark. There is no obvious explanation for the small scale of the figures
on board the bark.

Apart from the pictures of the naval engagements of the middle years of the
eighteenth century, Scott, one of the English followers of Canaletto, also
produced topographical paintings, including views of London and the River
Thames. He was no doubt well acquainted with the busy life of a port and the
many visiting craft. In 1732, with a group of friends including William
Hogarth, he made an excursion in a sailing boat to the mouth of the Thames,
recorded in the *Five Days Peregrination*.

Plate 32. An English Fleet coming to Anchor. Peter Monamy, c.1715

Peter Monamy is now known to have been born in London in 1681, although
his family originated in Jersey. In 1696 he is recorded in the Register of the
Company of Painter-Stainers as having been apprenticed for seven years to
William Clark, and his professional training seems to have been as a house
painter.

The principal ship in the picture, that of the admiral of the fleet, Union flag
at the main, is flying a striped ensign from its ensign staff as a signal to anchor.
Also present in the background is a vice-admiral of the red and a rear-admiral
of the blue: the small vessel in the foreground is a royal yacht, a number of
which served as despatch vessels.

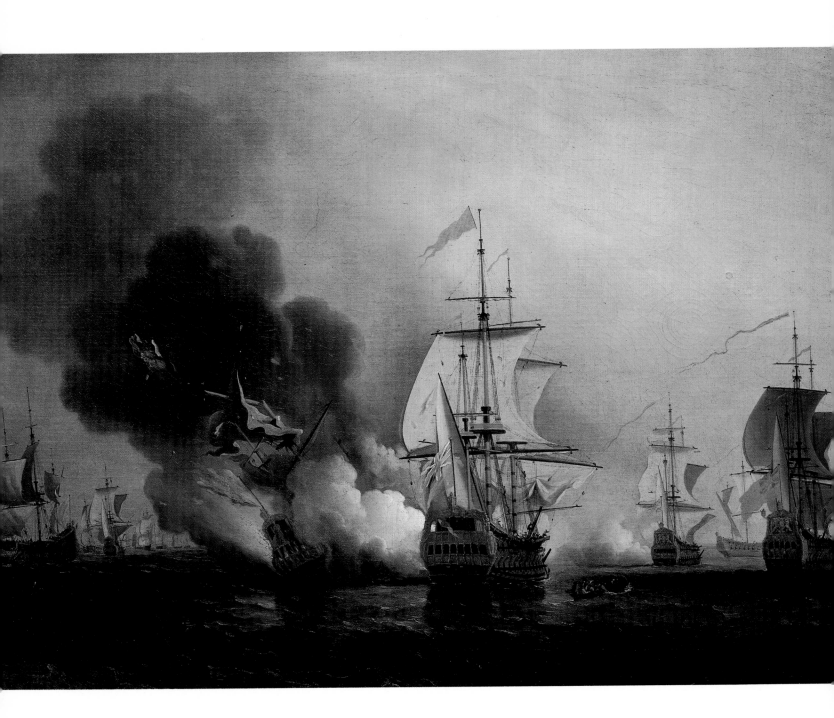

Plate 33. Wager's Action off Cartagena, 28 May 1708. Samuel Scott

Appointed to the West Indies Station in 1707, Commodore Charles Wager conceived the idea of attacking the Spanish galleons which he knew would be returning from Puerto Bello to Spain. On 28 May 1708 he eventually sighted and, with only four ships, intercepted a Spanish treasure fleet of seventeen vessels sailing off Cartagena on the coast of what is now Colombia. Wager himself in the 70-gun *Expedition* tackled the 64-gun *San Josef*, which was carrying the bulk of the treasure. At dusk, after one and a half hours of fighting, the *San Josef* unfortunately blew up. The 60-gun *Kingston* and the 50-gun *Portland* had disobeyed orders to attack two Spanish ships of 64 guns and 44 guns at the rear and head of the Spanish line respectively. Wager himself then tackled and captured the latter, which carried no gold but was nevertheless a valuable prize. At dawn the next day a large ship was sighted and pursued, but she escaped into Cartagena, and another carrying treasure went aground and was burnt by her crew.

The *Expedition* is in the centre of the picture, starboard quarter view, firing to port at the *San Josef*, which is blowing up. To the right are three English ships, and on the left the Spanish fleet is making its escape.

naval assistance, resulted in the capture of Sardinia and Minorca, and at the Treaty of Utrecht which ended the war in 1713, Gibraltar and Minorca were retained by Great Britain—no longer England alone after the Act of Union with Scotland in 1707—as overseas possessions.

One other naval lesson for Britain emerged from these two wars, that the demands of worldwide trade protection and expansion required positive naval backing on a permanent basis.

In earlier wars, the national fleets and squadrons had been laid up in port during the winter months and were recommissioned each spring for the conventional fighting season of summer and autumn. The Mediterranean operations had proved that a British fleet could be maintained in those waters without the usual winter withdrawal, and a permanent force in the Mediterranean now became an accepted feature of British naval policy in its exercise of sea power around the world.

9. THE WARSHIP: *classification, decoration, design*

The division of warships into six rates according to the number of guns they carried was not officially introduced until 1751, but it is a convenient way of classifying earlier warships as an indication of size and importance. Using the 1751 method, a first-rate of the end of the seventeenth century carried 90 guns or more [fig. 55], a second-rate from 70 to 90 guns, a third-rate from 50 to 70 guns, and fourth, fifth- and sixth-rates progressively less. First-, second- and third-rate ships were known as 'ships of the line', as they were the ships mounting enough guns to be considered powerful enough to lie in the line of battle. Fifth- and sixth-rates [fig. 53] after 1751 came generally to be classed as frigates, and they filled a long-felt need for a small, fast, well-armed ship to act both as a reconnaissance vessel for the battle fleet and a strong enough escort for mercantile convoys.

The generic name of frigate was a great deal older than 1751, originally used to describe the oared tender to a big war galley, lightly armed to intervene in the battle if an opportunity presented itself. Later, the name was applied to the despatch vessels which accompanied fleets and which were used to pass orders and information between ships during battle, but in no sense were they comparable to the real frigates of later years.

The first warship which has been widely considered to be entitled to the description of frigate was the *Constant Warwick* of 379 tons. She was built as a privateer in 1646 by the Earl of Warwick and was bought for the navy three years later. Originally mounting 30 guns, her armament was later increased to 42. Her claim to be the first frigate may rest on the fact that she was the prototype of a change in English naval architecture, favouring a longer keel and a lower freeboard. This produced a ship with finer lines and lying more snugly in the water to provide more speed and stiffness.

But the first real frigates, mounting 28 guns on a single gun-deck, were built in 1748. The largest guns they could carry were 9-pounders. By 1757 a 36-gun frigate, with 12-pounders substituted for the smaller guns, was built. Her long keel gave her a good turn of speed for fleet reconnaissance, and she had a heavy enough armament to defend convoys against attack by privateers.

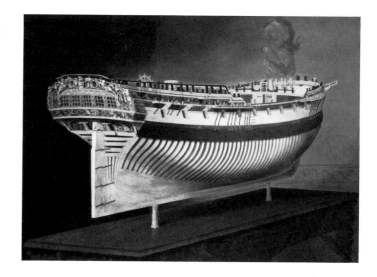

Each nation developed its own design of frigate, and it is an oddity of national prejudice that the British design was much admired by French naval experts and the French design [fig. 54] considered superior by the British. An opportunity came to compare the two with the capture in 1758 of the French 36-gun frigate *Aurore*. She was built in the year of her capture, brought into port as a prize and carefully measured in dry dock for comparison with the British 36-gun frigate *Brilliant*, built in 1757.

53. The 'Enterprise'. J. Marshall, 1777
This unusual painting, one of a set by a little-known artist in the employ of King George III, depicts a model of the *Enterprise*, a sixth-rate ship of 28 guns. The model was built around 1770 and the ship herself in 1774.

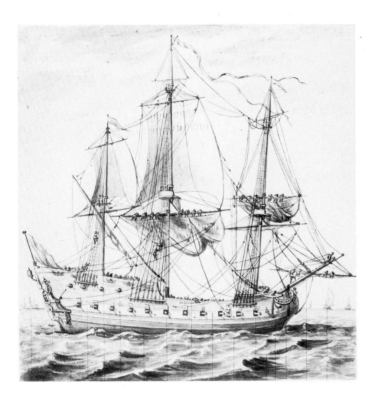

The French ship came out at 946 tons compared with the *Brilliant*'s 718 tons, and all other measurements, keel, beam, depth, length of gundeck, were substantially larger. Their capabilities, speed, weight of broadside, and weatherliness were virtually identical.

A ship smaller than the frigate, adopted into most navies, was the sloop, known in the French navy as a corvette. The require-

ment for such naval ships arose from the huge numbers of privateers licensed in time of war to operate against merchant ships, and sloops were built in large numbers in an attempt to limit the damage to trade during periods of hostilities. With a displacement of about 400 tons, they were either ship-rigged or carried a two-masted square rig and were built with a length-to-beam ratio of better than 4 to 1, giving them long fine lines and a good speed. Their normal armament was from 14 to 18 guns mounted on the upper deck. During the wars of the late eighteenth century they were frequently built of fir rather than oak, partly as an economy measure and partly, with their lighter hull, to enhance their performance in stays.

One of the features of warships of all nations, and to a lesser extent of merchant ships, was the amount and richness of their decoration. In England, it began to flower in the reign of Henry VIII, reached its peak of elaboration at the end of the seventeenth century, and became more sober and restrained during the eighteenth and nineteenth centuries. The same pattern of lavish ornamentation was to be seen in the ships of Spain, France and Holland.

Ship decoration had a very old and very natural history, for every true seaman likes a bit of embellishment for his vessel. Lucian, it will be remembered (see p. 10), described the elaborate decoration of the Roman grainship he saw in Piraeus; Viking longships were frequently decorated with a snake's head on the bow, its body stretching the length of the ship, its tail forming the stern. But by the seventeenth century decoration had been carried to ridiculous extremes. When Phineas Pett and William Bright designed and built the *Prince Royal* [plate 4] for James I, her total cost was £20,000, but included in this was £441

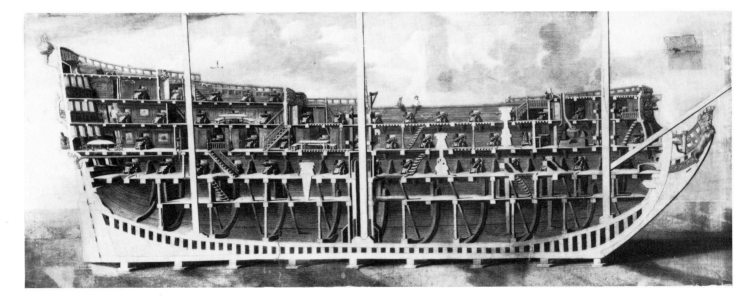

54. French Frigate of the Early Eighteenth Century. French School, *c.*1720

Frigates were a late development in national navies, arising from a requirement for a relatively lightly armed (a 30-gun example is shown here), fast warship for fleet reconnaissance and the escort of mercantile convoys as protection against privateer attacks. This called for a ship lying lower in the water for extra stiffness, and a longer length-to-beam ratio for speed.

55. The Section of a First-Rate Ship. Thomas Phillips

A longitudinal section of a first-rate ship of the line of the late seventeenth century. These wooden warships were vessels of immense strength: their hulls were double-skinned of oak up to 18 inches thick, and they were further strengthened with oak wales up to 8 inches thick running from bow to stern below the gunports.

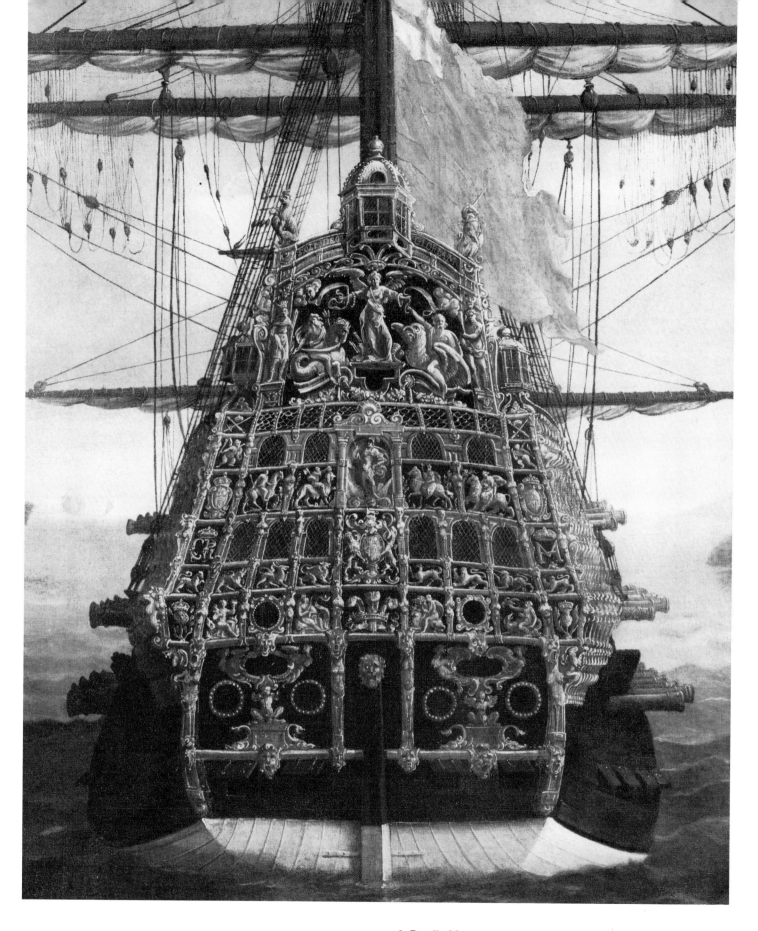

56. Detail of fig. 35

This detail of the famous painting by Lely and others illustrates the richly decorated stern (following in part designs by the painter van Dyck) of this royal showpiece of the English navy. The 100-gun first-rate ship, built at Woolwich by the Pett family, was renamed *Royal Sovereign* after the Restoration; she was accidentally destroyed by fire at Chatham in 1696.

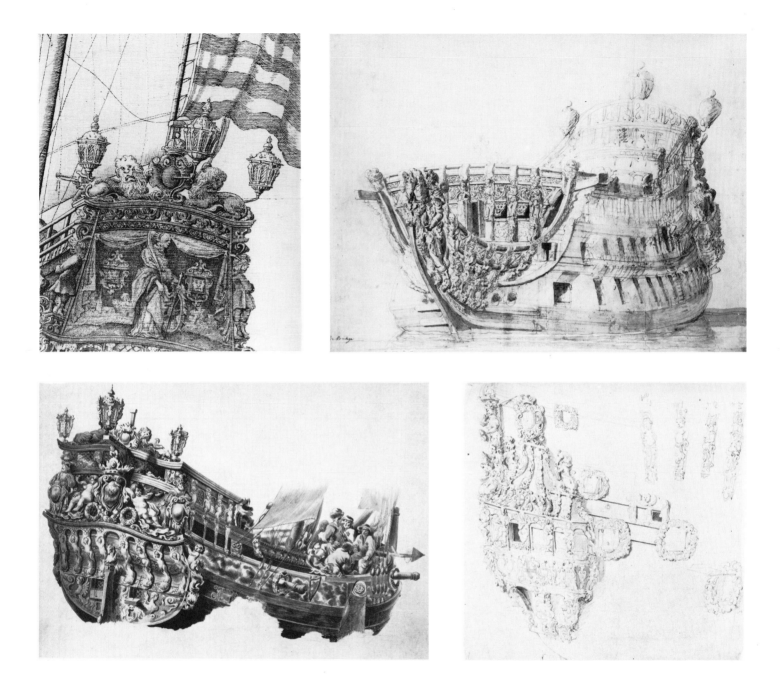

57. Dutch East Indiaman. Willem Van de Velde the Elder

On the tafferel is a full-length figure of St. Catherine with her wheel on her left, and on the upper transom is inscribed *Anno Catarina 1649*, suggesting that the ship was built in 1649.

59. Starboard Quarter View of a Dutch-Built Yacht, *c.*1675. After Gerard Valck

The lavish use of rich carving, which was fashionable at this time, is shown very clearly in this drawing. Valck was a Dutch printmaker who specialized in portraits; he frequently worked in mezzotint.

58. The 'Britannia'. Willem Van de Velde the Elder, *c.*1684

The *Britannia* was a celebrated first-rate of 100 guns, built in 1682 and rebuilt in 1700. This large drawing, showing details of the bow decoration and the figurehead, was probably executed during Van de Velde's visit to Chatham to watch the launch of the *Royal Sovereign*. It is done in isometric perspective.

60. Quarter Gallery of the 'Suffolk'. Willem Van de Velde the Younger, *c.*1685

The *Suffolk* was launched in 1680. The present drawing is a good example of the care lavished by the younger Van de Velde on the sculptural details of ship decoration. It may have been drawn from a model rather than from the ship herself.

paid to Sebastian Vicars for carvings and £868. 7s. to Robert Beake and Pane Isackson for painting and gilding, an extravagantly high proportion to be spent on decoration which made no contribution to the ship's fighting efficiency. A later ship, Charles I's *Sovereign of the Seas* [fig. 56], built for his Ship Money fleet, cost a total of £65,586. 16s. 9½d., and of this her carving, gilding and painting accounted for no less than £6,691. Her high stern was carved and gilded to a design by van Dyck. It is true that these two were special ships designed to enhance the prestige of the English navy, but the embellishment of ordinary warships was scarcely less elaborate. The classical figures on the stern and bow of the Swedish *Vasa*, which sank on her maiden voyage in

1628, were part of an elaborate iconographical and decorative programme. Shipwrights lavished the same care on the decoration of ships as craftsmen lavished on buildings. The increasing exuberance of design during the baroque period is mirrored as much in ship decoration as in the other decorative arts [figs. 57–60].

Once the fashion for decoration got into its full swing, the urge to expand it knew no bounds, and the carvers applied their art to virtually every piece of wood in sight. Hancing pieces (the wooden brackets used to finish and support the end of a deck where it dropped to the deck below) were carved often in the form of a naked woman; chesstrees (the fairleads through which

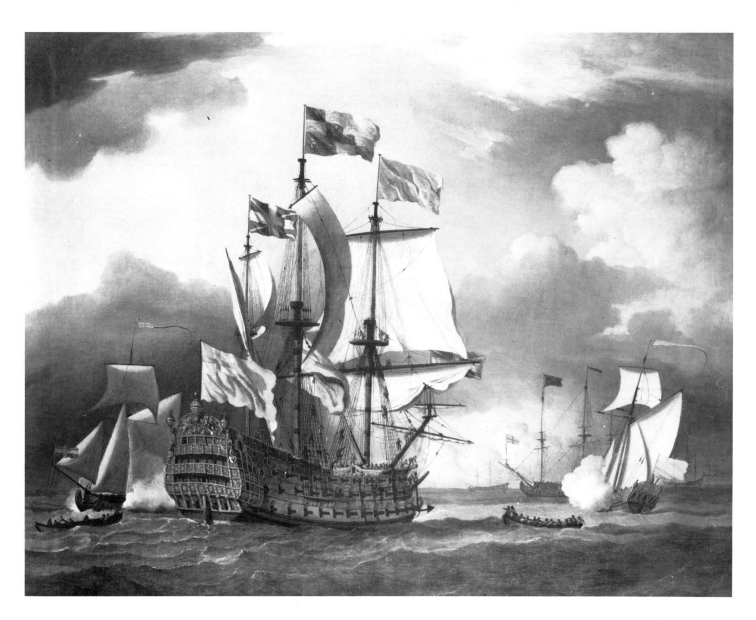

61. The 'Britannia'. After Willem Van de Velde the Younger

One of the largest and most powerful ships of her time, the *Britannia* proved to be top-heavy and cumbersome to sail. Nonetheless, as the flagship at Barfleur in 1692 she held her own against the French and certainly contributed to victory.

were led the bowlines with which the main tacks were hauled down) were elaborately carved in the form of a sun in splendour or a human or animal face, with the bowline being led through the open mouth. In the first half of the seventeenth century much of the carving was covered in gold leaf until, during the years of the Commonwealth, it was discovered that gold paint glistened just as much as gold leaf and at a fraction of the cost. The peak of warship decoration was reached during the reign of William III, and though the costs varied between ships, the Pipe Office (Admiralty) accounts for those years show an average cost varying from £896 for a first-rate to £52 for a sixth-rate.

With the exception of the ships of the East India Companies, particularly of France, Holland, and England, which generally equalled the splendour of the warships, merchant vessels were more modest in their decoration. Yet all of them sported a figurehead of some sort, set off by carved trailboards. Their rounded sterns gave carvers an opportunity of blending their work with the natural beauty of stern lights (windows) and galleries. So widespread was the urge to decorate that even the smallest and humblest vessels had something to show, were it only a little carved scrollwork on either side of the bow.

In order to try to contain the expenses of warship decoration the English Navy Board issued an order in 1703 limiting the amount to be spent on carving and painting to £500 for a first-rate down to £25 for a sixth-rate. Three years later another order tackled the problem of cost from the other end, specifying the actual carvings which a naval ship should carry. It gradually put an end to the extravagance of earlier years, and the more restrained Palladian style of the early eighteenth century also contributed to the change.

Although throughout the seventeenth and eighteenth centuries the basic design of the larger ships, whether warship or merchant ship, varied little, they more than doubled in size. Warships of over 1,000 tons had been built by 1600 and by the mid-seventeenth century the largest were around 1,600 tons. They reached 2,000 tons in the mid-eighteenth century and by 1800 some French and Spanish ships were measured at over 2,700 tons. Most merchant ships were considerably smaller, although many of the East India Companies' ships were not all that far behind the warships in tonnage.

The most important change in square rig had come early in the eighteenth century [fig. 62]. Triangular jibs had been used in Holland in the mid-seventeenth century, almost entirely in small coastal craft, and were known in England after about 1660. A painting of the royal yacht *Bezan*, a gift from Holland to Charles II after his restoration, shows her with one of these sails. Triangular jibs and staysails set on the forestay and foretopmast stay replaced the upper and lower spritsails set above and below the bowsprit in the smaller English warships in 1705, and a few years later in the larger warships as well. Additional staysails were also set between the masts.

One other considerable advance during these years around the turn of the century was the introduction of the steering wheel in place of the tiller. As ships had grown larger, so of course had their rudders and the tillers that controlled them. In rough seas and high winds it could take as many as six men on the tiller to control it by means of tackles rigged to the ship's sides, and even at its best it was not a precise instrument with which to hold a steady course. A still bigger disadvantage was that it had to be on the same level as the rudder head and in all but very small vessels this meant that the helmsman worked between decks and could not see the sails of the ship he was steering. The steering wheel, geared to the rudder head by ropes or chains, did not necessarily have to be on the same level and was normally placed on deck at the break of the quarterdeck, where it gave the helmsman a clear view of the sails.

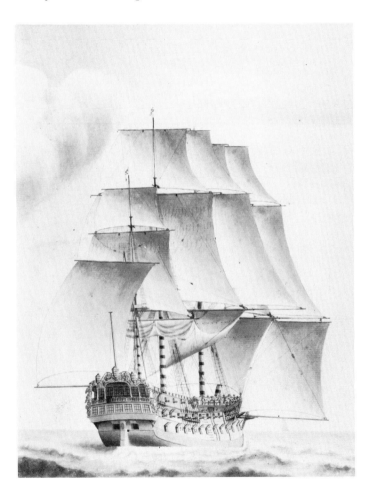

62. The 'Worcester'. Attributed to John Hood, *c.*1745
A fourth-rate of 60 guns, launched from Portsmouth in 1735, the *Worcester* is shown under full sail, quarter stern view. She took part in the successful siege of Porto Bello in 1739, and captured a Spanish frigate in April 1741.

10. MERCHANT SHIPPING AND THE EXPANSION OF TRADE

The huge surge of world trade of the sixteenth and seventeenth centuries, which followed the opening of direct sea routes both to the east and the west, continued throughout the eighteenth century. It is difficult to discover precise figures which can indicate the volume of this growth. Holland's merchant fleet has been estimated at 10,000 ships at the beginning of the seventeenth century. If this seems large, it must be remembered that the Dutch dominated the carrying trade for the next twenty-five years until in the twenties Holland was troubled by war. With peace again after 1648, the Dutch made considerable inroads into the carrying trade again. However, the English Navigation Act of 1651, and the three Dutch Wars which resulted, broke the Dutch competition for ever. Except in specific and localized circumstances the Dutch were never again a threat to the merchant fleets of England.

Merchant ships increased in size throughout the eighteenth century. Those trading to far distant places, the east or across the Atlantic to the West Indies, were still armed. In design they were a compromise, having lines less sharp than warships, and therefore more commodious, but still fine enough for respectable performance. Ships trading nearer home were true merchant-

men, unarmed, with bluff bows and flat floors to give the greatest cargo space.

Of the smaller merchant ships, those used to cross the North Sea or Baltic Sea, the commonest were the Dutch fluyt [fig. 64] and the English pinnace, both three-masted though the fluyt had a round stern and the pinnace a square one. In the Mediterranean the equivalent short sea ship was the bergantina, lateen-rigged on two masts. For coastwise trade, the variety of designs was enormous, depending largely on the type of trade carried and the characteristics of the coast along which they traded.

For many of these small coastal vessels, particularly those sailing mainly in shallow waters, the Dutch evolved the gaff rig, much easier to handle than square rig and much more economical in the number of men required as crew. The earliest known example of a full gaff rig set on two masts is the Dutch jacht, used in inland waters and fitted with leeboards in place of a keel because of its shallow draught. It was soon realized that two masts were unnecessary on so small a ship and in later designs the foremast was removed and a triangular fore staysail used to retain a balanced rig [fig. 63]. This version was known as a bezaan jacht. In England the smack rig, a loose footed gaff

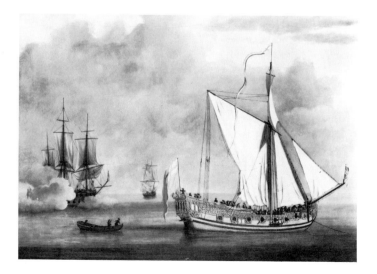

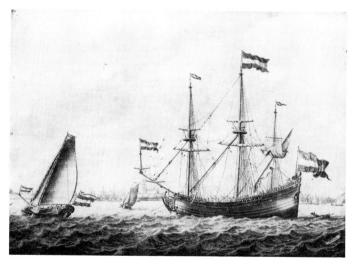

63. The 'Portsmouth'. Willem Van de Velde the Elder, 1675.
Though most of the elder Van de Velde's surviving work consists of drawings and grisailles, after his emigration to England he occasionally, and perhaps rather awkwardly, painted in oils. As in this portrait of the English 8-gun yacht *Portsmouth* (built in 1674), lying at anchor in shallow water and receiving a salute from the ship to its port quarter, his oil paintings are characterized by an intriguingly static air most unlike the work of his son.

64. Dutch Ships off Rotterdam. Adriaan van Salm
The potential elegance of the Dutch merchant fluyt, or fluitship, is emphasized here by the busy smaller craft around her in Rotterdam harbour. This grisaille, or *penschilderen* picture, is a good example of van Salm's painstaking if somewhat uninspired approach to marine subject-matter.

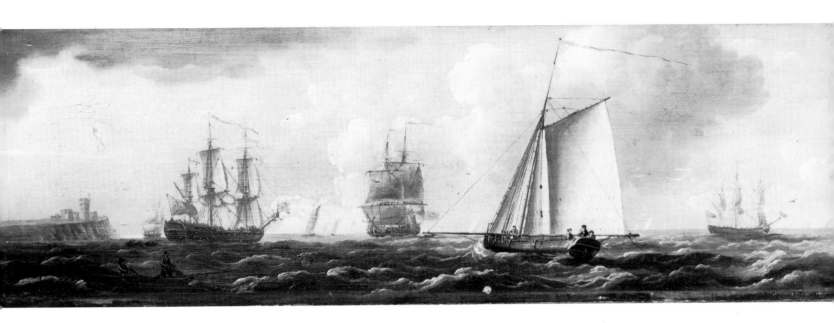

rig, was adopted for yachts after the Restoration, before the development of the cutter rig [fig. 65].

Throughout the eighteenth century and for most of the nineteenth, all the European nations used snows, brigs, brigantines and ketches for their coastwise trading and for shorter sea voyages. All of them were two-masted though the rigs varied slightly from nation to nation mainly to suit the particular trade needs for which they were built.

The equivalent Mediterranean trading vessels for the shorter sea crossings were the xebec and the polacre [fig. 66], types of ship not found anywhere else in the world. The xebec was developed from the 'brigantine' used originally by Mediterranean pirates, and had no relation whatsoever to the brigantine used in northern European waters. The normal xebec rig was square on the foremast and lateen on the main and mizen, but was variable depending on the strength and direction of the wind. It was a very complicated rig and though it certainly produced extra speed through the water, it needed a very large crew to handle it. Nevertheless, the xebec had a good cargo capacity and with its speed could expect to outsail any attacker.

The other Mediterranean trading ship was the polacre. This had three masts, square-rigged on the main and carrying lateen sails on fore and mizen, though occasionally it might be lateen-rigged on all three. The polacres were usually larger than xebecs, some of them built up to a tonnage of about 1,200. Their name came from their pole masts, single spars without topmasts.

The rest of the world was as prolific as Europe in the types of vessels used for trade. The standard ship of the Arabs was the dhow, lateen-rigged on a single mast [fig. 67]. For larger cargoes there was the baghla, quite a large ship whose hull design had been influenced by the Portuguese, Dutch and English ships which traded in Arab waters in the seventeenth and eighteenth centuries. Another was the ghanja, again a European-influenced hull but built with a quarterdeck which extended aft over the rudder head by a considerable distance. Both the baghla and the ghanja used the full lateen rig on two or three masts. Further east still the trading ship was the junk, which must be by some centuries the oldest ship design still in use. Marco Polo, in his account of his voyage to China in 1298, describes the ships he saw there, and even though he did not go into much detail, they

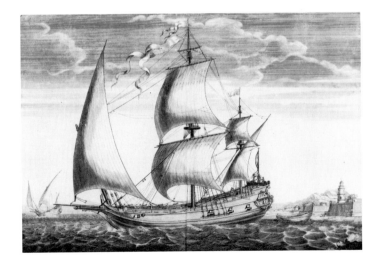

65. A Cutter Close-Hauled on the Port Tack. Attributed to Charles Brooking

This small painting on panel depicts a variety of craft off the English coast. The sea in particular is painted with great freedom.

66. Polacre de la voile. Claude Randon, *c.*1700

A polacre, three-masted and lateen-rigged on fore and mizen, square-rigged on the main. The rig varied according to the whim of the owner, many polacres being lateen-rigged on all three masts. Polacres were virtually exclusive to the Mediterranean. They were sometimes built up to 1,200 tons.

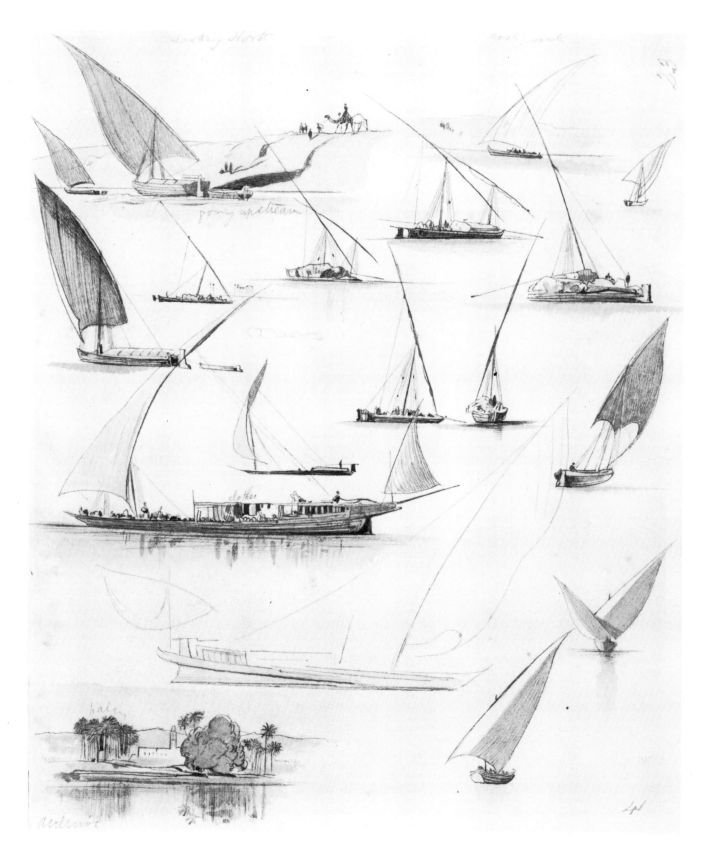

67. Nile Craft. Edward Lear

Lear travelled widely around the Mediterranean, filling his sketch-books with
details drawn on the spot. Here he portrays a variety of sailing craft, and, at
the bottom left corner, the palm trees of Antinoc.

were unmistakably junks. The other far-eastern trading ship was the lorcha, a European hull shape with the Chinese junk rig. It first appeared in Macao when the Portuguese set up a trading station there in 1557.

Of smaller vessels built for the coastwise trade, there was an almost infinite variety. In the Baltic were the jagt and the galea, though there were some differences in hull design and rig according to the nation or even the port in which they were built. In Holland the tjalk was the best known but it had many derivatives, such as the kof and the bezaanschuit, all adaptations to suit particular trades. Barges, keels and ketches carried most of the coastwise trade of England, though for the coal trade a particular design was evolved known as a cat, which spread through most of the nations of northern Europe. This was based upon a Norwegian model, with a canoe stern with projecting quarters and a deep waist, very strongly constructed to carry a cargo of about 600 tons of coal. For his voyages of discovery in the mid-eighteenth century, Captain Cook chose Whitby cats as the ships best suited for his purpose, mainly because of their strong construction but also because they were suitably small and weatherly.

In France the chasse-marée was the most popular of the smaller types and was built in large numbers with a second role in view. Their original rig, three-masted with the conventional square and lateen sails, gave way to a lugsail rig on all three masts, with very large sails set on masts raked aft. This rig made them quite a bit faster than most other contemporary vessels of their size and they were used extensively for smuggling and for privateering in wartime. The small merchant ship of Portugal was the fregata, of Spain the felucca and the tartane, of Greece the sacoleva and the trekandini. All these were comparatively small ships, and all were subject to local variations so that, for example, a felucca built in one port might have slight differences in hull design and rig from a felucca built in the next port along the coast.

Although this large number of types of smaller trading vessels might argue a conflict of practice and opinion on the part of merchants as to the most efficient small ship to further their economic interests, it was the variety of local shipbuilding skills, the demands of the particular trades they followed, and more particularly the average of local weather conditions and depths of water in which they operated that were responsible for the wide variations. The contribution they made to the phenomenal growth of trade during the sixteenth and seventeenth centuries is inestimable. Without them the bigger merchant ships, which carried the trade between continents, would have been stifled through the lack of a local means of distribution. Humble little ships they may have been in comparison with their ocean-going sisters, yet on them rested the reality of spreading the riches of the world to the peoples of the world. They expanded a hundredfold the profitable markets on which national wealth grew and prospered.

II. THE PATTERN OF SEA POWER

That sea power was the key to prosperity and the growth of national wealth was well enough understood by all the maritime nations of Europe. That its exercise depended on a fleet of warships to ensure the freedom of the merchant ships to trade on their lawful occasions was equally well understood. The term 'lawful' was what had to be fought for, and in the atmosphere of the scramble for world trade in the seventeenth and eighteenth centuries it was apt to have two meanings. Another nation's claim of monopoly of trade on account of prior discovery or later conquest was not lawful and had to be challenged, by force if necessary; one's own similar claim was lawful and had to be defended, again by force if necessary.

Throughout most of the eighteenth century Europe virtually dominated the world. In the twin continents of America, France, Britain, Spain and Portugal enjoyed colonial rights which, in theory, brought with them exclusive rights of trade if those nations possessed adequate sea power to enforce them. In Africa, France, Spain, and the Arabians, led by the Turks, battled for control of the Mediterranean shore, while in the remainder of the continent the British, Dutch, and Portuguese controlled the trade. In eastern waters the trade of India, China and Japan was held firmly in the hands of the East India Companies— British, French, Portuguese and Dutch. The growth of maritime enterprise called for a never-ending supply of new ships, both merchant ships and the warships to defend them, and the ship-yards of Europe echoed to the sounds of new building almost without cease.

The pattern of sea power was in a state of constant change. The European giants at the start of the century were Britain, France and Spain, with a large number of smaller navies trying to dominate their local waters. Holland, one of the giants of the seventeenth century, had been exhausted at sea by the three Anglo-Dutch wars and on land by the ambitions of Philip of Spain and Louis of France to absorb her border provinces. Her navy had lost the race for sea power and her policy was based somewhat hopefully on the possibility of maintaining her eastern interests as a sort of 'piggy in the middle' of the more vicious conflicts between Britain and France for supremacy in those waters.

Of the smaller navies, that of Genoa in the Mediterranean had virtually disappeared by the beginning of the eighteenth century, worn out by her many earlier wars against Venice. The Venetian navy, once dominant in the eastern Mediterranean, soon followed her into oblivion. Two wars against the Turks had exhausted her and both her trade and her empire in eastern Europe were eagerly absorbed by Spain, Portugal and Turkey. She no longer existed as a sea power of any account and her great and busy port of Venice [fig. 68] fell empty and silted up.

A new navy was beginning to appear in northern Europe, to challenge Sweden for the rich trade of the Baltic. In 1696, the new Tsar of Russia, Peter I (the Great), had built a small fleet of sailing warships and galleys on the banks of the Don River, sailed it down river under his own command, and won a toehold in the Sea of Azov against Turkish resistance.

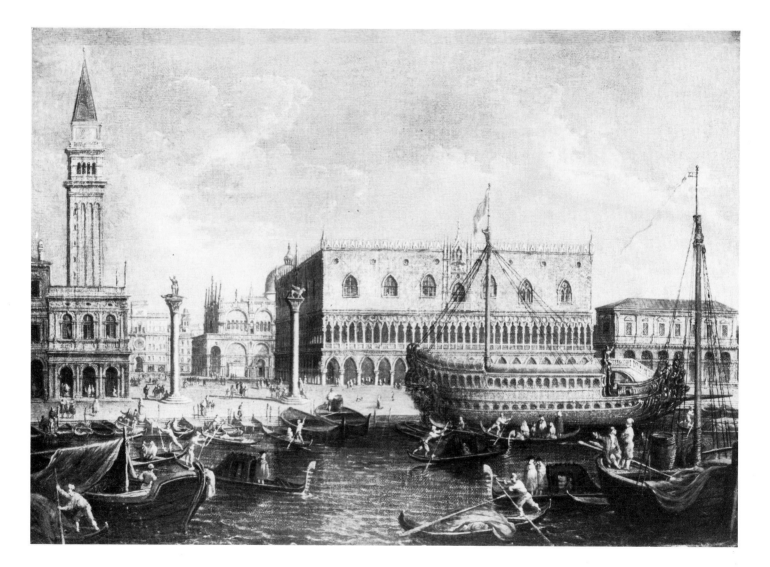

68. Doge's Palace, Venice. Unidentified artist
In this late-seventeenth-century painting there is little hint of the actual and contemporary decline of Venetian commerce. Indeed, contributing to a genre whose best-known and most capable exponent was Canaletto, the artist places deliberate stress on the foreground bustle of trade which, by implication, finances the splendour of the city beyond.

Determined that the Tsar should not repeat this adventure in the Baltic, Charles XII of Sweden declared war on Russia and defeated her in a land battle at Narva, a victory which made him confident that Peter the Great was sufficiently discouraged to leave things as they were in the Baltic.

But it was not to be. When Peter the Great became Tsar of Russia at the age of twenty-two he was wise enough to realize that his country needed an outlet to the sea if she were to prosper. After his success in the Sea of Azov he travelled round Europe to study the naval arts of gunnery, navigation and shipbuilding, and on his return raised an army and advanced to the Gulf of Finland. There he planned the construction of a naval base and dockyard and began to build a navy, with which to challenge the sea power of Sweden. He had the better of a series of battles against the Swedish fleet and at the peace that followed Sweden not only lost her Baltic provinces to Russia, giving her the outlet to the sea she needed, but also lost her naval mastery of the Baltic Sea to Peter the Great's new navy.

Even before the war in the Baltic had come to its end, a new conflict had broken out in the Mediterranean. In 1718 Spain, in an attempt to regain some of her losses in the War of the Spanish Succession, sent her fleet to cover a military assault on Sicily which, with the exception of the port of Messina, was quickly occupied, a significant change in the balance of maritime power in the Mediterranean. A Spanish fleet operating from Sicilian ports would have little difficulty in controlling all the Mediterranean trade routes. An immediate coalition of England, France, Holland and Austria was formed to restore the previous balance. That France, traditionally Spain's closest friend and ally in Europe, should so quickly join the opposition against her was no more than a reflection of how greatly the interests of a nation counted in the safeguarding of her seaborne trade when set against traditional ties of friendship with a former ally.

Britain, with wide trading interests in the Mediterranean, had kept a fleet permanently in those waters since the start of the

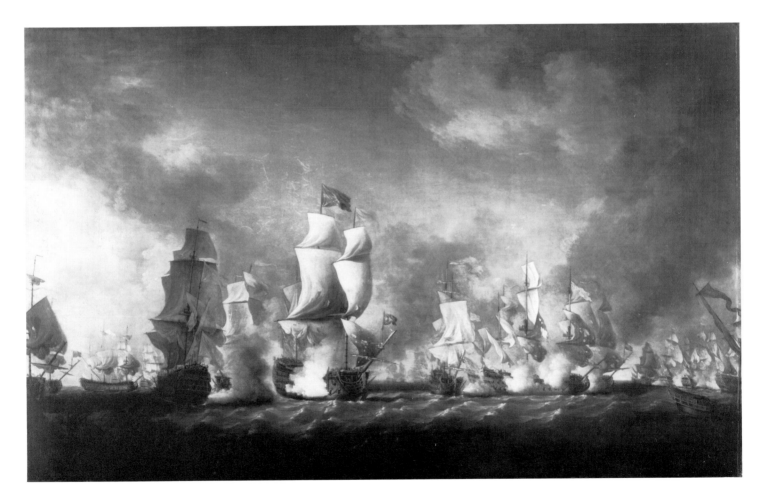

60 THE GREAT AGE OF SAIL

69. Battle of Cape Passero, 11 August 1718. Richard Paton
The theme of Paton's incident-packed painting is the defeat of the Spanish fleet near Messina, which prevented Spanish reoccupation of Sicily. Sir George Byng's flagship *Barfleur* (foreground, left of centre) is seen firing her starboard broadside at a Spanish rear-admiral's ship, which returns fire. To the right of the picture the chief incident is the capture of the Spanish flagship, *Real San Felipe*.

century. Quickly on the scene, it met the Spanish fleet off Cape Passero [fig. 69], and put it to flight, capturing seven and sinking four of the twenty ships of the line which formed the Spanish fleet. In a separate attack from the Atlantic another British squadron devastated the Spanish coast from Vigo to San Sebastian, burning or capturing every Spanish ship found in the ports along that stretch of coast. It was enough to convince Spain that she could not sustain her ambition to dominate the Mediterranean trade routes against the interests of the other trading nations, and the war came to a quick end with the naval power of Spain substantially lessened through her heavy losses.

A quarrel between Britain and Spain in the West Indies was enough to start the next war, a small affair in which trade with the Spanish West Indies was the immediate cause. Under the Treaty of Utrecht signed in 1713 Spain had granted Britain the right of sending one ship a year to the West Indies, with a cargo of manufactured goods for sale in each of two annual fairs. In the aggressive temper of the times, there is no doubt that this right was abused and a good deal of illicit trade found its way from Britain to the Spanish islands in the Caribbean. The Spanish customs, operating in small, fast, and well-armed ships known as guarda costas, did what they could to stop this contraband trade and there is equally no doubt that their methods, when they caught a British ship, were arbitrary and brutal. In

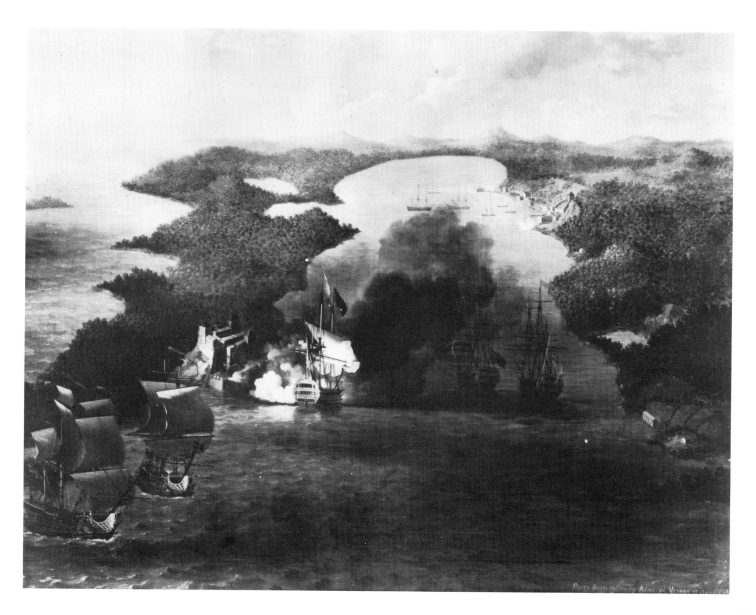

70. The Capture of Porto Bello, 22 November 1739. Samuel Scott
A large picture, drawn with a curiously attractive but certainly awry sense of perspective, showing Admiral Vernon's action from the south-west of the harbour. In the left middle distance lies the Castillo de Ferro (Iron Castle), which is assaulted by Vernon's flagship, the *Burford*. In the left foreground are the *Strafford* and the *Princess Louisa*.

1731 they stopped the British brig *Rebecca*, tortured the crew and, it was alleged, cut off the ear of her captain, Robert Jenkins. Although this was, perhaps, but a small thorn in the ample flesh of British trade as a whole in those waters, it festered over the years and came to a head in 1739 with British merchants clamouring for retribution over the excesses of the guarda costas. In a dramatic debate in Parliament, Jenkins displayed his severed ear to the Members, who, against the wishes of the Government, voted for war, inevitably to be known as the War of Jenkins's Ear.

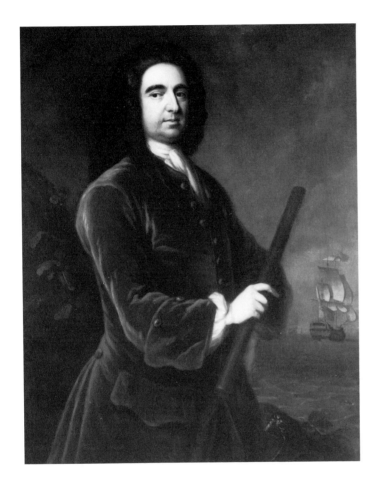

Admiral Edward Vernon [fig. 71], a Member of Parliament, declared that if he were given six ships he would go to the West Indies and teach Spain a lesson. The Government took him at his word, gave him his six ships, and sent him out to the West Indies expecting him to make a fool of himself and extricate them from a war they did not want. However, he captured the port of Porto Bello [fig. 70] with considerable ease and extracted a sizeable ransom. There was no holding him now and he planned

a new attack on the great Spanish port of Cartagena. His capture of Porto Bello had aroused so much enthusiasm in Britain that the Government had no option but to send him reinforcements in ships and an army to capture the port. The expedition proved a disaster, partly because an epidemic of yellow fever swept through both fleet and army, but mainly because admiral and general distrusted each other so much that they were not even on speaking terms. Tobias Smollett was in the fleet at Cartagena serving as a surgeon's mate and has left us, in his novel *Roderick Random*, a grim picture of the conditions of life on board British warships and their attendant hospital ships. Perhaps the only good thing to come out of this War of Jenkins's Ear was the training and taste for battle of a young British captain, Edward Boscawen. He distinguished himself both at Porto Bello and at Cartagena, and was to distinguish himself still further in the war that was even then raging in Europe and as an admiral in the subsequent war.

The ensuing war in Europe was fought over the succession of Maria Theresa to the throne of Austria and to the rest of the Habsburg possessions. Supported by Britain and Holland, her claim was disputed by a powerful coalition, including France, Spain and Prussia. At pains to preserve the balance of power in Europe, Britain was concerned to preserve her maritime supremacy from the threat of a Franco-Spanish fleet.

The war at sea was, in a way, peripheral to the war fought on land, though in the longer term its influence on the still developing pattern of world trade was immense. French sea power, seriously weakened by the loss of twelve ships of the line in the two actions off Cape Finisterre, was never able fully to regain its strength. Britain was now universally regarded as the dominant sea power in Europe. In addition to her warships France had lost over 3,500 merchant vessels during the wars, mainly to British privateers, and her overseas trade was in ruins. Britain's fleet, nearly twice the size of the French when the war started, had increased considerably during the eight years the war lasted, partly through the building of new ships, partly through the absorption of most of the captured French ships into her own navy. But beyond that the loss of those 3,500 merchant ships at a time when trade was expanding so fast that the ships could hardly keep up with it threatened France with virtual bankruptcy. It is true that Britain had lost nearly as many merchant ships during the war as had France but, serious as such a loss was to her, she had a larger economic base from which to absorb her losses and a vigorous rebuilding programme reduced the impact on her capacity to trade around the world.

There was one naval battle in the Mediterranean off Toulon [fig. 72] between the British Mediterranean fleet and a Franco-

71. **Portrait of Edward Vernon, Admiral of the White.**
Charles Phillips

Painted before the audacious expedition of Edward Vernon (1684–1757) to the West Indies in 1739, the portrait includes a background representation of a two-decker, with a red ensign, a commissioning pendant, and a blue flag at the fore. The likeness of Vernon captures something of his arrogant personality.

Spanish fleet, unremarkable except that the rigidity of the orders governing the line of battle caused a difference of opinion between the British Commander-in-Chief and his second in command, so that a possible chance of success was missed. In two convoy battles off Cape Finisterre [fig. 73] the two British admirals concerned, George Anson and Edward Hawke [fig. 85], showed what personal initiative could do to circumvent the sterility which so often accompanied a strict adherence to the

attacking the centre with his leading ships—a modified version of the *Fighting Instructions*. Admiral Richard Lestock, in the rear, made no attempt to bring his ships into action but kept the line, following the *Fighting Instructions* to the letter. The Franco-Spanish fleet escaped, and in the courts martial which enquired into the reason for this Mathews was cashiered and Lestock acquitted. It is of interest that one of Mathews's captains in the centre squadron was Edward Hawke who, only three years later,

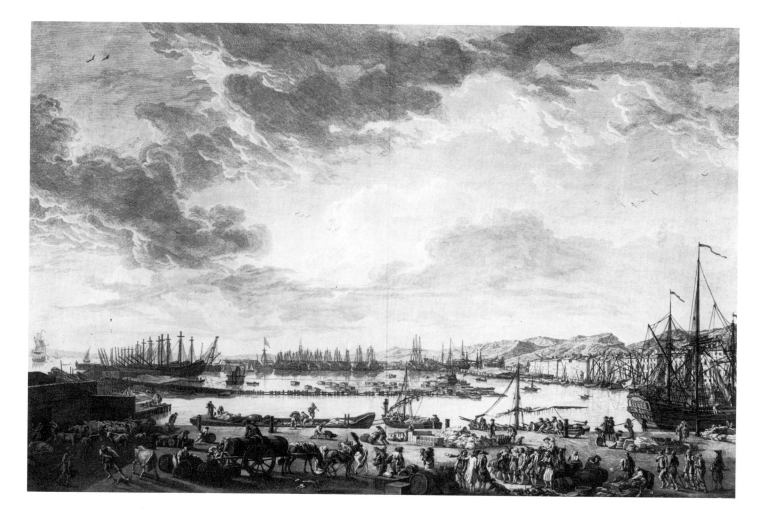

Fighting Instructions. The latter, originally introduced to bring some element of control over the fleet in action, had become as great a handicap as the confusion they had been designed to counter. Unfortunately they had now become Holy Writ, to be ignored, or even modified, at one's peril.

The sterility of blind adherence to the *Fighting Instructions* was exposed at Toulon in 1744. In brief, Thomas Mathews, one of two admirals, had attempted to bring the enemy to action by

broke the rule with conspicuous success, and that one of the senior officers sitting in judgment at the courts martial was John Byng who, during the next war, discovered that too strict an adherence to the line of battle led to his execution on the quarterdeck of HMS *Monarch* [fig. 83].

The two actions that were fought off Cape Finisterre in 1747 show the beginning of the break-out from the rigidity of the line of battle. They were, perhaps, not naval battles in the strict

72. Toulon—Old Town. Charles Nicolas Cochin the Younger after Claude Joseph Vernet, 1762

Toulon in south-western France was founded by Romans. For centuries it has been the most important naval base in the country, with an arsenal, dry docks and shipbuilding yards. It has a well-sheltered harbour and is surrounded by mountains, which make it a superb defensive site.

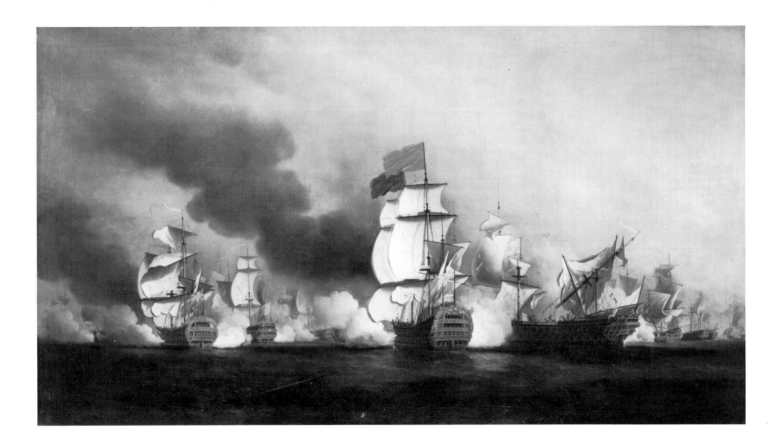

meaning of the word since both were attacks on large convoys escorted by ships of the line. This inevitably threw the French on the defensive, to try to hold up the British attack long enough for the convoys to escape. The two British admirals, George Anson in the first action and Edward Hawke in the second, could not afford to waste time forming a line of battle before making their attacks, and hoisted the signal for a general chase under which each ship made all sail possible and attacked individually, the first ship to arrive going for the nearest enemy and subsequent arrivals passing her on her disengaged side and making for the next nearest. It was not a tactic that would be applicable to every naval battle but it did restore the initiative to an admiral by providing him with a legitimate licence to abandon the line of battle whenever speed of action was essential for success.

73. First Battle of Finisterre, 3 May 1747. Samuel Scott
Lord Anson's family celebrated his victory off Cape Finisterre by commissioning this picture from Scott. In the foreground, the Vice-Admiral's flagship the *Prince George* features prominently if rather fraudulently, for she was not in fact deeply involved in this action. To her right lies the stricken *Invincible*, and beyond appear more captured French ships.

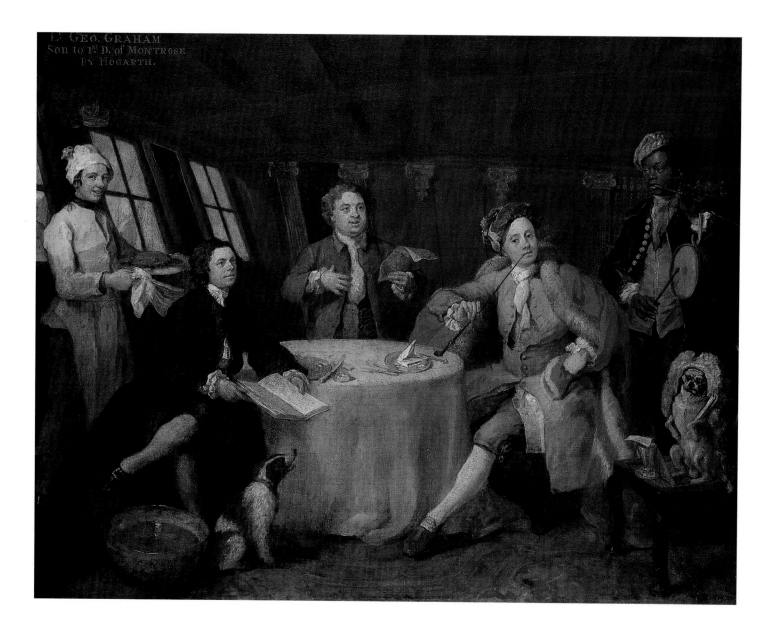

Plate 34. Lord George Graham in his Cabin. William Hogarth

Paintings of shipboard scenes are rare in any period of history, and few are so charming or informal as this one by Hogarth. The seated figure, wearing a fashionable fur-lined cape and smoking a pipe, is Captain Lord George Graham, son of the Duke of Montrose. The other figures are thought to include Graham's purser and clerk, and the painting may celebrate his successful action off Ostend in June 1745, when he captured several French privateers. The dog to the right, provided with a wig and song sheet, is Hogarth's pug, Trump. Hogarth's sharp wit, careful observation and belligerent attitude to the ills he saw around him have left us with a rich legacy illustrating many facets of eighteenth-century life.

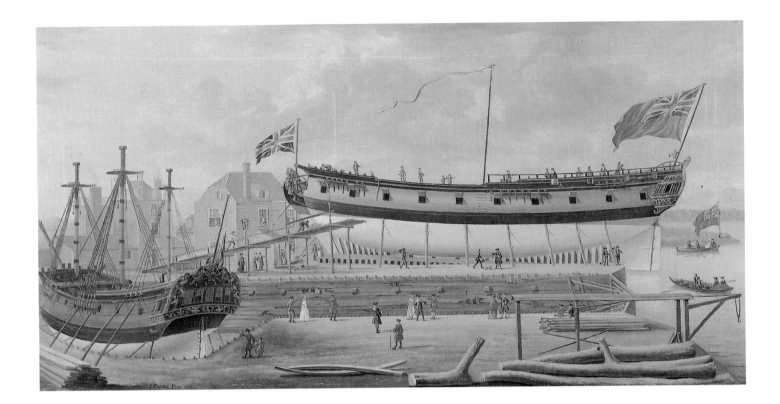

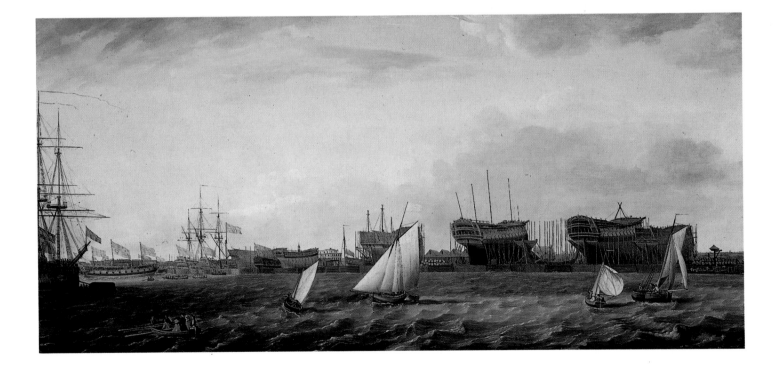

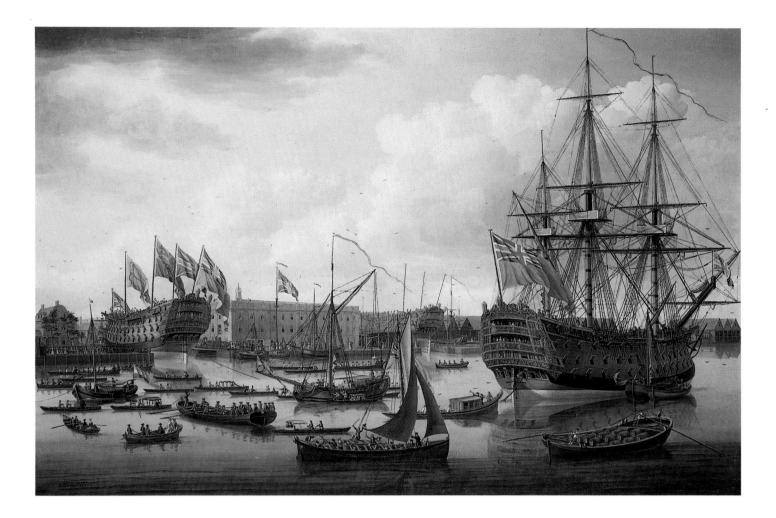

Plate 35. A Sixth-Rate on the Stocks. John Cleveley the Elder, 1759

John Cleveley received no formal training as an easel painter, and we do not know exactly how he developed his skill. He was born the son of a joiner at Southwark, London, and he in turn became a joiner's apprentice. He worked in the Royal Dockyard at Deptford, which was to become the backdrop for many of his paintings, but he also painted some battle scenes and ceremonial events. The shipyard in this painting was probably the one owned by William Wells at Rotherhithe. The vessel to be launched is a 24-gun ship.

Plate 36. Blackwall Yard. Francis Holman, 1784

At the time when this view of the Blackwall shipyard was painted it had become the largest private shipyard in the country. It had been owned by the Perry family since 1708, and was a major contractor to the Royal Navy. The smaller vessel which has just entered the water to the left of the picture, flying the white ensign and the royal standard of the Hanoverians, is the 44-gun *Adventure*.

Plate 37. A Launch at Deptford. John Cleveley the Elder, 1757

Though it is dated 1757, Cleveley evidently brought together in this painting details from a number of different events he had witnessed in earlier years. For, despite its wealth of detail, giving the impression that it is an eye-witness account of a ship launching ceremony, this is a composite, showing two warships which could not in fact have been present at the launch of each other. The three-decker being floated out on the left is the *Cambridge*, with 80 guns, launched on 21 October 1755. The ship on the right appears to be the *Royal George*, of 100 guns, launched at Woolwich in 1756 (and destined to attain notoriety when, on 29 August 1782, she foundered at Spithead, with appalling loss of life). It is known, however, that the *Royal George* never went to Deptford, nor would her draught have allowed her to do so. Nevertheless the essentially fictitious nature of the scene does not compromise its scrupulous accuracy in terms of ship portraiture and topography.

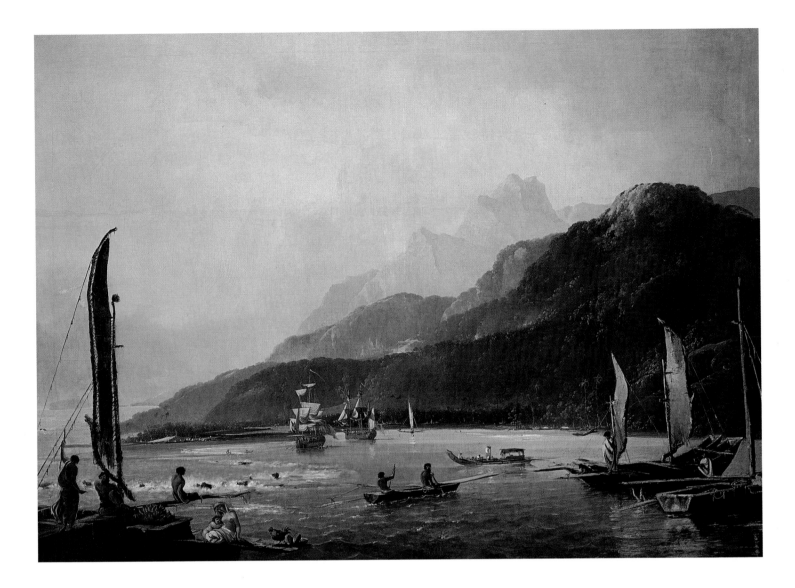

Plate 38. 'Resolution' and 'Adventure' in Matavi Bay, Tahiti, *c.*1773. William Hodges, 1776

Hodges was the last-minute replacement for Johan Zoffany on Cook's second great voyage of exploration. Zoffany was a portrait painter, and it is unlikely that he would have painted the glorious landscapes with the beauty and grandeur that were to characterize Hodges' canvases. This is one of a number of large paintings commissioned by the Admiralty from sketches made on the spot. Hodges has created a scene of peaceful co-existence between Cook's encampment in the distance, with his two vessels at anchor drying their sails, and the Tahitians, depicted in classical poses, with a variety of canoes of different types. The brilliance of the colours and the beauty of the landscape are breathtaking. Hodges had been the pupil of Richard Wilson, and, like his master, specialized in landscapes. His style was too raw and freely painted to suit conventional tastes. He later tried his hand at banking, but failed to make a success of it and eventually committed suicide.

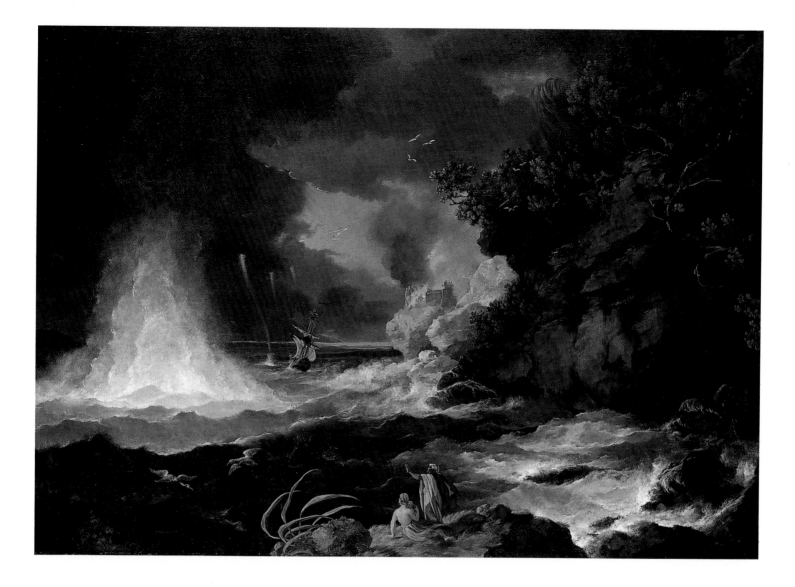

Plate 39. A View of Cape Stephens in Cook's Straits, New Zealand, with Waterspout. William Hodges, 1776

Here the terrifying power of the sea is shown with great drama. All the elements of nature—earth, air, fire, and water—are perturbed. Humanity is dwarfed, and even the *Resolution* looks like a toy ship tossed in the waves. On the headland in the middle distance a deserted *Pa* or Maori stronghold, burns fiercely. Both Captain Cook and George Forster, the natural historian, wrote vivid descriptions of the waterspout they had observed in May 1773, and three years later Hodges produced this magical painting of the phenomenon from sketches he had made on the spot.

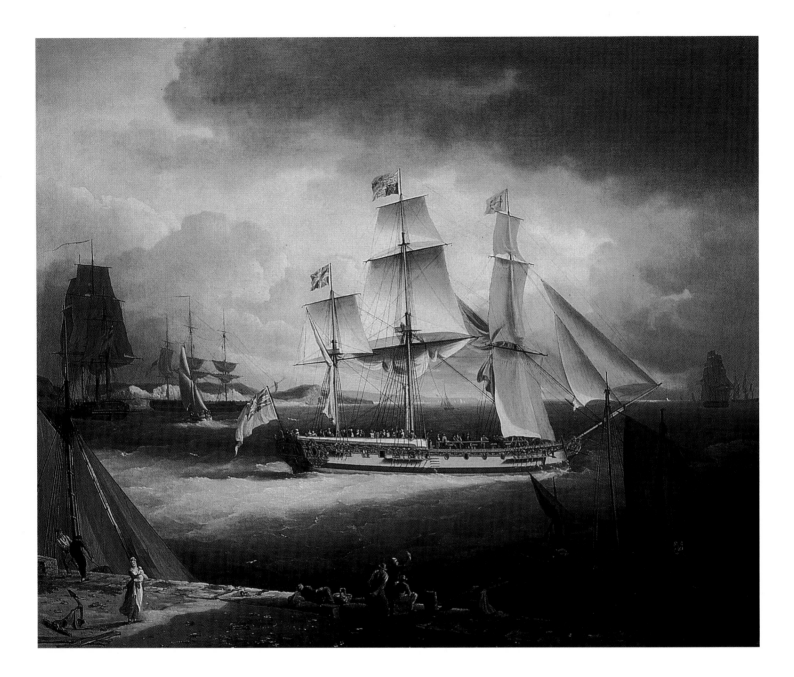

Plate 40. The Royal Yacht 'Royal Sovereign' (1804).
John Thomas Serres, 1809

A most charming painting of one of the royal yachts, which had been built in
a long succession since the seventeenth century. The *Royal Sovereign* was
designed by Sir John Henshaw and launched at Deptford in 1804. She was
considered to be one of the best of the royal sailing yachts and remained in
royal service until 1832. Here she is probably shown at Weymouth when
George III visited in 1806.

   In 1793 John Thomas Serres succeeded his father, Dominic Serres the Elder,
as marine painter to the king. He had been taught by his father, and was a
great admirer of the work of Philippe Jacques de Loutherbourg but, unlike him,
did not attempt many battle scenes, preferring ship portraits and views of
shipping. He taught drawing at the Chelsea naval school and published the
Liber Nauticus in 1805 as an aid to drawing ships for students.

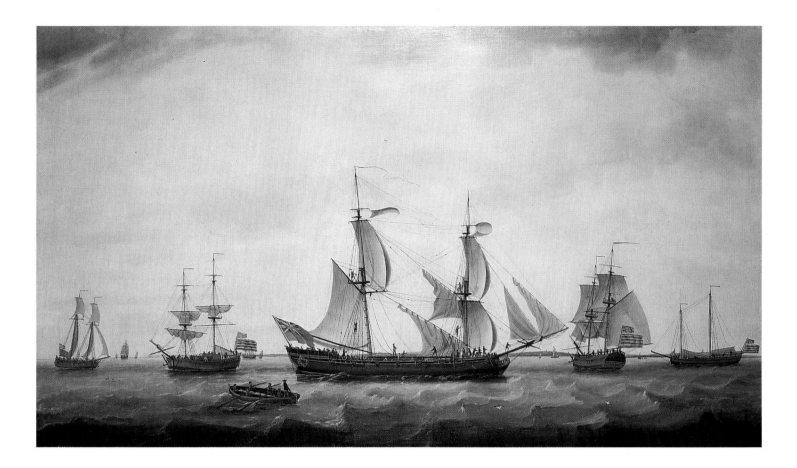

**Plate 41. A British Brig with Four Captured American Merchantmen.
Francis Holman, 1778**

Attempts have been made, with little success, to identify the subject as a
particular incident in the American Revolutionary War. The British vessel in
the centre is surrounded by four American prizes, which fly the Union flag over
the rebel striped flag. Francis Holman was one of the most important British
marine painters of the eighteenth century, exhibiting regularly from the late
1760s until the 1780s, yet his origins are obscure and the known details of his
life are very sparse. It is believed that Thomas Luny was one of his pupils. He
produced paintings of actions, ship portraits, and many delightful scenes of
shipyards.

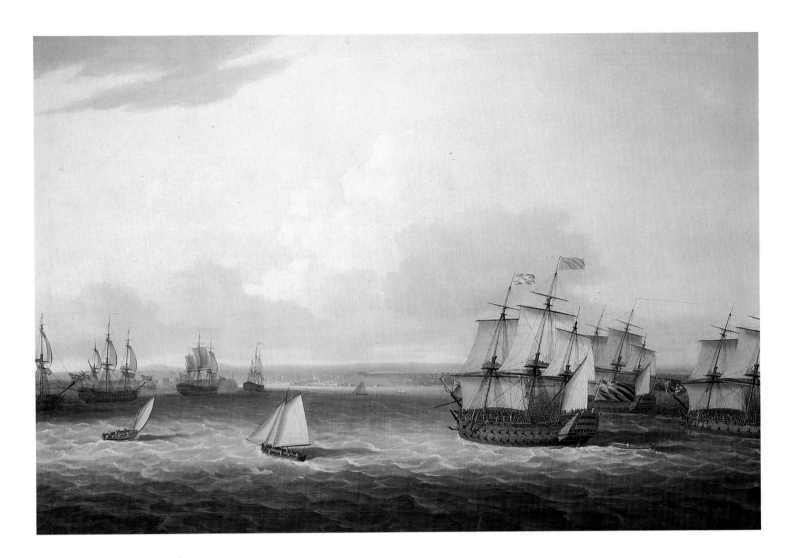

**Plate 42. The British Fleet entering the Harbour at Havana,
16 August 1762. Dominic Serres, 1775**

One of a series of paintings by Serres which describes the six-week siege,
bombardment and eventual capture of Havana, which was the last major
operation of the Seven Years War. Here in the later stages, after the fall of
Havana, the British fleet enters the harbour to take possession of the Spanish
ships. To the left, passing Morro castle, is the *Valiant*, commanded by
Commodore Augustus Keppel leading the red squadron. On the right is the
Namur under Admiral Sir George Pocock, the commander-in-chief of the naval
squadron. Three members of the Keppel family were involved: the Earl of
Albemarle, who commanded the army and was in overall command; his
brother William, as a general; while Augustus was second-in-command of the
naval squadron. Serres was probably commissioned by Augustus to paint this
series, which he may have based on a set of prints.

Dominic Serres was born in Gascony; rebelling against his parents' choice
of career, he went to sea. Eventually he settled in England and took up painting
as his profession. The combination of his knowledge of seamanship and skill
as a draughtsman make his works valuable as historical documents.

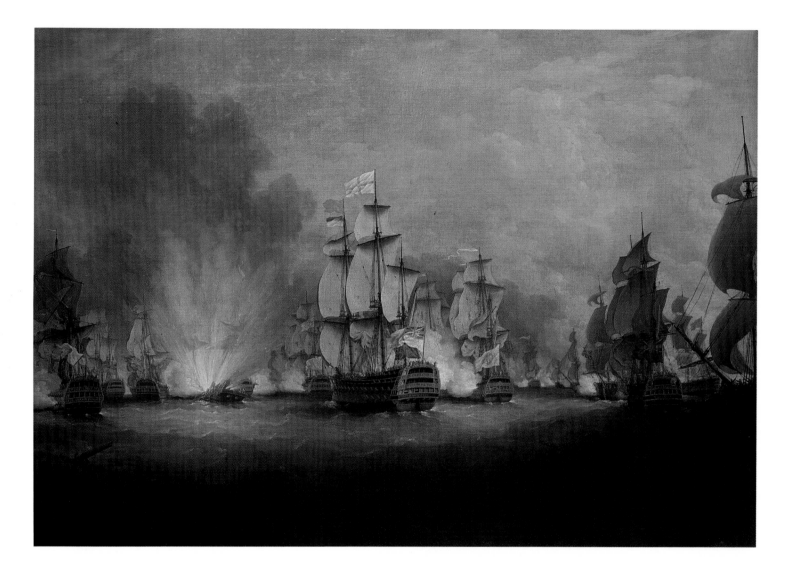

**Plate 43. Moonlight Battle off Cape St. Vincent, 16 January 1780.
Richard Paton**

Paton has chosen to portray the dramatic moment when, at 4.40 p.m., the
Spanish ship the *San Domingo* blew up with the loss of all her crew. The British
commander, Sir George Rodney, in his flagship the *Sandwich* (in the centre of
the painting), was escorting a convoy which was shipping supplies to the
besieged outpost at Gibraltar before proceeding to the West Indies. The battle
was called 'Moonlight' because it continued through the night until 2.00 a.m.,
when most of the Spanish squadron had surrendered.

Richard Paton, like a number of other eighteenth-century marine artists,
took up painting relatively late in life; for the greater part of his career he also
worked for the Excise. His work varies in quality but this painting shows a
strong sense of drama and rich colour.

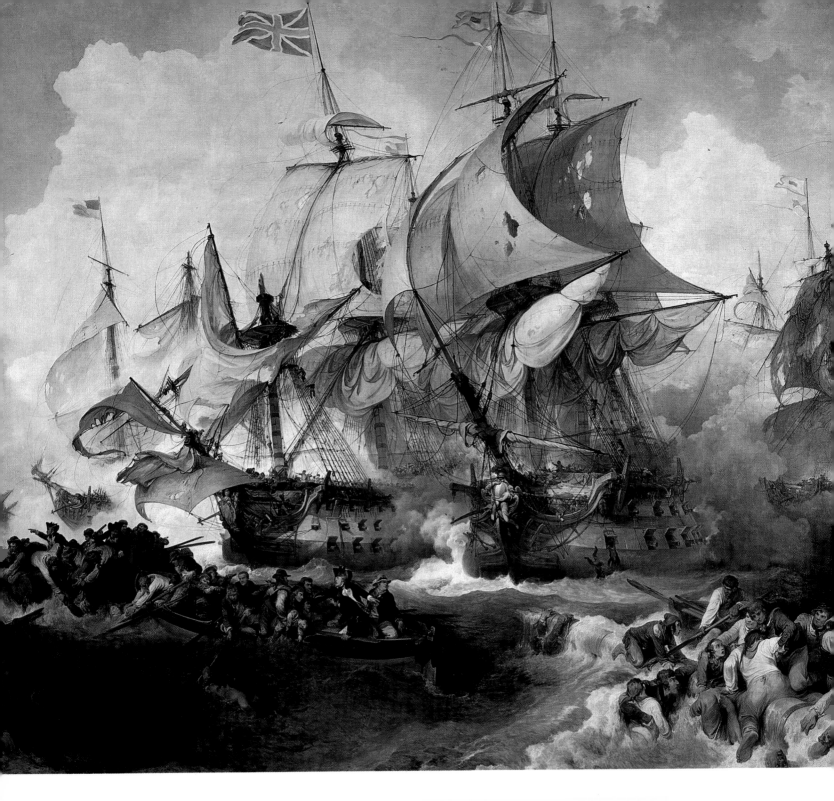

Plate 44. Battle of the Glorious First of June.
Philippe Jacques de Loutherbourg

De Loutherbourg was one of the most precocious, prodigious and prolific artists
of his generation. He arrived in London aged thirty-one, having achieved
considerable critical and financial success in Paris. He started work designing
stage sets for David Garrick at Drury Lane and in the 1760s he received
commissions to paint military battles as designs for prints.

Here de Loutherbourg has produced one of the most dramatic
interpretations of a sea battle ever to be painted. Unlike his contemporaries,
he has shown the human drama of war at sea, an arresting image of men and
ships pitched both against one another and the force of the sea. In the
foreground, where English sailors rescue their French opponents, he places
notable (if idealistic) stress on the humanitarian episodes which punctuate war.
It was, in all senses, a powerfully nationalistic image, and this may have
contributed to the Royal Family's decision in 1812 to buy the painting.

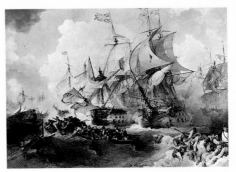

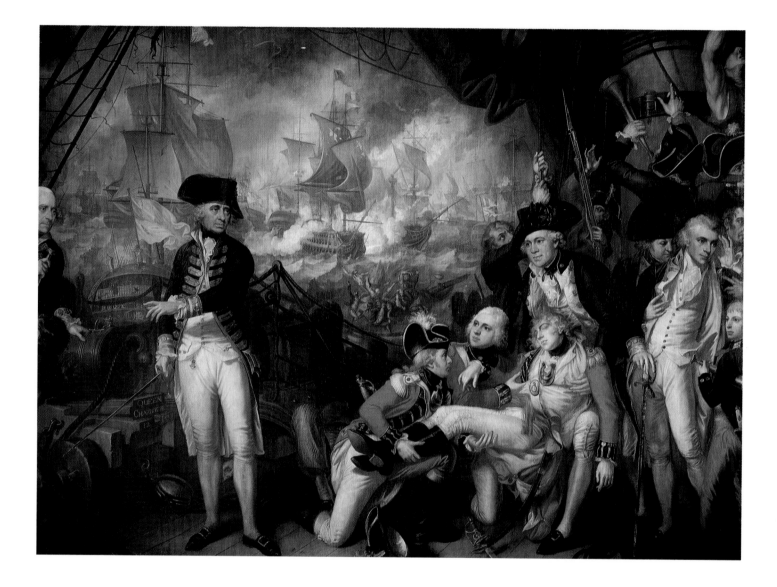

**Plate 45. Lord Howe on the Quarterdeck of the 'Queen Charlotte'.
Mather Brown**

This large canvas, not so much a battle piece as a rather bizarre group portrait,
depicts an incident from the 'Glorious First of June'. The picture has a
somewhat 'stagey' appearance: the action between the *Brunswick* and the
Vengeur in the background is like a theatre backdrop. The principal figure on
the left is Lord Howe, who somewhat inappropriately wears full-dress uniform;
in reality he had worn the blue coat and fur hat befitting a sailor. The swooning
figure on the right is the dying Captain Neville of the Queen's Regiment, whose
members were acting as marines on board. When the *Queen Charlotte* returned
to England, Mather Brown was given access to the ship and made sketches of
the participants.

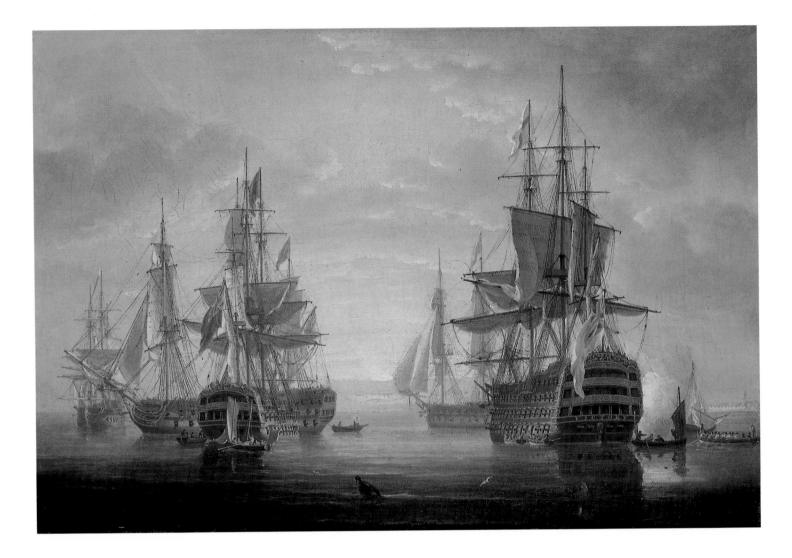

Plate 46. Nelson's Flagships. Nicholas Pocock, 1807

This serene little picture with its delicate colouring shows ships of the line
associated with some of the great actions of the wars with France. On the left
of the group is the *Agamemnon*, 64 guns, which Nelson had commanded at the
beginning of the French revolutionary wars, and which is always supposed to
have been his favourite ship. Next, broadside to the viewer, is the *Vanguard*,
74 guns, which was his flagship at the Battle of the Nile in 1798. In front of
the *Vanguard* is the *Elephant*, which became his temporary flagship at
Copenhagen in 1801. The *Victory* is shown as originally built, and beyond is
the *Captain*, 74 guns, Nelson's ship at the Battle of St. Vincent.

As the master of a merchant ship, Nicholas Pocock had considerable
experience of the sea before he took up painting as a profession in his forties.
His log-books had been carefully illustrated with views of harbours and ships.
He witnessed the 'Glorious First of June' from the frigate *Pegasus*, and was often
commissioned to paint scenes of naval engagements, which he executed with
meticulous detail.

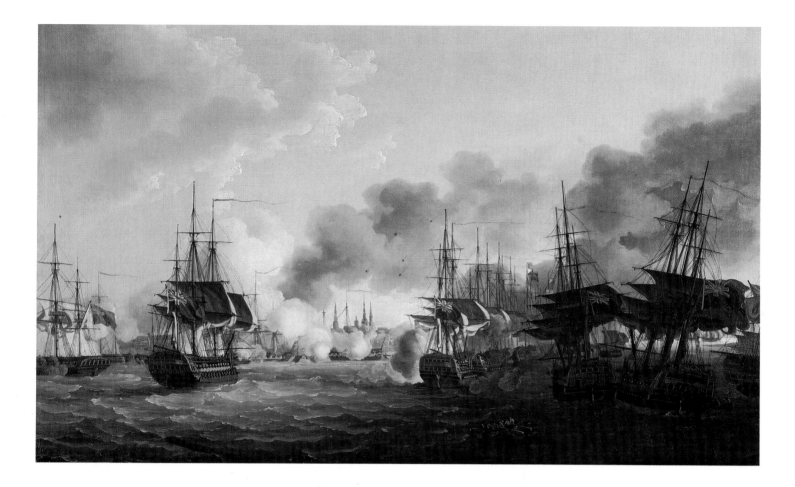

Plate 47. Battle of Copenhagen, 30 March–2 April 1801.
John Thomas Serres, 1801

This battle is perhaps most famous for the words 'I really do not see the signal', Lord Nelson's response to Commander-in-Chief Sir Hyde Parker's signal to break off the action. Nelson continued the fight and won a victory at the price of great loss of life on both sides. The shoals in the approaches to Copenhagen made the British attack hard to plan and execute, since the three-deckers could not be brought into such shallow water. The difficulties can be seen from this painting, as the line of British ships, with very little room to manoeuvre, fire at the Danish line and the smoke of gunfire billows out around the spires of Copenhagen beyond them.

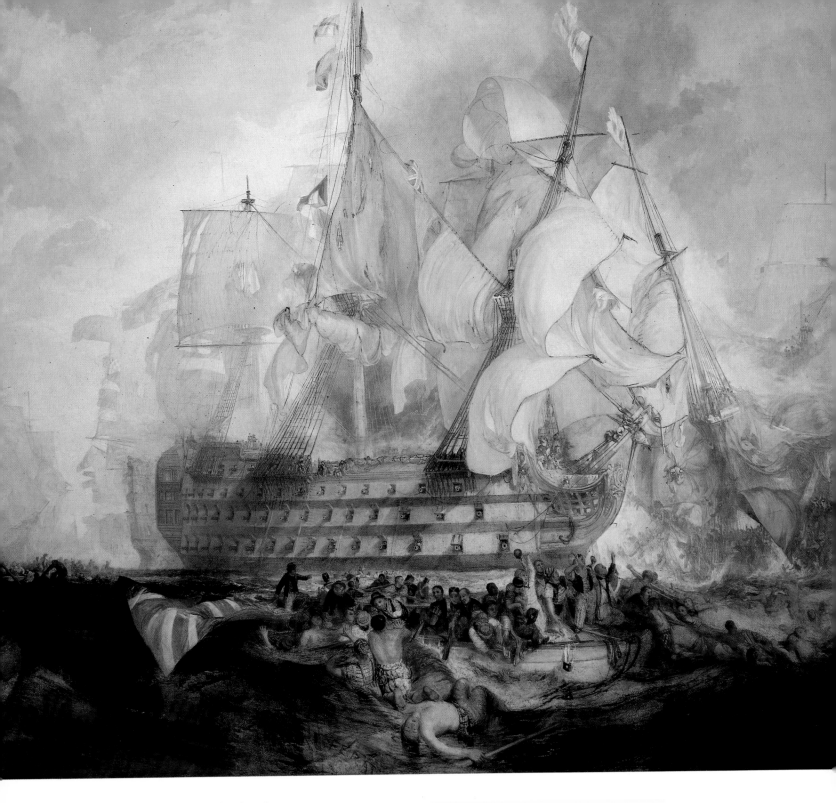

Plate 48. Battle of Trafalgar, 21 October 1805.
Joseph Mallord William Turner, 1824

In 1823 George IV commissioned Turner to paint *Battle of Trafalgar* to hang
in St. James Palace as a companion to de Loutherbourg's *Glorious First of June*,
in a series of paintings of British victories. The commission was one of Turner's
most important; he took great trouble to get the details right and wrote to the
marine painter John Christian Schetky to obtain sketches of the *Victory*. His
composition was clearly influenced by de Loutherbourg's great painting, with
its Romantic view of the clash of elements, human and natural, in the drama
of battle. Turner's painting was completed in 1824, but, despite the pains he
took, it has been criticized by naval experts from his time to ours as an
inaccurate view of the battle, and drew disparaging comment from the
Greenwich pensioners when it hung in the Painted Hall. Turner clearly did
not attempt to paint the battle with documentary accuracy; rather, he
produced a Romantic vision of the *Victory* as a bulwark of strength as the swell
of battle rages around her.

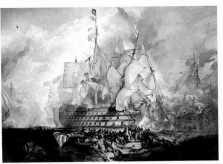

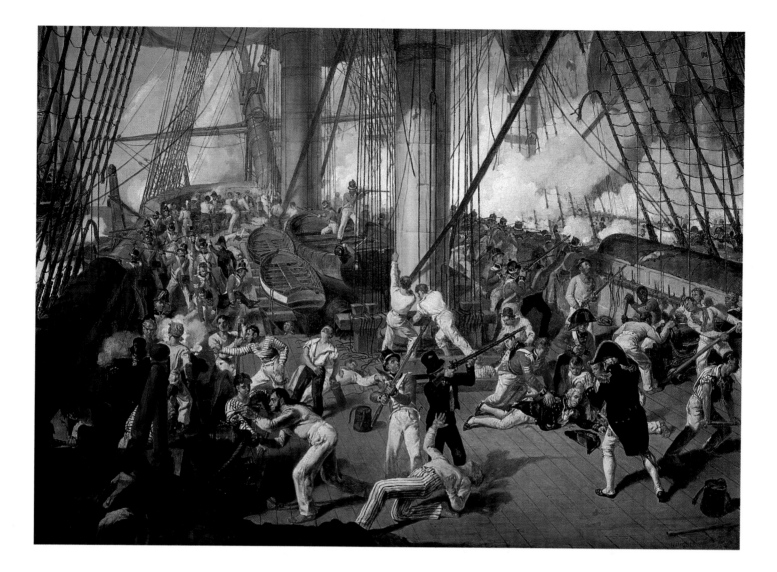

Plate 49. The Fall of Nelson. Denis Dighton

The wounded Lord Nelson has fallen to the deck, the fatal shot piercing his
right shoulder, lodging in his spine. Running to his assistance is Captain Hardy.
With a marine by his side, Midshipman Pollard takes aim towards the French
snipers in the tops of the *Redoubtable*, one of whom had shot the British admiral.
The artist has shown the *Victory* with solid gunwales, which were not introduced
until some time after Trafalgar. The *Victory* suffered severe losses during the
battle; 57 men and officers were killed and 102 were wounded, more than any
other vessel.

   Denis Dighton was primarily a painter of military battle scenes and of
military men, and at one time held a commission in the army. He was
appointed military painter to the Prince Regent, and his wife was fruit and
flower painter to Queen Adelaide.

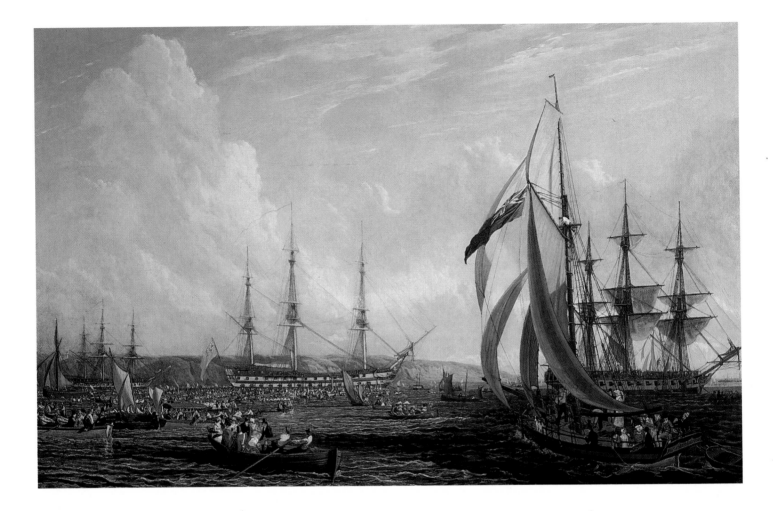

**Plate 50. Napoleon on the 'Bellerophon' at Plymouth, August 1815.
John James Chalon, 1816**

This lively crowded scene shows, in the distance, the portly figure of the
deposed emperor standing at the gangway of the *Bellerophon*, acknowledging the
sightseers anxious to catch a glimpse of 'Old Boney'. Ordered by the French
provisional government to sail for America, Bonaparte embarked on a British
ship whose commander was under contrary instructions from the British
government not to proceed there. Instead they anchored in Plymouth Sound,
and while the British government continued in its indecision about his fate,
Bonaparte was willing to appear to the crowds, who rowed out in their
hundreds to see him. This painting was exhibited at the Royal Academy in
1816, with the following description:

Scene in Plymouth Sound in August, 1815.
On Wednesday, 25 July, 1815 the BELLEROPHON 74 guns, Captain Maitland,
in company with the EUROTAS and LIFFEY frigates anchored on Plymouth
Sound within the breakwater. The point of the time chosen is half past six in
the evening the [time] at which Bonaparte usually made his appearance at the
gangway.

Chalon, who together with his brother Alfred Edward helped to found the
Sketching Society, painted a wide variety of subjects in watercolours and oils.

12. EARLY ENGLISH MARINE ARTISTS

Like landscape painting, early marine art in England was an import from abroad. Vroom and Willaerts in the early seventeenth century had worked on commission for English clients, but they do not appear to have visited the country, nor did they inspire any native talent. The obscure Isaac Sailmaker (*c.*1633–1721) is said to have moved from Holland to London in the 1650s. But the significant exodus of Dutch artists to England took place in the 1670s. Jan van Beecq (1638–1722) was painting competent pictures of English warships by that date, while Jacob Knyff (1639–81) from Haarlem was making a speciality of port scenes [fig. 74].

The arrival of the Van de Veldes in 1672 acted as a catalyst.

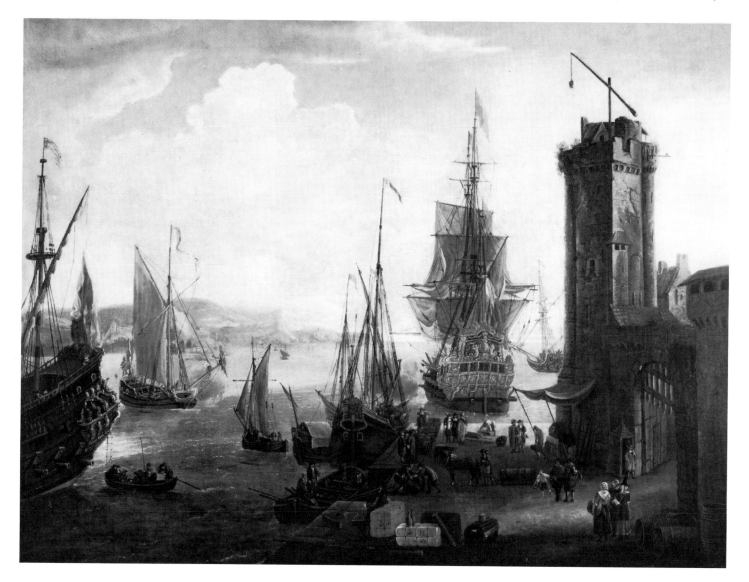

74. Dock Scene at a British Port. Jacob Knyff, 1673

Signed works by Knyff, such as this fine but largely imaginary port view, are exceptionally rare. Here the artist responds with evident enjoyment to the potential magnificence of a crowded pierside scene. Beside the pier is an English ship, possibly Dutch-built; beyond is an English flagship, whilst a royal yacht arrives from the left.

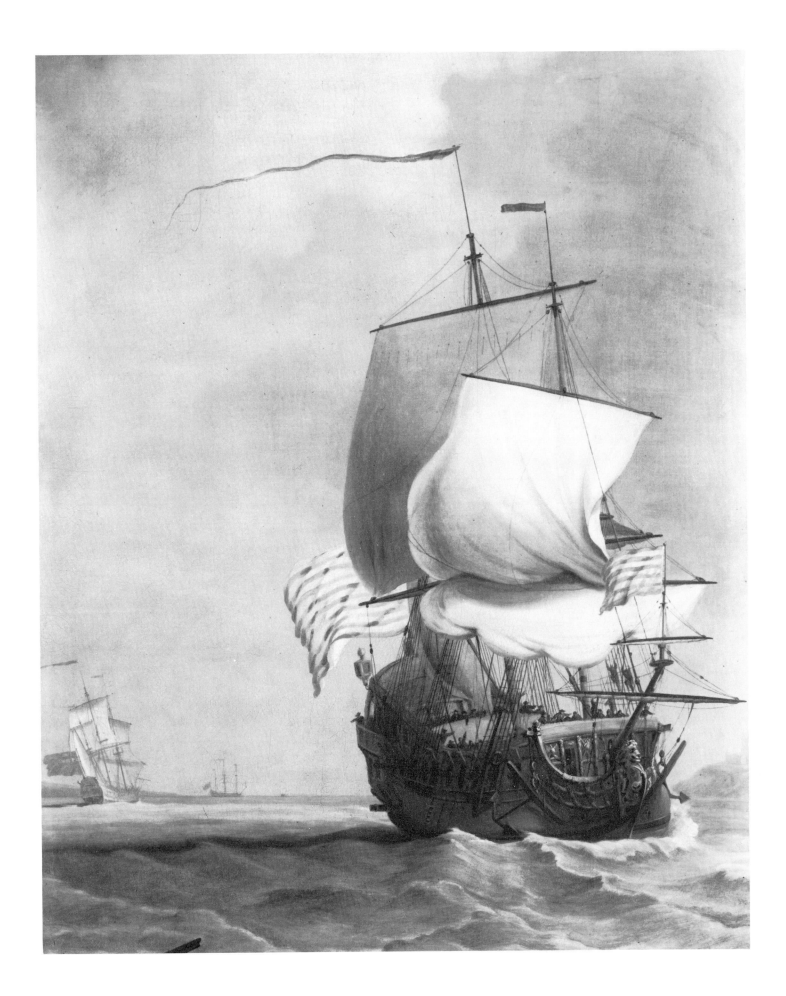

Here were two artists of European importance painting magnificent works for a wide range of patrons. The message was clear. A market for seascapes existed if anyone cared to exploit it. Many early English marine paintings are unattributed or by artists who exist only as names: H. Vale, for example, who painted *The Relief of Barcelona* [fig. 52], and his presumed relative, R. Vale. The first English-born marine artist of any substance was Peter Monamy (1681–1749), whose family came from Jersey. Apprenticed to a member of the Painter-Stainers Company in 1696, he gradually established himself as successor to Willem Van de Velde the Younger, who had died in 1707. Monamy

was a friend of Sir James Thornhill and William Hogarth, and he was appointed a governor of the Foundling Hospital. He became a considerable figure in the London art establishment.

The relatively large number of works attributed to Monamy or bearing his signature point to a successful studio practice. His favourite themes, such as the evening gun [fig. 76] and the ship burning at night, were repeated again and again, and vary greatly in quality. According to George Vertue, there were many unfinished pictures in his studio at the time of his death, 'his work being done for dealers at moderate prices kept him but in indifferent circumstances to the end'.

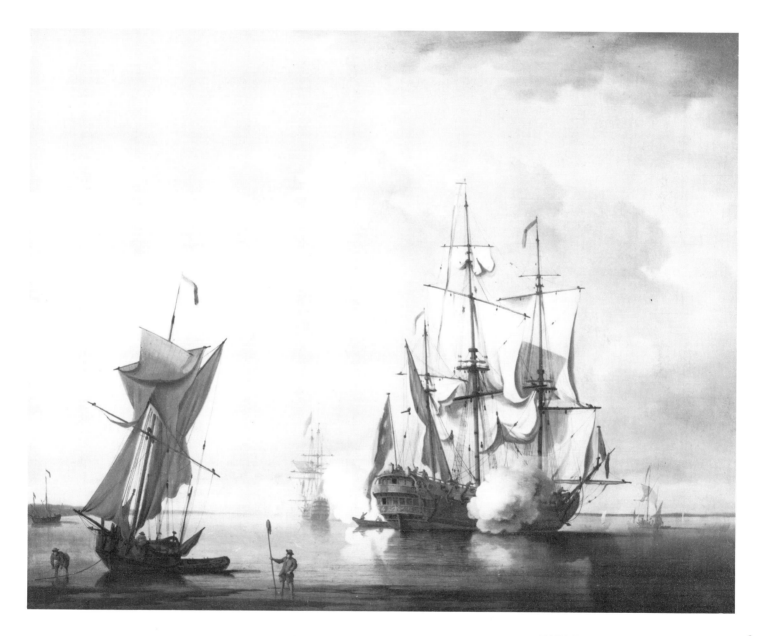

75. An English East Indiaman. Peter Monamy, *c.*1720
She flies the striped jack of the Honourable East India Company. The unusual composition of this picture suggests that it was originally part of something larger, and indeed there is a tradition that it was once included in the decorations for Vauxhall Gardens.

76. Man-of-War firing a Gun at Sundown. Peter Monamy
Working safely within the traditions established by his Dutch predecessors, Monamy depicts a two-decker coming to anchor (probably at the Nore) and saluting the admiral whose flagship is in the background. The beached vessel is a trading hoy.

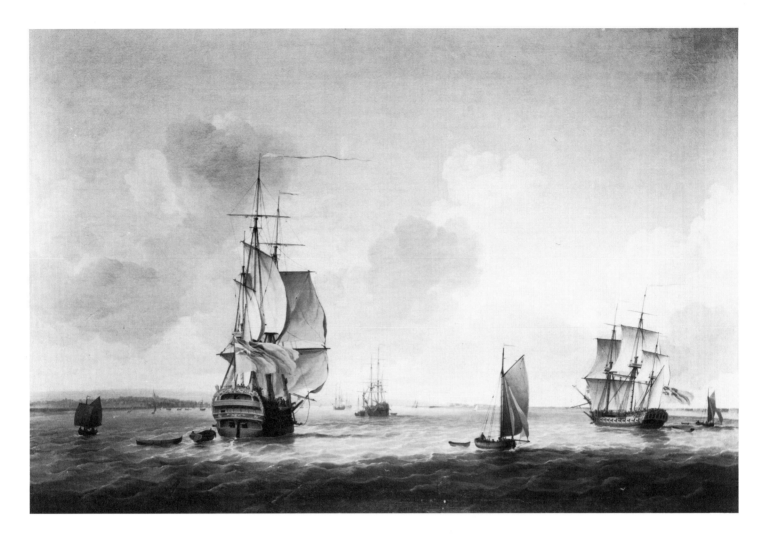

Monamy would not have happened without the Van de Veldes. Though the inspiration for many of his subjects came from their work, Monamy's style is quite distinctive, broad and painterly in handling, if sometimes coarse, warm and full in colour. Vertue speaks of him visiting coasts or seaports 'to improve himself from Nature and those observations for his future improvement', and his best work bears evidence of careful study of ships and the sea [plate 32; fig. 75]. No doubt as he got older and lazier, he allowed his work to degenerate into repetition and formula.

Monamy was not the only marine painter to fall into the clutches of unscrupulous dealers. It is said that signatures on the works of Charles Brooking (1723–59) were removed by a shopkeeper near Leicester Square who sold prints and pictures, so that potential buyers would not discover the identity of the artist. It was only when the dealer's wife accidentally exhibited a signed example that Brooking's admirer, Taylor White, learnt

his name, and subsequently helped to promote his career. With few influential patrons, poor, and, according to a contemporary, 'of sickly appearance', Brooking had an uphill struggle to establish himself. He was beginning to do so at the time of his tragically early death in 1759. Like Monamy, he had become a governor of the Foundling Hospital, to which he contributed one of his grandest marine compositions. Of his background and training little is known, but his acute knowledge of ships and rigging suggests that he had firsthand experience of the sea. His pictures [plates 29, 30; figs. 65, 77] possess such freshness and verve that he must have painted his work from nature. One has to wait for Turner and Constable before finding marine pictures that match his work in the directness of their response to the accidents of light and weather. His drawing of ships is impeccable, and so is his eye for detail; the little figures of his sailors are to be seen actually working the ship, not standing idly about.

Brooking was impecunious and obscure. Samuel Scott (1702–

77. A Ship running into Harwich. Charles Brooking

A two-decker (left), a frigate (right) and several smaller craft are seen off a coastal town which closely resembles Harwich. Some topographical inaccuracies suggest that the landscape of this fresh and invigorating picture was drawn from memory.

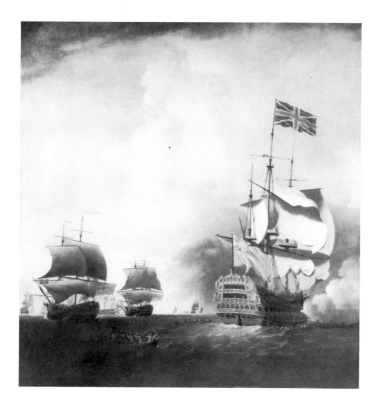

rather flat, his ships mechanical (he is said to have painted from models), but it is clear from letters and drawings that he made every attempt to portray events as accurately as he could. His most successful compositions are often those with fewest ships [plates 31, 33; fig. 78]; the large area of surrounding space throws them into sharp relief and accentuates the intervals between them.

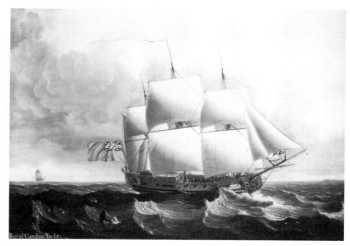

72), the third of the early English marine masters, was neither. Well connected, he was patronized by several leading admirals, and more importantly by a number of aristocratic families, chief among them the Walpoles and the Earl of Sandwich. His decorative sea-pieces and views of the Thames hung in the drawing-rooms of country houses, along with hunting pictures by John Wootton and Italian scenes by William Marlow. Scott's major achievement as a sea painter was to chart the sea battles of the War of the Austrian Succession and the Seven Years War. Though he had competition from Brooking and Richard Paton (1717–91), an artist of independent means who emerged in the 1760s, Scott was the dominant figure. His pictures often appear

One last painter from this early period deserves mention. This is John Cleveley the Elder (c.1712–77), founder of a dynasty of marine artists, who specialized in dockyard scenes and ship launches [plates 35, 37]. He also painted ship portraits [fig. 79] and a few ceremonial events. Based in Deptford, with no aspirations to academic honours, he appears to have worked for a small circle of shipowners and dockyard owners. His dockyard scenes combine an enormous amount of documentary information with an engaging elegance and command of figure composition, akin to the contemporary conversation-piece. They are an entirely original contribution to the imagery of marine art, and their rare quality deserves wider recognition.

13. CHANGES IN SHIP DESIGN

As noted earlier, by about the middle of the eighteenth century the large ships, whether warship or merchant ship, had roughly doubled in size from those of the previous century. They were beginning to approach the maximum which the strength of their

building material, wood, would bear. Yet the general design had changed very little and they were still bluff-bowed, somewhat stubby vessels. No naval architect during these hundred years had seriously studied the science of hydrodynamics in relation

78. A First-Rate shortening Sail. Samuel Scott, 1736

This ship, shortening sail to reduce her speed, is probably intended to be the *Britannia*, for she flies the flag of Admiral of the Fleet Sir John Norris, Commander-in-Chief in the Channel in 1735. Characteristically, Scott based his representation on a ship model—probably one of the several made for the rebuilding of the *Royal William* in 1719.

79. The 'Royal Caroline'. John Cleveley the Elder, 1750

The *Royal Caroline* was built in 1749 at Deptford by Joshua Allin—the site of Cleveley's well-known views of ship launches. Here she is shown under sail off the coast. She was an adapted sixth-rate, and replaced the *Caroline* as the principal royal yacht.

to the shape of a ship's hull or the effect of skin friction on the speed of a ship through the water. Although every shipowner naturally appreciated speed, there were at the same time more important aspects. Nations wanted warships strong enough to carry as many guns as possible and wide enough to provide room for their recoil when they were fired; merchants wanted as large a rectangular box as possible in which to stow their cargoes. Both added masts as tall as possible to carry as big an area of sail as would push the ship through the water.

Yet changes were in the air. A Swedish naval architect, Frederik af Chapman, built a tank for testing ship models, which were drawn through the water by a system of drop weights. The results of these tests convinced him that the basic hull shape of existing ships was hydrodynamically inefficient and that to achieve the best speed possible any ship's hull needed a fine entry and a clear run aft. These were the two qualities of contemporary shipbuilding which were noticeably absent. In 1768 he published the results of his studies in a book, *Architectura Navalis Mercatoria* [fig. 80], with many designs for merchant ships and

small warships which proved the relationship between hull form and speed through the water. He followed this in 1775 with his *Tractat om Skepps Buggeriet* (Treatise on Ship Building), which over the years had a profound effect on the design of ships in all the European countries and, indeed, as far away as Canada and America. Although it was a relatively slow process to convince all naval architects of the value of some of af Chapman's new designs, such as the hollow bow and the tapering run of the hull aft, the main features of his studies were too obvious to be long delayed. The days of the tubby ship with her wide bow and a length-to-beam ratio of 3 or 3½ to 1 were numbered, and the longer ship with a sharper bow and a streamlined hull was to become the model which all shipowners most admired.

One new type of ship, born on the east coast of America and designed to take advantage of the prevailing westerly winds which blew steadily at right angles to the north-south coast, was the schooner, of which the first example was built at Gloucester, Massachusetts, in 1713. She was an example of a vessel whose design, completely radical in relation to the generality of mer-

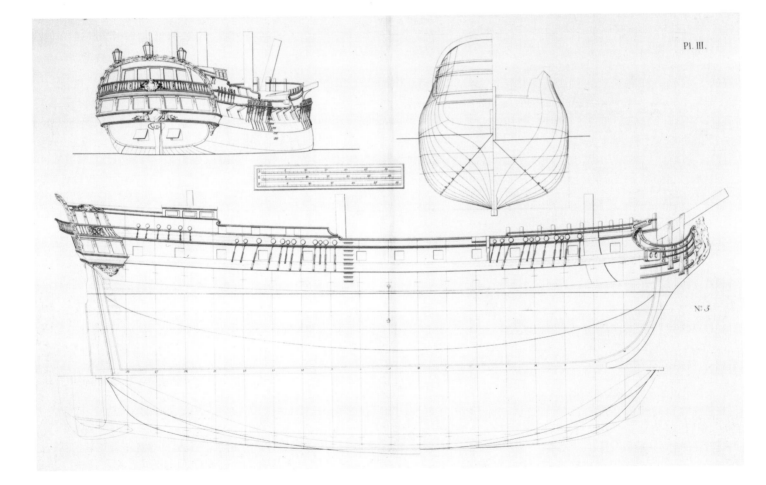

80. Plate from 'Architectura Navalis Mercatoria'.
Frederik af Chapman, 1768

Chapman was the first naval architect to use a water tank in which to test design models. From these experiments he was able to produce ships' draughts incorporating a fine entry and a clear run aft to the hull form, qualities which were missing from almost all contemporary designs.

chant shipping, was adopted purely for the conditions of the waters in which she would spend her serving years. She was two-masted with fore-and-aft gaff sails on both masts, a rig popular with shipowners as it required a smaller crew than a square rig. The schooners were very fast and weatherly, ideally suited for carrying cargoes in and out of the many ports along the coast, particularly as the prevailing wind was a reaching wind whether they were sailing north or south. Perhaps the most famous of the American schooners were those built in the nineteenth century to harvest the huge cod fishery of the Grand Banks lying south and east of Newfoundland.

A version of the schooner was also adopted for use in the stormier waters of northern Europe. Often with three masts, and almost invariably with square topsails, the topsail schooner became very popular in the nineteenth century, vying for the coasting trade with the hundreds of smacks, brigs and ketches.

14. THE GROWTH OF FREE TRADE

By the middle of the eighteenth century there was beginning to grow a new doctrine of the liberalization of trade in an effort to curb the vicious excesses of monopoly trade claims. It had started some fifty years earlier with various national attempts to wage war on piracy and buccaneering, and except in far eastern waters these scourges on the legitimate voyages of innocent ships had been largely suppressed. In times of war, of course, all nations licensed private shipowners to prey on the trade of an enemy by the issue of Letters of Marque, but in peacetime the thought was growing that every ship should have the right to expect an unhindered passage across the oceans to her destination if she was engaged in honest trade and prepared to obey the customs laws of the country in which she hoped to sell her cargo. It was a doctrine which came to be known as the 'Freedom of the Seas'.

It was the almost inexhaustible growth of trade around the

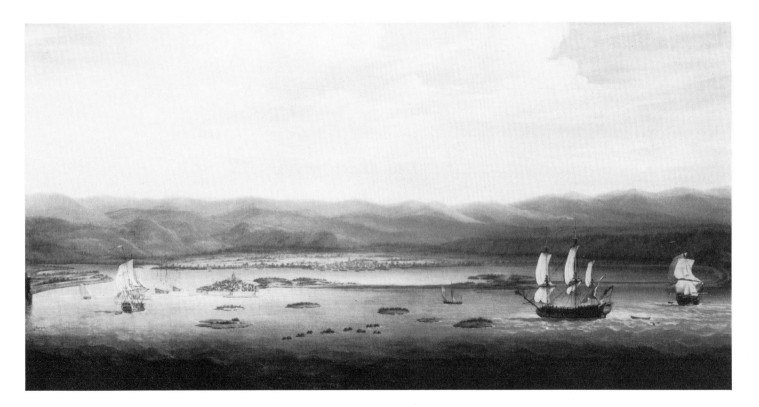

81. Port Royal, Jamaica. Richard Paton
Paton's view, in which the curiously awry scale of proportions does not detract from its visual appeal, shows merchantmen and other vessels at the approach to Port Royal (left, middle distance). Kingston, Jamaica's capital today, lies towards the right of the picture.

world which proved to be the main spur towards acceptance of this doctrine among the nations. The colonial empires which had their birth with the voyages of discovery of the late fifteenth and early sixteenth centuries had been consolidating and expanding ever since. The days of stark plunder, of the extermination of native civilizations to lay hands upon their wealth of gold and silver and precious stones, had given place to ordered colonial government. The descendants of the original settlers had set up their own businesses and needed to trade just as much as their European originators [fig. 81]. In many cases their primary products—tea, coffee, spices, cotton, hardwoods such as teak and mahogany, fir trees for ships' masts, sugar, tobacco—were the only source of supply for Europe's demand. In return the expanding populations and increasing wealth of these colonies called for goods from Europe, agricultural tools for their farms and plantations, fine furniture for their houses, woven cloth for their clothing and household needs, tea from India via London—everything that a steadily improving standard of life could demand.

It all had to be carried across the oceans in ships, and although some European nations still hankered for monopoly trade with their own colonial possessions, the sheer volume and variety of production and demand made it more and more an impossible dream. Gradually the various nations came to realize that the only way of maintaining and increasing the trade on which their national wealth depended was to relax their restrictive rules on the carriage of goods to their colonies and to liberalize their trade. The colonials themselves were beginning to use their financial muscle to enjoy the fruits of a much wider trade than the narrow selection which national restriction inevitably forced on them.

Only with the East India Companies were the monopolies still strictly enforced. They were autonomous organizations with the military power to enforce their own rules irrespective of any decisions of their home governments. Yet even for these companies the writing was beginning to appear on the wall. The French company lost all its Indian trading ports to Britain during the Seven Years War. At this time the Government in London stepped in to exercise some control over the British East India Company, requiring it to accept Government approval of all its senior

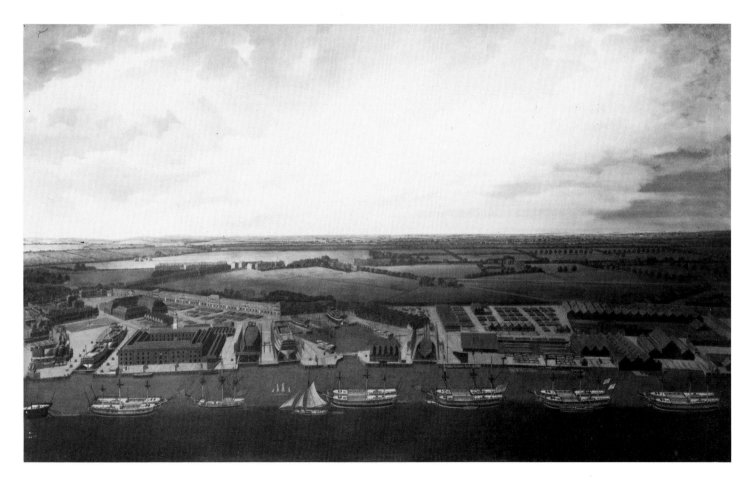

82. Deptford Dockyard. Joseph Farington
In this panoramic landscape of Deptford and the Thames, Farington, perhaps better known as a diarist, draws consciously on the 'bird's-eye view' tradition of the late seventeenth century. The picture, one of a set of four (of which two are by Nicholas Pocock), was painted during Deptford dockyard's greatest period of activity and prosperity.

appointments. A few years later, the Dutch company collapsed under the financial burden of maintaining sufficient forces to police its monopoly trade rules, and its empire in the East Indies was thrown open to the ships of all nations. A few more years, and once again the British Government stepped in and abolished its own company's monopolies, that of trade to India in 1813 and to China and Japan in 1833, throwing these, too, open to any ship of any nation.

The growing freedom to trade in waters previously restricted was matched by a new demand for ships, and the eighteenth century saw all the shipyards, both in Europe and in the colonies, trying to keep pace with the demand [plates 35, 36, 37; fig. 82]. Most of the ships they built were the familiar types, though towards the end of the century the new designs of af Chapman were producing altogether more graceful ships, longer and faster though with the same cargo capacity.

15. THE SEVEN YEARS WAR 1756–63

The War of the Austrian Succession, which ended in 1748, left a legacy of tension and distrust between Britain and France. The loss of France's best battleworthy squadron in Hawke's action off Cape Finisterre in 1747 rankled deeply and the severe setback in the trade war had brought the threat of ruin to many ship-owners. The tension spread to North America where the French in Canada viewed with alarm the steady westward colonization of a vigorous British population in the original thirteen colonies. To deter the British expansion a chain of forts was built from Montreal to the headwaters of the Ohio River and in 1755 information was received in London that a fleet, with six of France's best regiments on board, was about to sail from Brest to reinforce the French in Canada. This, combined with the building of the forts, was more than the British ministers could stomach, and Admiral Boscawen was ordered to sail with a fleet to Canadian waters with instructions to stop them.

The French fleet became dispersed in a fog off the Newfoundland banks and Boscawen sighted only three ships, of which he captured two. It was, at once, too little and too much, too little to cripple French sea power, too much for them to overlook in time of peace. War was officially declared the following year.

It began with a British reverse. Minorca, with its secure harbour at Port Mahon, had come to Britain as part of the spoils of the War of the Spanish Succession. With Gibraltar, gained in the same war, it gave British sea power a commanding position in the western Mediterranean, and a military garrison was stationed at Port Mahon in view of its importance as a naval base. With the declaration of war a French fleet sailed from Toulon and landed troops on the island, remaining in those waters to prevent any British attempts to bring reinforcements to the garrison. A British fleet under the command of John Byng

was sent out post-haste from Britain. In an engagement with the French fleet, very much a repeat performance of the battle of Toulon in the previous war, Byng stuck rigidly to the line of battle. His centre and rear squadrons were content to fight a long-range battle, which could never do any serious damage to the enemy, while the van squadron was severely mauled. After the battle Byng called a council of war of his admirals and senior captains, put some distinctly loaded questions to it, and on its advice returned to Gibraltar, leaving Minorca to inevitable capture by the French. The public outcry was such that Byng was court-martialled, found guilty, and executed [fig. 83].

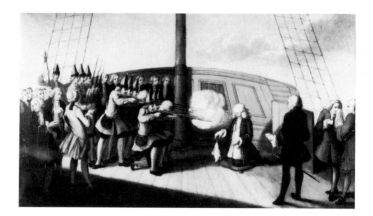

Facing the destruction of her seaborne trade from a British blockade of the Biscay coast, France was forced into desperate measures to try to retrieve her fortunes, and she assembled an army of 30,000 men north of the Loire estuary. The plan was for the French Mediterranean fleet to break out from the British blockade of Toulon, sail up to Quiberon Bay, join forces with

83. Execution of Admiral Byng. Unidentified artist

The demand for a scapegoat after the humiliating Minorca episode in the Seven Years War was satisfied by Admiral Byng, as this painting graphically records. Byng, kneeling on the quarterdeck, drops his handkerchief as a signal for his executioners to fire. In the right foreground, a man holds the execution order; further to the right, Byng's supporters (one of them perhaps George Lawrence, his secretary) mourn his demise.

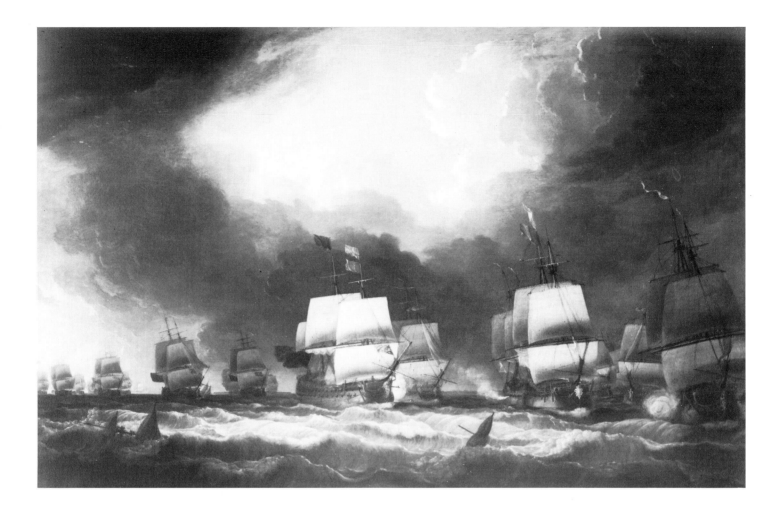

the squadrons at Rochefort and Brest, and hold the English Channel long enough to land the army in England. All was ready by the summer of 1759. For the British, Hawke [fig. 85] commanded the blockading fleet off Brest, Boscawen that off Toulon. With Minorca no longer available as a base, Boscawen had to rely on Gibraltar, and it was while he was refitting there in August that the French fleet, commanded by Admiral de la Clue, slipped through the straits. Although several of his ships had their yards down on deck, Boscawen was in chase within two hours. After sinking the French *Centaure*, which briefly held up the British fleet, he set off for the remainder through the night to discover in the morning that half the French fleet was making for Cadiz and the other half for Lagos to try to take advantage of Portuguese neutrality. Four French ships made it into Lagos Bay. Boscawen followed them in, burned two and towed the other two out as prizes.

Later that year Hawke was driven off his blockading station in a severe gale and the French admiral Conflans seized the opportunity of slipping out of Brest and sailing to Quiberon Bay where the French army lay in readiness. Hawke, making his way back during a lull in the storm, was just in time to sight the French about to enter the bay. In spite of a rising wind from the west-north-west threatening the fleet with another gale and the rock-bound waters of Quiberon for which he had no accurate charts, Hawke hoisted the signal for a general chase and the British ships streamed in under full sail [fig. 84]. Seven French ships were sunk or driven ashore and later burned [fig. 86], seven more, jettisoning their guns overboard, managed to scrape over the bar at the entrance to the Vilaine estuary, some breaking their backs and all of them landlocked there for over a year. Eight others broke off the battle and escaped south to Rochefort. Two British ships were wrecked on the Le Four shoal during the night, and next morning their crews were taken off and the ships were burnt to prevent them falling into the hands of the French.

The effect of the battle on French trade was catastrophic.

84. Battle of Quiberon Bay, 20 November 1759. Dominic Serres, 1766
Serres's dramatic interpretation of an action during the Seven Years War, painted several years after the event, features the *Royal George* (centre, starboard bow view), the 100-gun flagship of Admiral Sir Edward Hawke, firing to port at the *Soleil Royal*. In the background can be seen the captured *Formidable*, an 80-gun French ship, and the spars of a sunken vessel.

85. Portrait of Edward Hawke, First Baron Hawke, Admiral of the Fleet. Francis Cotes
This three-quarter-length portrait of Edward Hawke (1705–81), in which he wears the flag officer's undress uniform of 1767–83, tie wig, and ribbon and Star of the Bath, was painted in the late 1760s—shortly after Hawke's retirement from a highly distinguished naval career. He was best known for his service in the Seven Years War.

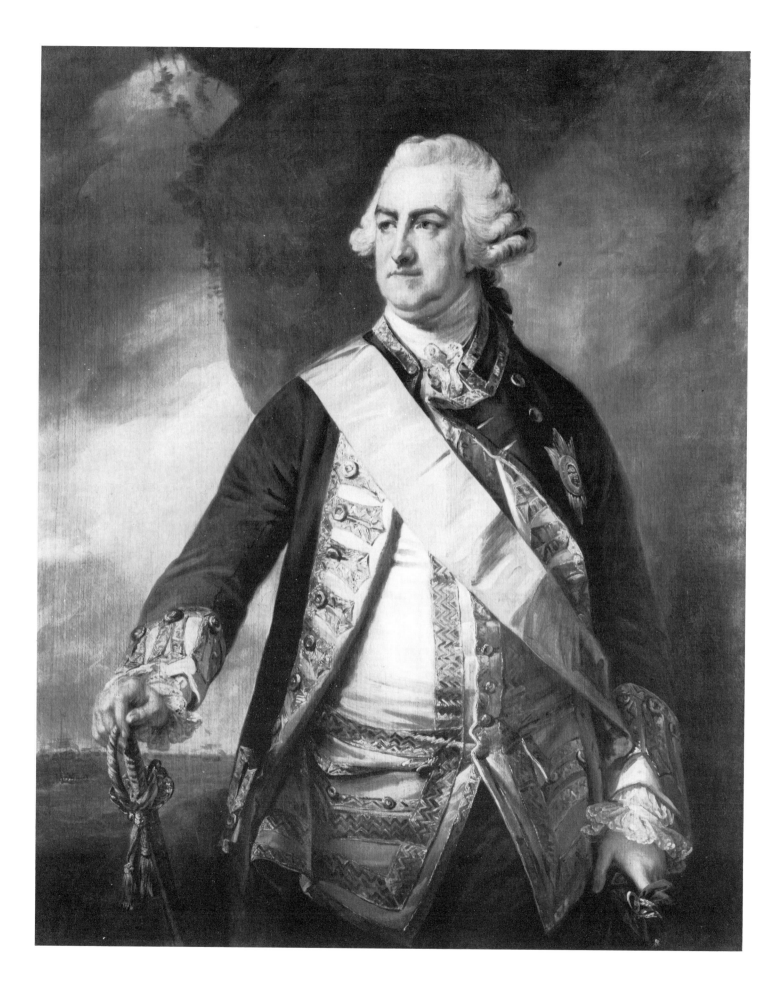

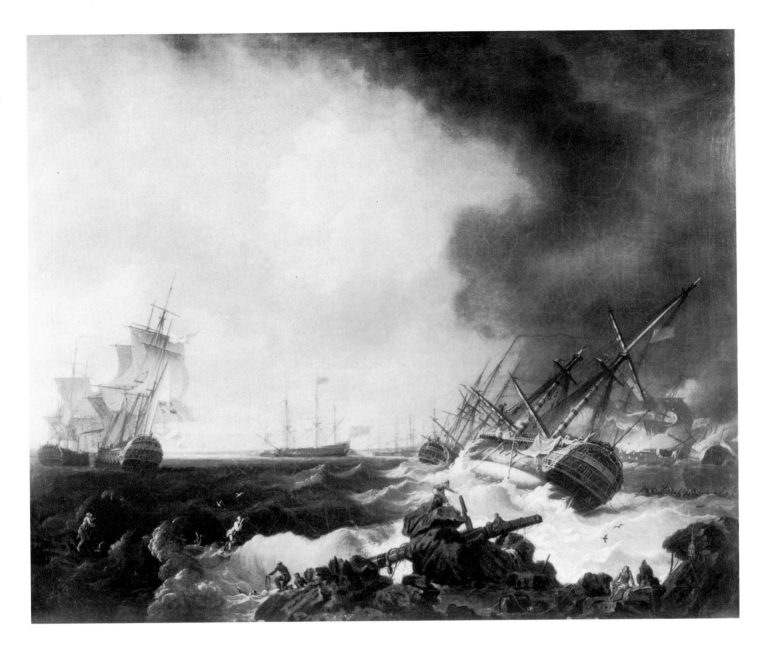

With the French fleet no longer effective as a fighting force, the British blockade tightened. Few French merchant ships managed to penetrate it, and all neutral ships trading to France were stopped and searched for contraband. Equally catastrophic was the plight of the French colonies. As the war spread and embraced them, there was little hope of reinforcements in ships and men from the home country. Left bare, they were ripe for the plucking.

In India, the fleet commanded by Admiral Pocock captured Calcutta and Chandernagore, and in so doing removed the two naval bases on which the French admiral, Count d'Aché, relied to refit and replenish his ships. Three indecisive actions were fought between the fleets and d'Aché was forced to leave Indian waters. In surrendering command of the sea to the British, there was no hope left for the French. The whole of India fell into British hands, or, more accurately, into the hands of the British East India Company, and the French East India Company ceased to exist. The additional wealth of trade created by this absorption of the French part of India was immense and, with the British command of the sea guaranteeing their safety, new fleets of merchant ships were able to exploit it to the full.

In Canada, too, affairs were going badly for the French. In

86. The Day after the Battle of Quiberon Bay, 21 November 1759. Richard Wright, 1760

The wreck of the 74-gun *Resolution* lies on her starboard side, mizen-mast gone. To the left of the picture is the captured *Formidable* (see fig. 84) and in the central background lies the *Royal George* with other English ships. This is a powerful if pessimistic evocation of post-battle carnage, painted adeptly by a self-taught artist from Liverpool.

a carefully planned campaign the British Prime Minister, William Pitt (the Elder), aimed not only at the defeat of the French forces, but also at the final acquisition of the whole of France's North American possessions, most of Canada in the north and Louisiana in the south. With these, and possibly the Spanish settlement of Florida thrown in, the North American continent would be open to British expansion and development. In 1758 Pitt selected Boscawen to take the first step in his American plan, the capture of the French fortress port of Louisburg on Cape Breton Island, strongly held by a permanent garrison of French regular troops and a French squadron of warships. In a brilliant

to Quebec, a feat of seamanship supposed to be impossible for ships of that size. It is at this point that one of the most famous of British navigators steps into the pages of history. James Cook had been appointed master (navigator) of HMS *Pembroke* in Saunders's fleet, and with the masters of other warships he surveyed the river, producing charts which enabled the fleet to make the passage safely. That the ships reached Quebec without loss was almost entirely due to their careful and accurate survey. Once there, boats from the fleet landed Wolfe and his troops above the city, the ships' crews manhandling the guns up the cliffs. Quebec fell after a land battle, and the next stage of Pitt's

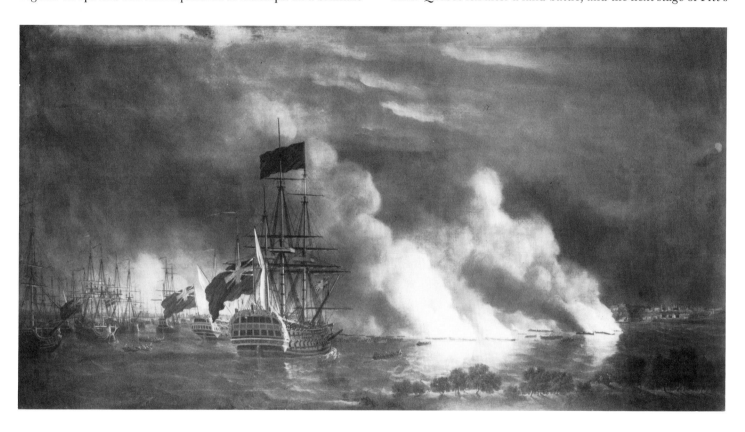

little campaign Boscawen landed British troops along the coast from Louisburg, supported their advance with gunfire from his ships, and when the surrendering French set fire to their ships in harbour to prevent their capture, sent in the boats of the fleet, doused the fires in two of them before much damage had been done, and towed them out as prizes. Commanding the British troops ashore was James Wolfe to whom the final French surrender was largely due.

Louisburg, dominating the entrance to the St. Lawrence river, was the key to the whole of Canada. In the following year Admiral Saunders, Boscawen's relief, sailed the fleet up the river

plan was successfully completed. The final stage, in 1760, was the capture of Montreal, the capital of French Canada, by troops brought up from New York.

With the surrender of French Canada to the power of British arms, Louisiana in the south also surrendered. Cut off from all hope of reinforcement from metropolitan France by the British blockade, Martinique and Grenada in the West Indies were also captured, falling easily into British hands with little more than token resistance.

Further afield still, British squadrons were consolidating their command of the oceans. In 1762 Spain entered the war on the

87. Fire Raft Attack on the English Fleet before Quebec, 28 July 1759. Samuel Scott

One of several pictures by Scott treating incidents in the Seven Years War. This records the launch of French rafts, laden with explosives, against Admiral Saunders' fleet; small English picket boats, seen here amongst the fire rafts, were able to tow them clear before any damage was done. Saunders' flagship, the *Stirling Castle*, is in the centre of the picture.

side of France but failed to inform her overseas dependencies until it was too late. The British East Indies squadron arrived off Manila with a small military force on board, and eight days later the town surrendered. By the terms of the capitulation, not only the town but the whole of Luzon and all the other Spanish islands in the Philippines were surrendered.

But Pitt had not done with Spain yet. The Spanish island of Cuba in the West Indies, the central pivot of its trade in those waters, was well worth capture as its return to Spain at the end of the war could be offered in return for the cession of Florida, the last part of the American mainland beyond British ownership and control. A fleet under Admiral Pocock, with a military force of 15,000 men commanded by the Earl of Albemarle, arrived off Havana and after a siege of six weeks and a heavy bombardment of its forts the city surrendered [plate 42], leaving the British in possession of a squadron of Spanish warships, and a large hoard of gold bullion.

The war left Britain virtually unchallenged over the oceans of the world. Her massive gains gave her possession of North America and the whole of India with all that they meant to a vigorous trading nation. Minorca, regained from Spain after the war, restored to Britain her commanding position in the Mediterranean. In terms of ships lost in battle the cost had been inconsiderable, particularly in comparison with France and Spain. In terms of ships gained, both warships and prizes from the harassing of trade, the results were prodigious. Raleigh's words that 'whosoever commands the trade of the world commands the riches of the world' rang loud in British ears.

16. THE SCIENTIFIC VOYAGES

It would be pleasant to think that what drove those early explorers, Diaz, da Gama, Cabral, Columbus, Verrazzano, Davis, Gilbert, Cartier, Magellan and the others, to push their small ships across unknown oceans was a curiosity to discover what new lands lay beyond the horizon. Possibly it might be true of one or two of them, but for the great majority it was the lure of riches and power that drove them onward. They went on their voyages armed to the teeth to enforce their determination to trade on their own terms, to hold to ransom whole nations and ancient civilizations for the delivery of their gold and precious stones.

During the second half of the eighteenth century and the first two or three decades of the nineteenth, a whole series of new voyages of discovery was made, not with any idea of an expansion of trade but to fill in the still unknown corners of the globe, to learn and record the anthropology, the flora and the fauna of its more distant corners, and to observe the magnetic variation of the earth, still vital knowledge in perfecting the art of navigation. They are known generally as scientific voyages, mainly because anthropologists, botanists, and, above all, artists were carried on board as expert observers to record and picture everything of interest. Most of these voyages were recorded in superb descriptive volumes illustrated with drawings and paintings, making the life of the sea an important part of the worlds of literature and art.

But all these voyages pale into insignificance in comparison with the three great circumnavigations of James Cook, that same navigator who had charted the St. Lawrence river for the fleet to reach Quebec in 1759. His voyages were planned to prove or disprove the existence of a vast southern continent, named *Terra Australis Incognita*, which most geographers believed to exist if only to balance the known land mass in the northern hemisphere. If there were such a continent, the British Government was anxious to get there before France or Spain stumbled on it and claimed it for their own. Cook was then to go to New Zealand, which the Dutchman Tasman had discovered in 1642 but which was still thought by many to be part of the great southern continent.

On his first voyage (1768–71), after a stay at Tahiti to observe the transit of the planet Venus across the face of the sun, Cook sailed south without sighting land and then west to New Zealand, circumnavigating and surveying both islands to prove that they were not a northern promontory of the mythical continent. Crossing to Australia, he sailed up its eastern coast, anchored for a refit of his ship in Botany Bay, and returned home round the Cape of Good Hope. Among the 'supernumeraries' embarked were Joseph Banks, a wealthy Fellow of the Royal Society interested in botany, Charles Green, astronomer, Daniel Solander, botanist, Sydney Parkinson, draughtsman, and Alexander Buchan, artist. The main purpose of the voyage was to

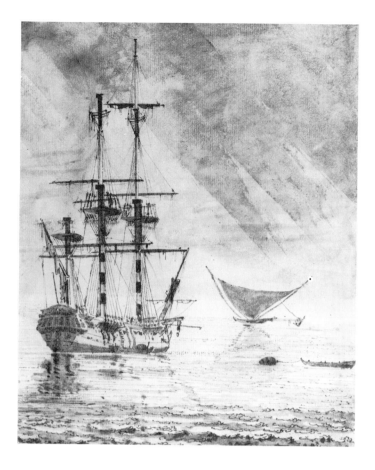

clear up doubts about *Terra Australis Incognita* and New Zealand, but science was not to be disregarded either.

Cook's second voyage round the world (1772–5) [plates 38, 39; figs. 88, 111] was in part the completion of his first, including a circumnavigation in high southern latitudes, frequently crossing the Antarctic Circle in search of land but always being turned back by ice. It was definite proof that there was no great unknown continent habitable by man in the south seas. He spent another year in the Pacific, accurately charting the positions of several islands hitherto only vaguely known, and discovering several new ones. He had with him on board two astronomers, William Wales and William Bayly, a botanist, George Forster, and a painter, William Hodges, whose sketches in watercolour and paintings in oils even today can re-create the excitement and mystery of discovery of new lands and new peoples.

Less than a year after his return from this second voyage, Cook was away again on his third (1776–9). His instructions included an exploration of the west coast of North America to try to find the Pacific entrance of that will o' the wisp of the first great age of discovery, the North-West Passage. He rounded the south-western extremity of Alaska [fig. 89], passed through the Aleutian Islands and the Bering Strait, to reach the latitude of $70\frac{1}{2}°$ North before the impenetrable ice wall forced him to abandon the search. He did not survive this voyage, being killed by the natives at Kealakekua Bay in the Hawaiian group of

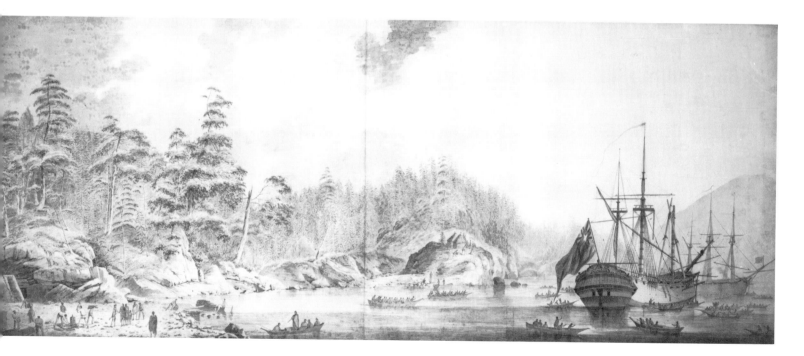

88. The 'Resolution' in the Marquesas Islands, 1774. William Hodges

The *Resolution* is seen at anchor, quarter stern view, with a Marquesan-type canoe on the right. It was probably drawn in Vaitahu Bay in April 1774, during the later stages of Cook's second voyage.

89. 'Resolution' and 'Discovery' in Nootka Sound, April 1778. John Webber

This drawing was made off the Alaskan coast during Captain Cook's third and final voyage, while searching for a North-West Passage. The scene records the peaceful relations established between the explorers and the native Red Indian population. The tents perched on an outcrop, right of centre, contain astronomical instruments.

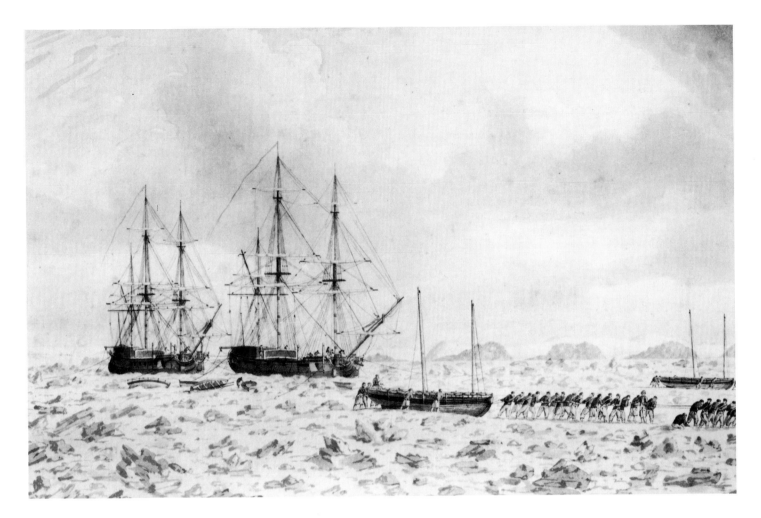

islands. William Bayly was once again astronomer for this voyage and a new painter, John Webber, replaced William Hodges.

These scientific voyages left little as yet undiscovered around the world. The accuracy of their surveys made safer the task of ships' navigators, and the observations of their astronomers, entomologists, botanists and painters hugely extended man's knowledge and understanding of the world. They created, too, a wider appreciation of the value to the seaman of careful hydrography, and at the end of this period of exploration the admiralties of the maritime nations set up hydrographic establishments to provide accurate charts of the world's seas and oceans for the use of any navigator of any country who needed them.

One unexpected result of Cook's historic voyages was the opening up of new and extremely rich grounds for the whale and seal fisheries. Whaling and sealing had, of course, been pursued for centuries, mainly in the colder waters of the northern hemisphere [fig. 31], growing in importance at approximately the same rate as the growth of worldwide trade. Whaling was carried out from ships of around 200 tons with a crew of about fifty, who pursued the whales in small boats, harpooning them with a harping iron before lancing them in the underbelly. The main European whaling ground was in the waters around Spitsbergen, where each nation active in the trade set up its own harbour. In the early years the Dutch were predominant in the whale fishing industry, and their harbour of Smeerenburg ('Blubbertown') in Spitsbergen is recorded as being visited annually from 1633 onwards by more than 1,000 whaling ships.

Cook's discovery of South Georgia in 1775 revealed the richness of those Antarctic waters, first in the immense numbers of fur seals which bred in the islands and, as the fishery developed, in the huge schools of whales there ready for the taking. This great expansion of the available fishing grounds was the signal for a new burst of activity as the seafaring nations expanded their whaling fleets to reap their shares of this prodigious harvest.

90. 'Racehorse' with 'Carcass', 7 August 1773. John Cleveley the Younger after Philippe d'Auvergne, 1774
The two exploration ships are shown stuck in the ice, while the commander of the expedition, Captain Phipps, leads two parties of men who are dragging the ships' launches over the ice in an attempt to find free water. Eventually the ships broke through the ice, and although the explorers failed to find a North-West Passage they brought back much useful information.

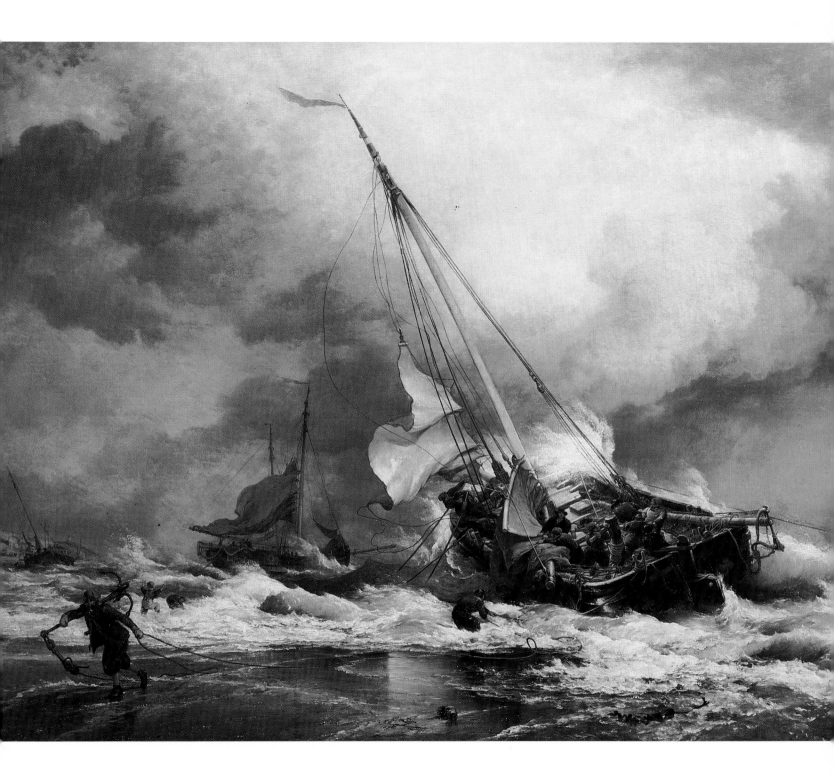

Plate 51. Beaching a Pink in Heavy Weather at Scheveningen.
Edward William Cooke, 1855

Cooke invests this commonplace scene of a humble fishing pink being hauled up the beach with all the drama of a titanic struggle against the elements. The little Dutch vessel dominates the sombre composition. A central golden area of sky, sail and sand, with the red caps of the sailors and the pennants, provides the only relief. The rigging and gear is meticulously rendered and the short, steep waves so characteristic of shallow water, with flecks of spray whipped away by the onshore wind, all contribute to the excitement of the scene.

Cooke's early interest in ships was fostered by Captain Burton of the West Indiaman *Thetis*. He was trained as an engraver by his father, and took up oil painting in 1834 with the encouragement of Clarkson Stanfield, whose principal follower and successor he became. Cooke's work is in the English tradition (based on the Dutch) of Scott, Brooking and Pocock, and his marines were more acceptable to sailors than those of Turner because he focused on the ship rather than on the atmospheric effects of sea and sky.

This painting, based on sketches made in 1837 during one of Cooke's frequent visits to Holland, was exhibited at the Royal Academy in 1855.

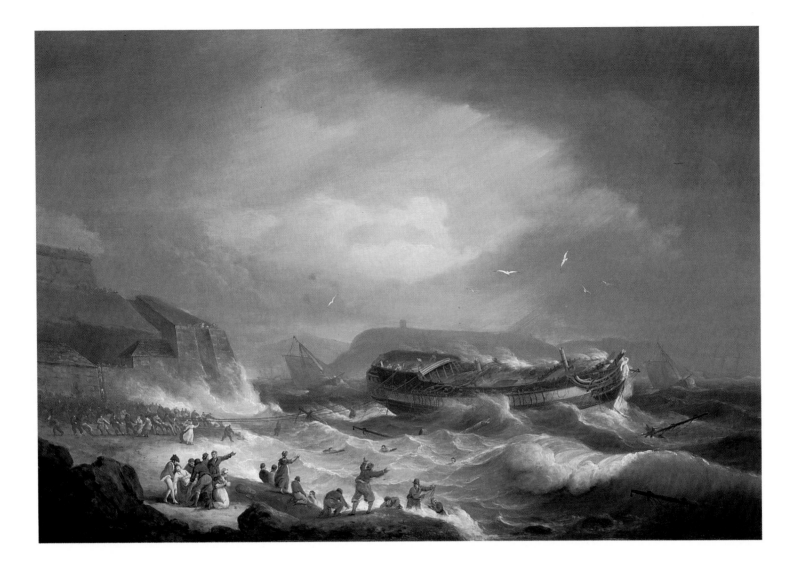

Plate 52. The 'Dutton' wrecked in Plymouth Sound.
Thomas Luny, 1821

When Thomas Luny was forced by ill-health to retire from the Royal Navy
he went to live at Teignmouth, Devon, where he was taken up by several of
the naval men in the town, including Sir Edward Pellew (later Lord Exmouth).
This painting, from a series depicting incidents in Pellew's career, is one of
Luny's most accomplished.

The *Dutton*, an East Indiaman bound for the West Indies with troops aboard,
was wrecked in Plymouth Sound during a gale on 26 January 1796. Thanks
to the heroic efforts of Pellew (then stationed at Falmouth, commanding a
squadron of frigates) in getting a line aboard, all but four persons were saved.

Although the scene is somewhat artificially dramatized with gesticulating
figures silhouetted darkly against the luridly illuminated surf, Luny's first-hand
knowledge of the sea and ships enabled him to bring great truth to his depiction
of the shipwreck, which was to become a favourite subject of the Romantics.

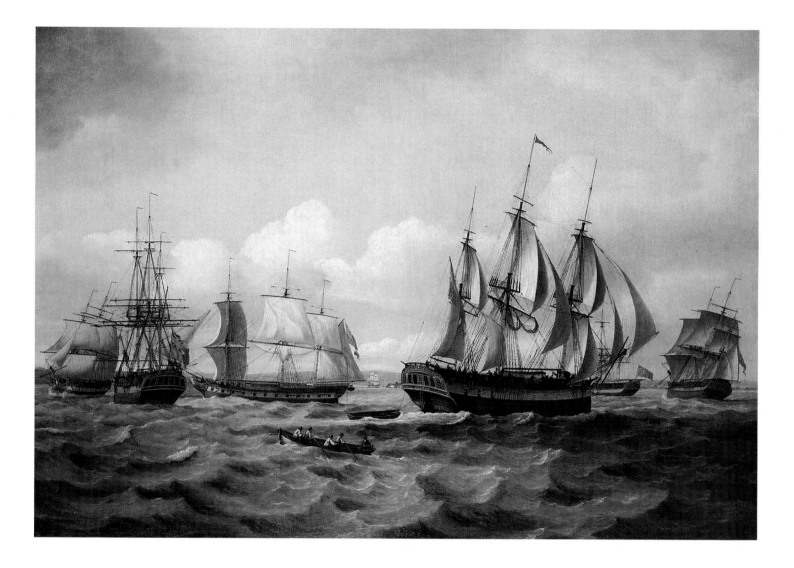

Plate 53. A Fleet of Merchantmen. Thomas Luny, 1802

This honest, well-crafted and knowledgeable painting is typical of Thomas
Luny at his best. Early in his career he was a pupil of Francis Holman and
at the date when this picture was painted he was serving in the Royal Navy.
When in 1810 he left the service and retired to Teignmouth, the influence of
his former captain (now Admiral) Tobin secured him many commissions and
his last days were prolific and prosperous in spite of increasing disability.

Luny was a skilled ship portraitist, and he exhibited at the Royal Academy.
At his best, his work is distinguished by fluid brushwork and attractive
colouring in the green of the seas and pearly translucent skies. Here he shows
the merchant ship *Castor*, probably of the Brocklebank Line and engaged in
the transatlantic trade, with the *Mars* at anchor on the left and the *Iris* and
Mariner on the right.

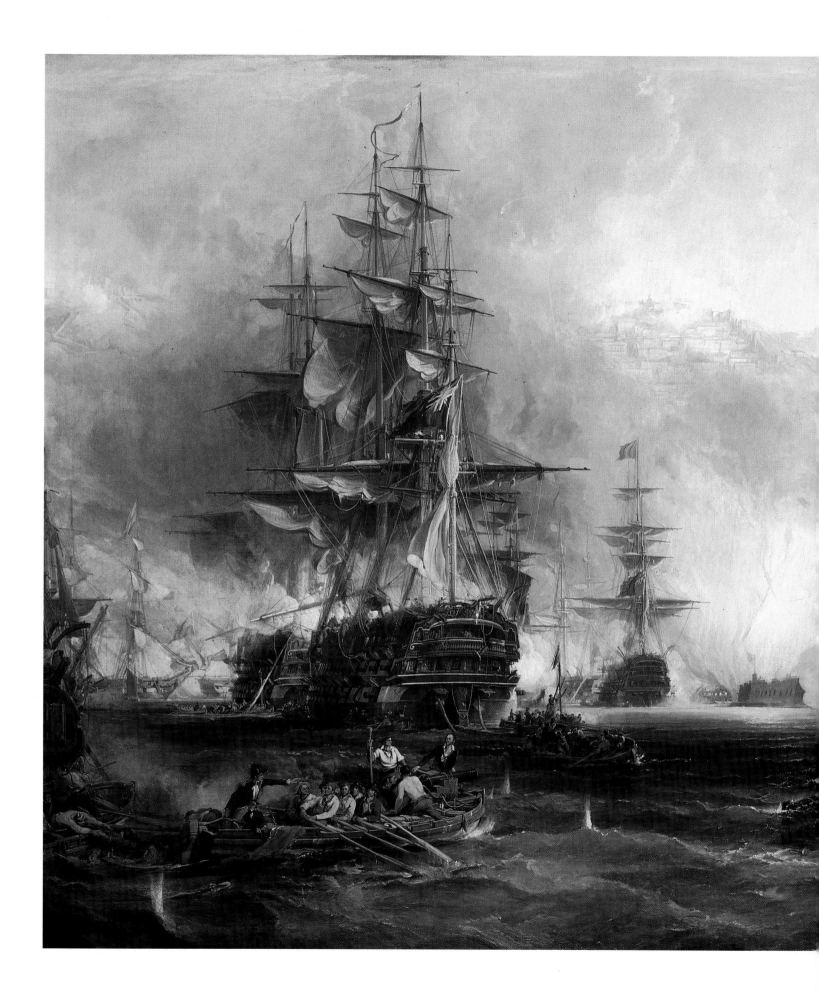

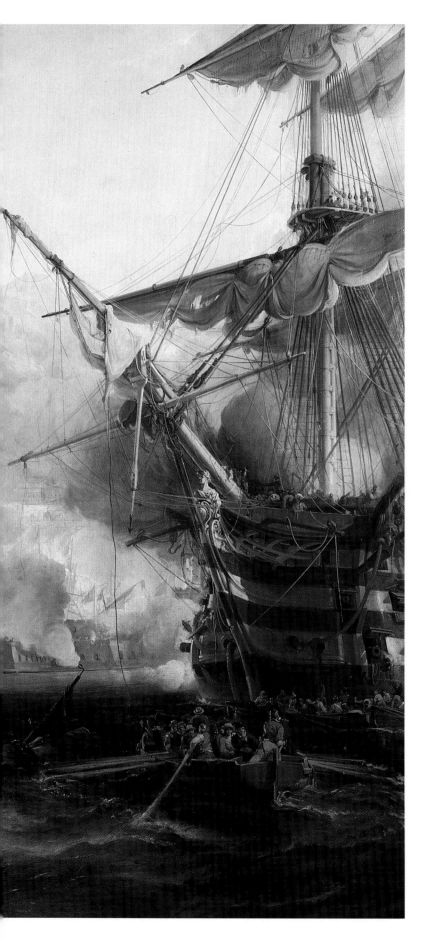

Plate 54. The Bombardment of Algiers. George Chambers, 1836

This picture, which hung originally in the Painted Hall at Greenwich, was commissioned by friends of Sir Edward Pellew to commemorate an action that secured the release of 3,000 Christian slaves held by the Dey of Tunis. This action severely weakened the ability of the Barbary states to attack shipping, which had been a menace since the seventeenth century. For his success in this battle Pellew was created Viscount Exmouth.

In the left foreground of this spirited reconstruction is a barge mounting a howitzer. To the left are two boats under the stern of the *Mutine*. In the right foreground is another barge with a carronade. Beyond her, more boats are sheltering under the *Impregnable*. In the left middle distance are the *Minden* and the *Superb*. In the left background is the forepart of the Dutch flagship *Melampus*, and ahead of her the stern of a British frigate. In the middle and right background are the *Queen Charlotte* and *Leander* and beyond are the batteries of the harbour, with Algiers behind.

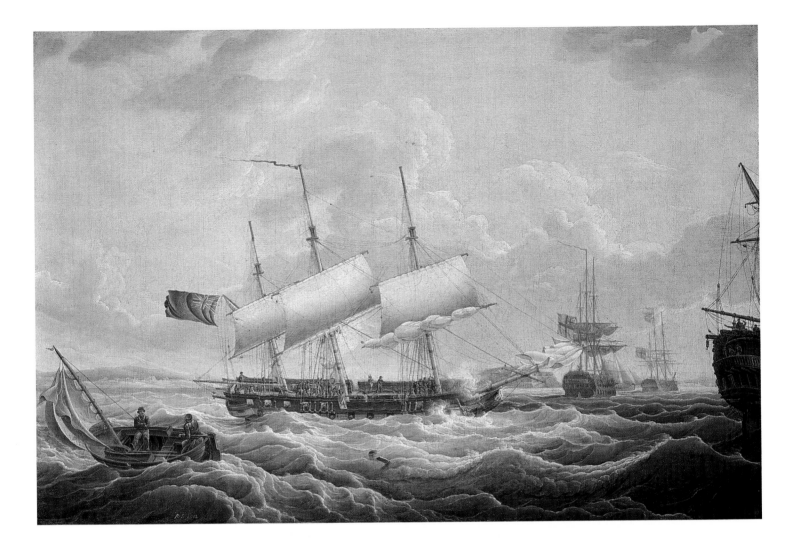

Plate 55. A Frigate coming to Anchor in the Mersey.
Robert Salmon, 1802

This is one of Robert Salmon's early works, painted some twenty-six years
before he left Britain to continue his successful career in America. Although
Salmon records that he arrived in Liverpool in 1806, this work, painted in the
year that he first exhibited at the Royal Academy, is thought to be a view of
the Mersey, looking directly upstream from the river-mouth with the Rock Fort
to the right and the Bootle shore to the left. In the centre a frigate, with
shortened sail and close-hauled, in Salmon's typically stylized choppy seas, is
coming to anchor.

It is not known where Salmon learned his impeccable craftsmanship and
technical accuracy but, like his other early works showing scenes around his
home in Cumberland, it has an already mature style influenced by the Dutch
and modified by later English and Italian painting. Salmon's work has self-
confidence, freshness and directness; his original technique and personal vision
give it a distinction which raises it above the level of more traditional
eighteenth-century marine painting.

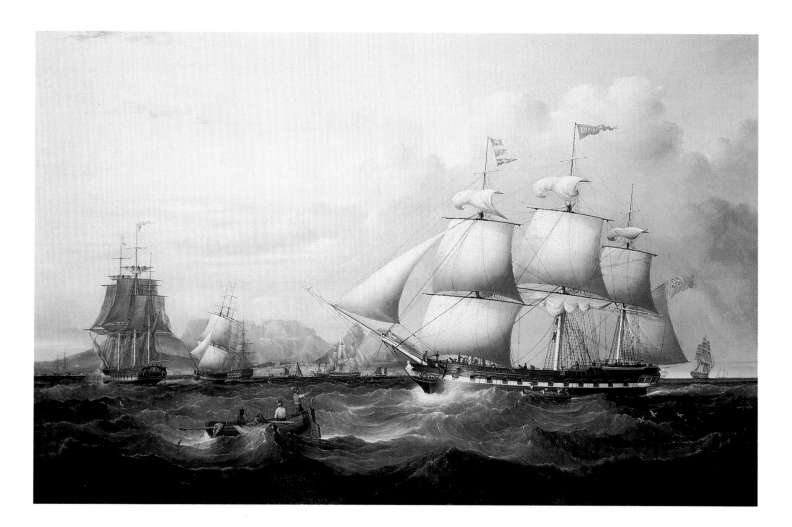

Plate 56. The 'Euphrates', Indiaman. Samuel Walters, 1835

Samuel Walters is typical of that host of ship portraitists who made their living in the great days of the British shipping industry by commemorating the elegant and profitable ships for their proud owners and masters. Walters was born at sea, the son of a marine artist, and by 1830 was an exhibitor at the Liverpool Academy Annual Exhibition. Between 1842 and 1861 he exhibited at the Royal Academy. Apart from a brief and unsuccessful period in London, he lived all his life in Liverpool and Bootle.

The *Euphrates* is shown off Capetown. As in most of Walters' ship portraits, the subject is seen in profile on a choppy sea, with a fresh breeze filling the sails. The details of rigging and flags are meticulously rendered.

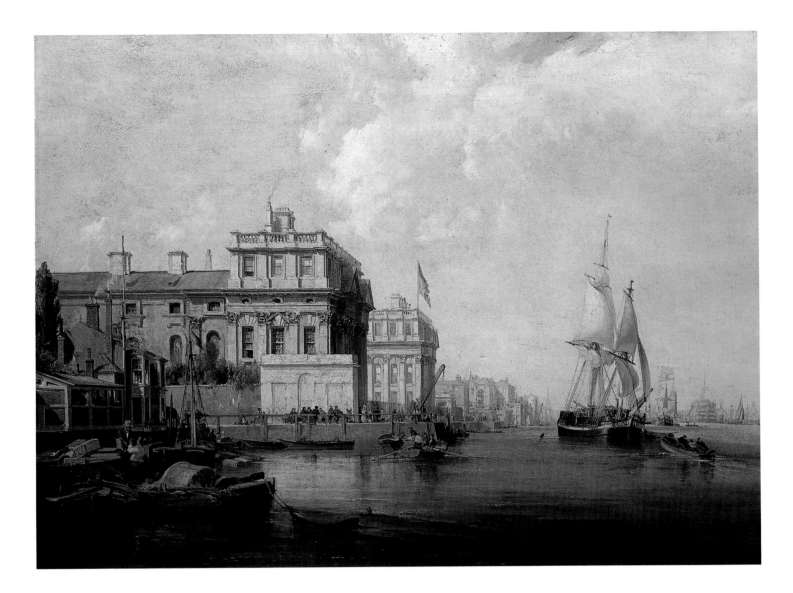

Plate 57. Greenwich Hospital. George Chambers, 1836

This view of Greenwich Hospital looks west across the river frontage towards
Fisher's Alley, Greenwich landing, and the Ship Inn, now the site of the Cutty
Sark dry dock. Beyond the brig sailing down river is HMS *Dreadnought*, moored
off Greenwich as a Seamen's Hospital in 1830.

    Chambers was a self-taught artist whose harsh early life left him a legacy of
ill-health. As a boy, his talent for drawing freed him from his apprenticeship
on a coastal trader; after many vicissitudes (and a period devoted to theatrical
scene painting) and as a result of the patronage of Lord Mark Kerr, his work
began to be recognized, one of his paintings being bought by William IV.

    Chambers' brushwork is fluid and he is able to suggest detail with a few deft
strokes. His early seafaring ensured that he drew shipping accurately and
naturally, a slightly 'stagey' composition being a reminder of his theatre
experience. Only Chambers' early death prevented him achieving the
recognition he deserved as a foremost British marine artist.

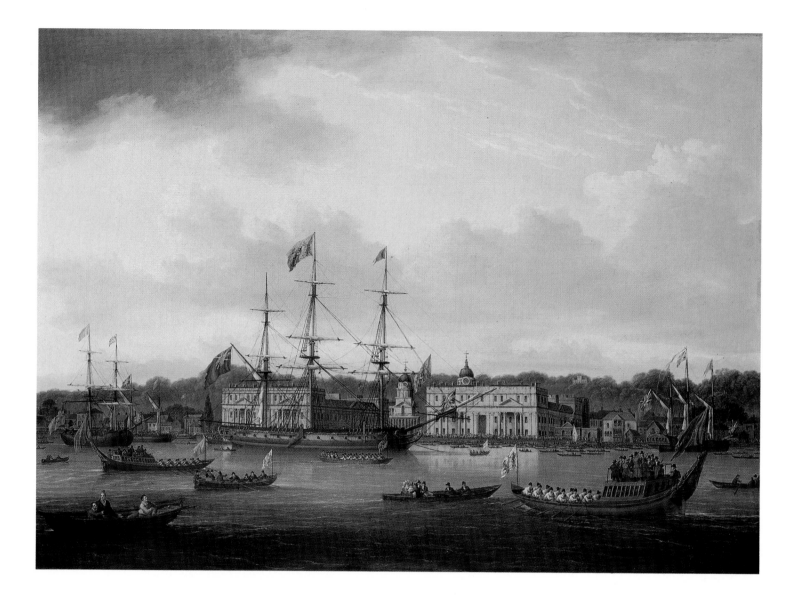

Plate 58. Return of George IV to Greenwich. William Anderson

The King's visit to Scotland in August 1822 was the first by a British monarch
since Charles II. This picture shows him being rowed in a barge to the
watergate at Greenwich on his return on 1 September. The *Royal George* (royal
yacht) is shown at anchor, starboard broadside view, in the left middle distance.
In the right foreground is the Lord Mayor's barge, complete with orchestra.
The hospital and riverside buildings and the slopes of Greenwich Park form
a backdrop to the busy scene.

Little is known of Anderson's early life or artistic education, beyond the fact
that he was born in Scotland, became a shipwright and moved to London at
the age of thirty to set up as a marine painter. He learned a finished style firmly
based on the Dutch seventeenth-century school and owing little to the influence
of the Romantics. The painting has a sparkling brilliance of colour and mastery
of brushwork which recall Canaletto's similar view of Greenwich.

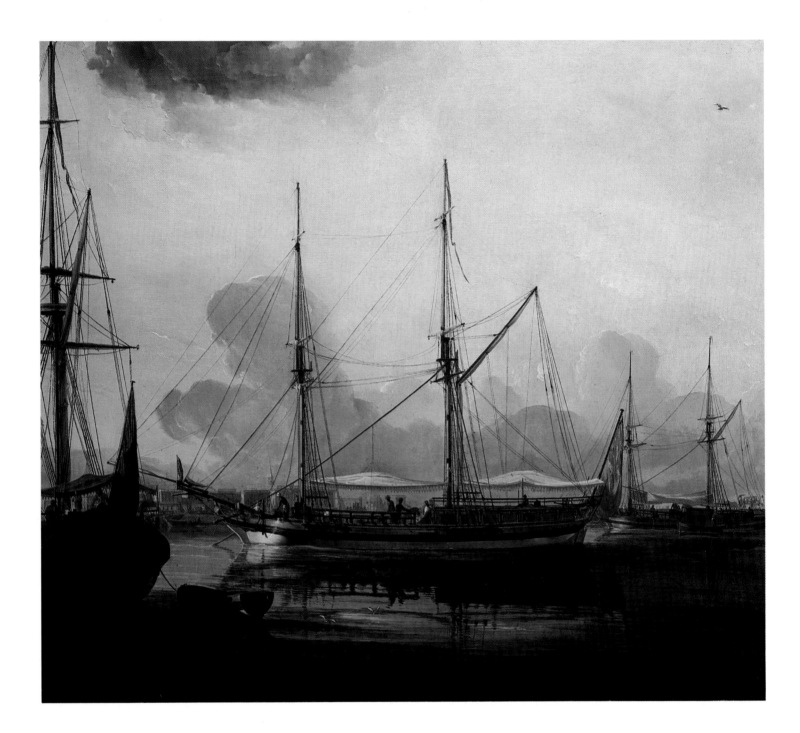

Plate 59. The 'Charlotte of Chittagong' and other Indian Government Vessels at Anchor. Franz Balthazar Solveyns, 1792

This panel shows the *Charlotte of Chittagong* lying in the Hoogli river off Calcutta with other Indian government despatch vessels. These snow-rigged craft, with large passenger accommodation, were used by the East India Company as despatch vessels and to carry the Company's servants around the coasts and up the great rivers of India.

Franz Balthazar Solveyns was born in Antwerp in 1760 and studied portraiture and history painting there and in Paris. He visited India and stayed to make many paintings of Indian life. He also published two series of etchings of local craft, *Pleasure Boats* and *Boats of Lading*, which are now valuable reference works. They sold poorly and he returned to take a job in the docks at Antwerp, where he died.

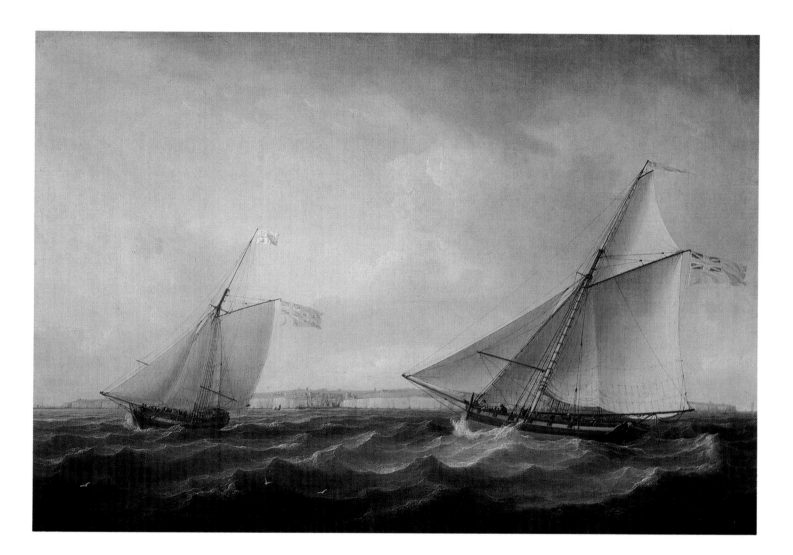

**Plate 60. Trinity House Yacht and Revenue Cutter off Ramsgate.
Thomas Whitcombe**

In this typical work Whitcombe depicts a Trinity House yacht (on the left)
flying the distinctive jack of that organization, composed of the red cross of
St. George between four ships. Trinity House was then as now responsible for
the lighthouses, lightships and navigational marker buoys around the English
coast. On the right is a cutter of the Revenue service, used to stem the tide
of smuggling at this time.

   Whitcombe was a prolific marine artist, particularly in the recording of the
naval side of the French revolutionary wars. He was a frequent exhibitor at
the Royal Academy, but little is known of his life. His ability to draw the stance
of ships in correct relationship to the elements, and his atmospheric use of
strongly-patterned cloud forms and seas full of movement, suggest that he had
some first-hand experience of the sea. At its best, his mature style is crisp and
fresh but his work is most valuable as an historical record.

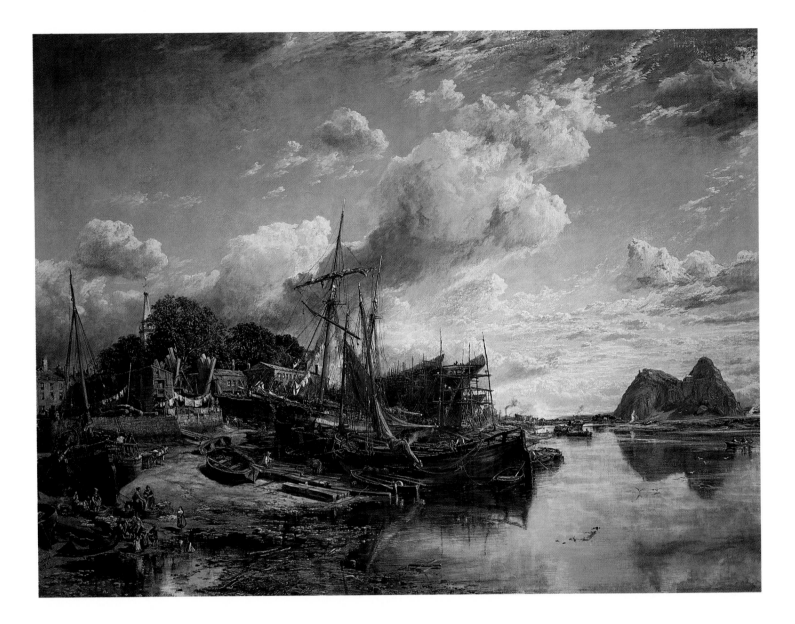

Plate 61. Shipyard at Dumbarton. Samuel Bough, 1855

This picture is both a landscape in the Romantic tradition and a painting of particular marine interest. It is an early work, painted while Bough was living in Port Glasgow, and it was exhibited at the Royal Scottish Academy in 1855. In it can already be seen the fresh natural sparkle which characterizes his later work. Bough, who was born into a poor family in Carlisle, became a theatrical scene painter and taught himself to paint in oils through studying the works of Turner and others.

In the extreme left foreground is the southernmost portion of Dumbarton Quay. In the middle distance is the shipyard belonging at that time to Messrs Macmillan & Son, later the site of the Dumbarton Distillery. The two iron-framed ships under construction are thought to be the *Ardbeg* and *Jane Jack Mitchell*; the inscription on the painting indicates that the yard also built gabbarts, a Scottish type of sailing barge. Visible through the trees on the left is Castlegreen House, belonging to the Denny family, and in the right background Dumbarton Rock is mirrored in the Clyde.

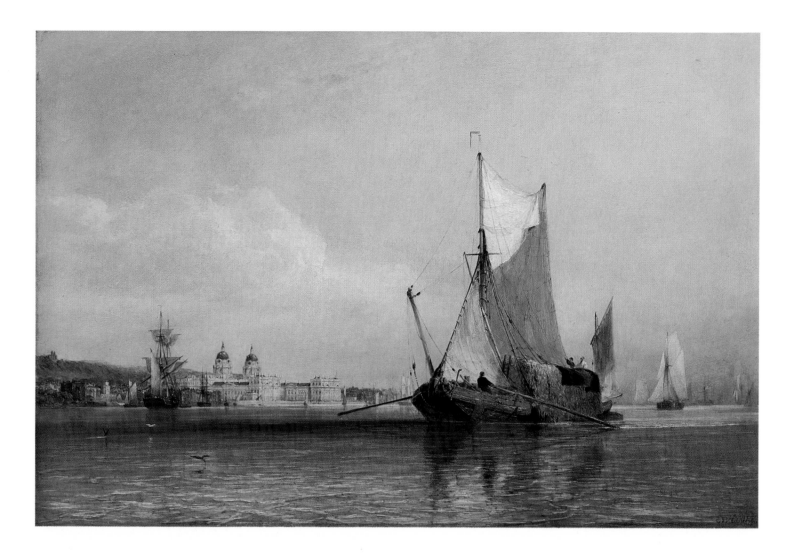

Plate 62. A Haybarge off Greenwich. Edward William Cooke, 1835

In 1828, at the age of seventeen, E. W. Cooke began publication of *Fifty Plates of Shipping and Craft*. His engravings were favourably compared with those of Cotman, with whom Cooke's family was on close terms.

Cooke was always admired for his colour and draughtsmanship rather than for his painterly qualities. This is one of his earliest oils. He took up the medium in 1834 under James Stark and this is one of two works exhibited the following year at the Royal Academy. The subject-matter and style relate closely to his work in *Shipping and Craft*.

Haybarges, particularly suitable (because of their shallow draught) to enter farm creeks, brought hay from as far as Suffolk and Margate on the Kentish shore to feed the thousands of horses in London, returning with loads of manure to spread on the fields.

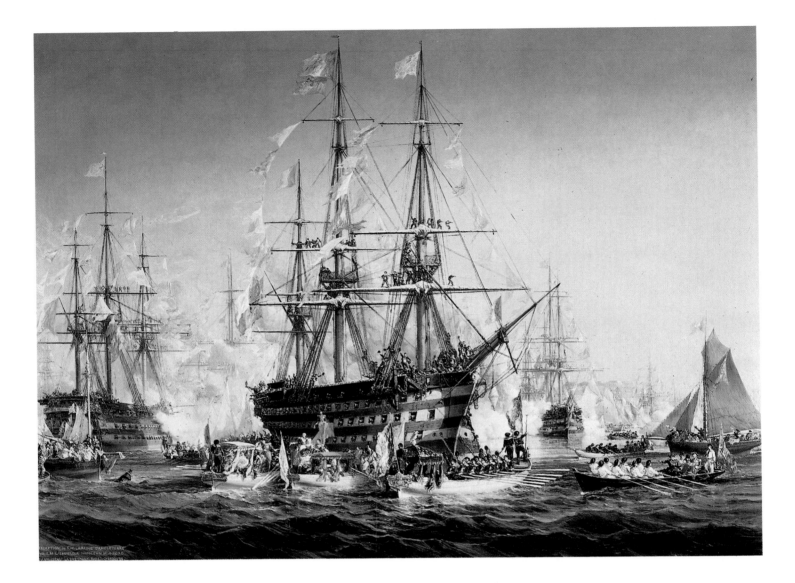

**Plate 63. Napoleon III receiving Queen Victoria at Cherbourg.
Jules Noel, 1859**

This painting commemorates the scene as the Queen went aboard the French
flagship to attend a banquet given by the Emperor and Empress to mark the
completion of the fortifications at Cherbourg.

The centre of this large decorative work is dominated by the French three-
decker *Bretagne*, dressed overall with the royal and imperial standards at the
main. The Emperor, in the full-dress uniform of a French admiral, awaits the
Queen in front of the entry port. She is about to leave her barge and ascend
the companion ladder. In the centre foreground are the royal and imperial
barges and other vessels, both French and English, some dressed overall. Small
boats, filled with sightseers, crowd the scene. In the background is Fort Roule.

Jules Noel studied at Brest and exhibited at the Salon from 1840 to 1879.
He was chiefly known for his coastal views of Normandy, which have been
favourably compared with the work of Eugène Isabey.

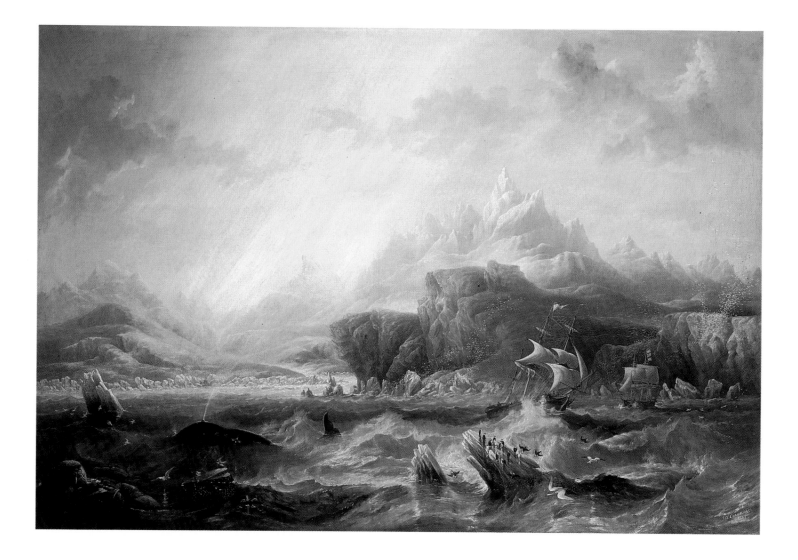

Plate 64. 'Erebus' and 'Terror' in the Antarctic.
John Wilson Carmichael, 1847

In this painting Carmichael adds a Romantic feeling to scientific endeavour
and human endurance. It is one of two—the other also in the National
Maritime Museum—inspired by the publication of an account of the British
Antarctic Expedition (1839–43) by its commander, Sir James Clark Ross.
Ross was an experienced ice navigator and was the first to locate the magnetic
North Pole.

The bomb-vessels HMS *Erebus*, 370 tons, and HMS *Terror*, 340 tons, specially
strengthened for ice conditions, were heavy and sluggish but of shoal draught
and maximum capacity for their size.

John Wilson Carmichael was born in Newcastle, a self-taught artist with
early seafaring connections. He was influenced by Turner, Callcott and
Clarkson Stanfield, and the fantastic landscape in this work, painted in the
year when he moved to London, shows the influence of John Martin.

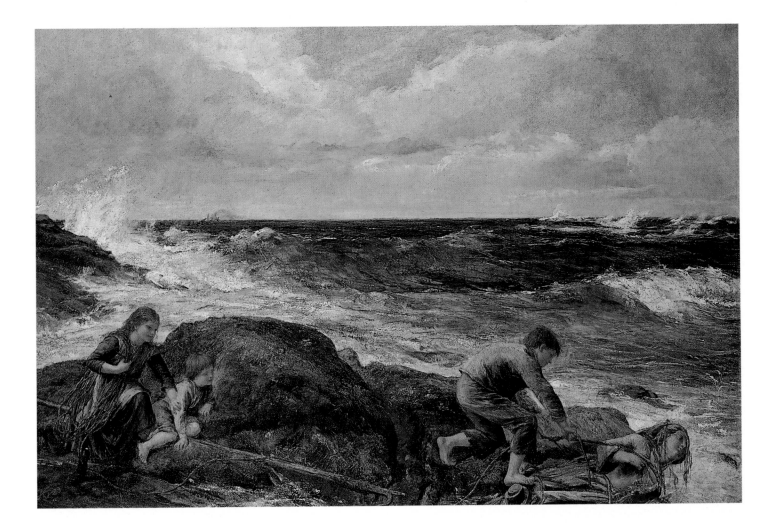

Plate 65. Catching a Mermaid. James Clarke Hook, 1883

This painting is a fine example of the imaginative work of a Victorian marine artist, designed to appeal to the emotions and to please wealthy purchasers rather than seafarers. (When it was exhibited at the Royal Academy in 1883 it was bought by a London merchant, Humphrey Roberts.) In this work the children provide an essential counterpoint to the seascape behind, and their vitality mirrors that of the waves. Without them, the composition would be empty, and the human interest they provide is introduced to engage the viewer's sympathies. It is upon this, rather than on the actual narrative content, that the effect of the picture as a whole relies.

James Hook came to marines by way of figure and history painting. His seascapes conform to three basic patterns: beach scenes; views from clifftops; boats at sea. 'Hookscapes' were part of the Victorian art scene, very often featuring idealized representations of the fisherfolk of Devon and Cornwall. This work is typically vigorous, with many touches of the luscious colour for which he was famous.

17. WARS AGAINST AMERICA AND FRANCE

In 1773 a cargo of 340 cases of tea shipped to Boston by the firm of Davison, Newman and Co. of London was tipped overboard into the harbour as a protest both against the taxation levied on the American colonies by the British Government and against some limitations on trade imposed from London on the settlers. Known as the Boston Tea Party, it began as a small, local affair but over the next three years grew to be a pointer to the future as attempts to reach some sort of compromise with Britain foundered against the obstinacy of George III and his prime minister, Lord North. In 1776 a Declaration of Independence was signed by the leading citizens of the thirteen colonies; George Washington took command of a hastily raised citizen army; and a first victory over the British garrison at Saratoga gained France as an ally for the rebellious colonies.

A year or two later Spain and Holland joined the alliance against Britain.

Apart from the military operations in North America [fig. 91], the American Revolutionary War was fought almost entirely at sea and for the first time for nearly 200 years Britain was in danger of being overwhelmed by the sheer numbers of ships ranged against her. She could count 130 ships of the line in her fleet, most of them in good fighting condition, but they had to be spread widely round the world to protect her trade interests. They had, however, some technical advantages to redress the balance. Most British warships had their bottoms sheathed in copper, mainly as a defence against the teredo worm, but at the same time it provided an increase in speed of a knot or two. A flintlock replaced the dangerous slowmatch as the means of

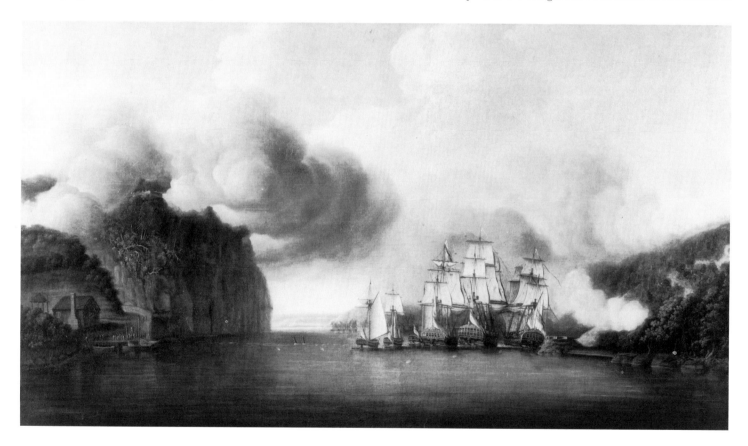

91. Forcing a Passage of the Hudson River, 9 October 1776.
Thomas Mitchell, 1780

This representation of the small but important operation undertaken by
Captain Hyde Parker during the American war was based on a painting by
Dominic Serres. The action is viewed at a point just north of New York. Parker
(in the *Phoenix*) and his squadron, viewed from astern, lie between Fort Lee
and Fort Washington.

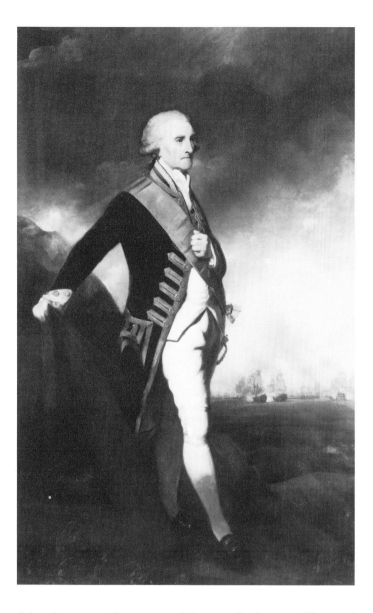

action off the Dogger Bank in 1781, the Dutch navy took little part in the war. However, the presence of her ships just across the North Sea tied down an equivalent British force to counter any movements they might make.

Although between them France and Spain had enough ships to dominate the English Channel and its western approaches and enforce a sea blockade, their separate national interests overrode this obvious chance of bringing Britain to her knees. Spain's war aim was the recapture of Gibraltar and Minorca; French eyes were on a naval offensive in the West Indies. Such naval actions as took place in French and Spanish waters were mainly convoy actions, involving French convoys from the West Indies and British convoys of supplies to Gibraltar, which was under siege for more than three years. They were mainly fought on conventional tactical lines and produced indecisive results, the only exception being an action off Cape St. Vincent in 1780, more generally known as the Moonlight Battle [plate 43]. A British fleet commanded by Admiral Rodney [fig. 92] was escorting a supply convoy to Gibraltar when it met a Spanish fleet under the command of Admiral de Langara which was blockading the colony. There was little daylight left when the two fleets met and although Rodney had a considerable advantage in numbers of ships, a formal battle fought by the rules of the *Fighting Instructions* would inevitably have ended in stalemate. On sighting the Spanish fleet Rodney hoisted the signal for a general chase. Six Spanish ships were captured, one blew up, two others were driven ashore, and Rodney delivered the supply convoy to Gibraltar before crossing the Atlantic to take command in the West Indies.

The main sea campaign of this war was fought against the French in West Indian and American waters. The land war had not gone well for Britain and by August 1781 the British army under Cornwallis was surrounded by Washington's army at Yorktown. Early in September the French Admiral de Grasse and his fleet reached Chesapeake Bay with reinforcements for Washington, at the same time effectively cutting Cornwallis's only supply route. Admiral Graves, with a British fleet, sailed from New York to drive the French ships off. Instead of attacking them as they emerged one by one out of Chesapeake Bay, Graves formed his fleet into a line of battle and, when de Grasse was clear of the land, hoisted the signal to engage the enemy, still keeping the signal for the line of battle flying. It was a repeat of the Battle of Minorca (see p. 73), with only the British van squadron getting within range of the French ships. At the end of the day Graves broke off the action and withdrew to New York. By leaving de Grasse in command of the sea around Chesapeake Bay, he sealed the fate of Cornwallis and his army.

firing the guns and gave a small increase in the rate of fire; and a new gun made its appearance as an auxiliary to the main armament in the yardarm-to-yardarm type of battle so eagerly sought by British admirals. Known as a carronade after its Scottish manufacturer, the Carron Iron Company, it fired a 68lb. shot and was familiarly known in the British ships as 'the smasher'.

The French navy, much improved since the Seven Years War, was built round a strength of eighty ships of the line, all in good condition and many of them new. The Spanish fleet equalled that of France in numbers, though there were some defects in the training of its crews. Holland could count fifty ships of the line, but because of the shoal waters along her coastline they were built smaller than those of other nations. Apart from a small

92. Portrait of Admiral Lord George Brydges Rodney. Studio of Sir Joshua Reynolds

A contemporary version of the portrait by Reynolds exhibited at the Royal Academy in 1789, this shows the sitter in Admiral's full dress uniform of 1783–92. Rodney's impeccable service record was exemplified by his successes in the West Indies, not least in his victory over Admiral de Grasse at the Battle of the Saints in 1782, represented in the right background of the picture.

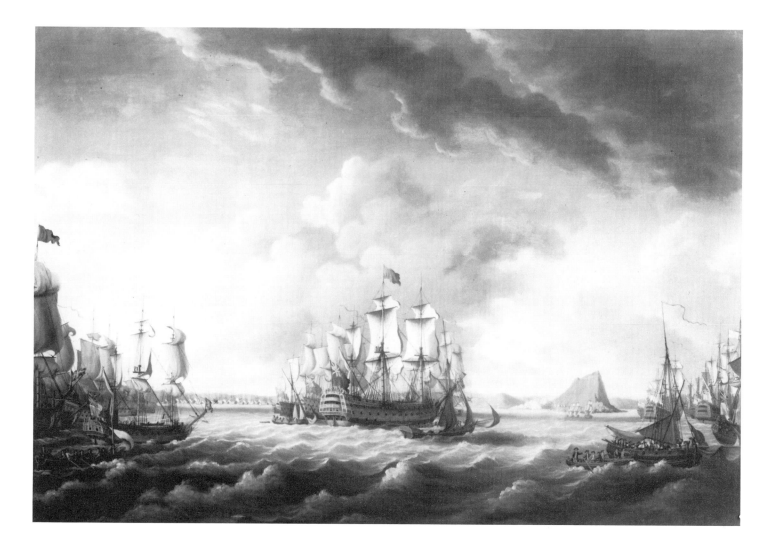

When Rodney and his fleet arrived in the West Indies after
the Moonlight Battle they joined the ships already there under
the command of Samuel Hood, which brought an approximate
equality in numbers with the French fleet. After various confrontations, the decisive battle took place two years later. Knowing
that de Grasse was engaged in bringing a large convoy from
Martinique to Cuba, Rodney set off in pursuit and the two fleets
met off the Saints, a small group of islands south of Guadeloupe.
They approached on opposite courses but a sudden change of
wind threw the French line of battle into disorder and enabled
Rodney to lead his squadron through a gap. One of the ships
in the van squadron also found a gap and Hood led his rear
squadron through a third. This cutting of their line at three
points paralysed the French plan of battle and five ships were
captured, one of them the 110-gun *Ville de Paris*, de Grasse's flagship with the admiral on board. The victory was decisive enough

for Britain to regain most of her naval prestige, and at the peace
to insist on the return of the West Indian islands she had lost
to the French in the earlier fighting. But of more significance
was the introduction of a new tactical thought in naval battle,
of breaking through an enemy line and throwing it into confusion. In the next war to be fought on a world scale, already
just around the corner, this was to become the dominant naval
tactic, refined as the war progressed by adding a concentration
of forces at the point of breakthrough.

The climax of the long series of wars between Britain and
France for command of the seas came when the French Revolution threw Europe into over twenty years of warfare. The trigger
that brought Britain into the onslaught was the execution of
Louis XVI and the consequent fear that French revolutionary
fervour might cross the Channel and infect Britain herself. On
the seas at least, Britain was ready. The backbone of the navy

93. Howe's Relief of Gibraltar, 11 October 1782. Richard Paton

In 1782 Admiral Howe was sent to deliver supplies to besieged Gibraltar, all
but neglected since Rodney's and Darby's similar expeditions of 1780 and 1781.
Here we see part of the English fleet running towards the straits, with the
Franco-Spanish fleet at anchor in Algeciras Bay. Howe's flagship, the *Victory*,
is nearest, with one cutter astern and another to starboard.

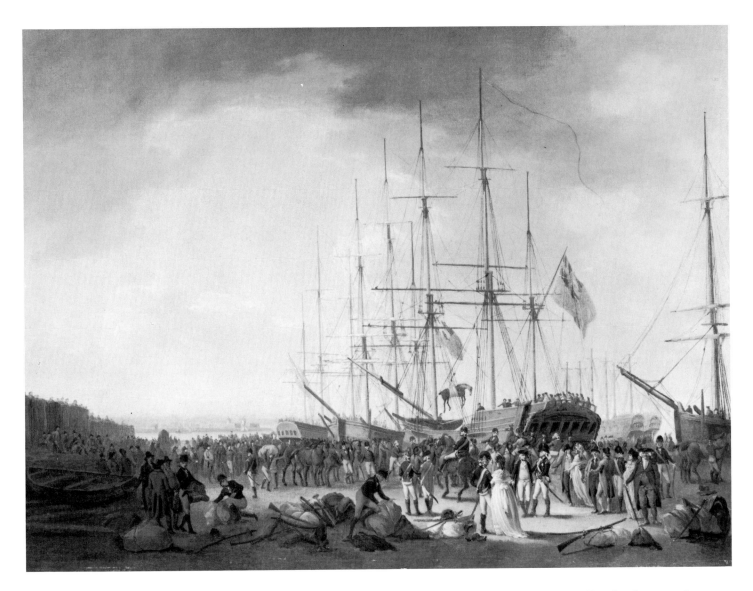

of 1793 was the third-rate 74-gun ship, around 1,850 tons, of which there were ninety-two in the fleet, with five 100-gun first-rates and sixteen 80-gun second-rates. A total of 114 frigates provided an adequate back-up. More important than the ships was the quality of the officers and crews, well-trained and experienced, and led by admirals who had studied and appreciated the new tactics.

Although the French fleet numbered eighty ships of the line, most of the pre-Revolution officers had been replaced by largely untrained men appointed politically, and the crews were generally undisciplined. Spain, entering the war on France's side in 1796, added another sixty ships of the line, though their crews too lacked training. Holland, occupied by France in 1794, brought fifty more ships of the line to add to the total but

although they were manned by well-trained crews, they were no match materially, rate for rate, with the ships of Britain.

French successes in the European land fighting were to some extent counterbalanced by their failures at sea. Toulon was temporarily occupied by the British Mediterranean fleet and when it was evacuated some four months later, Corsica was captured in its place. Meanwhile in 1794 the first major battle at sea, known by the British as the Glorious First of June [plates 44, 45], had been fought off Ushant against a fleet escorting merchant ships bringing foodstuffs essential to a beleaguered France. It was an action in which a variation of the new tactics was attempted, with only partial success as some of the British captains failed fully to understand the admiral's intentions. Lord Howe's plan of action was for each ship in the line of battle to

94. Troops embarking near Greenwich. William Anderson, 1793

During the spring of 1793 considerable numbers of English troops were shipped across the Channel to serve in the nascent war against post-revolutionary France. It is thought that this painting, which admirably describes the typical bustle (if not the emotion) of the moments before departure, may represent the embarkation at Blackwall on 9 May of the 11th Light Dragoons, bound for Ostend to join the allied army in Flanders.

turn simultaneously towards the French line and break through it in the gap astern of its opposite number. Six of them did so, the remainder followed each other round in a wide sweep which did little to bring Howe's bold plan the success it deserved. It was a tactical victory for the British, with seven French ships captured; strategically, however, it was a reverse as the convoy escaped to safety while the fleets were engaged.

The Spanish entry into the war in 1796 made British dominion of the Mediterranean no longer tenable, and the withdrawal of the fleet there, for the first time in nearly 200 years, left the Mediterranean bare of British warships. Yet this produced the conditions in which the next big naval battle was fought, when the Spanish fleet, in a joint venture with France, left its Mediterranean ports to unite with the French Atlantic squadron at Brest in preparation for an invasion of Ireland. It was intercepted by the British ships withdrawn from the Mediterranean [fig. 95]. Although the odds in numbers of ships were two to one in favour of the Spanish it was perhaps unfortunate for them that the two

greatest admirals in British naval history were both present in this action. In command was John Jervis, then at the top of his profession, a man whose greatness never rested on the noise and glare of popularity but on his total dedication and devotion to the British navy. The second great man, not yet an admiral but about to become one as a result of this battle, was Horatio Nelson, equally dedicated and devoted but relishing also the acclaim of the crowds. When the Spanish ships were intercepted they were sailing in two groups and Jervis led the fleet in line of battle between them, splitting the Spanish fleet. As the action developed it became obvious that the larger group would escape. Realizing this, Nelson, in the rear squadron, left his position in the line and placed his ship in the path of the escaping Spanish ships, capturing two of them. Two more were taken in the battle and several others were so badly damaged that the fleet retreated to Cadiz where it was blockaded in.

To leave the line of battle without a direct order from the admiral was a punishable offence, but so far had the new flexi-

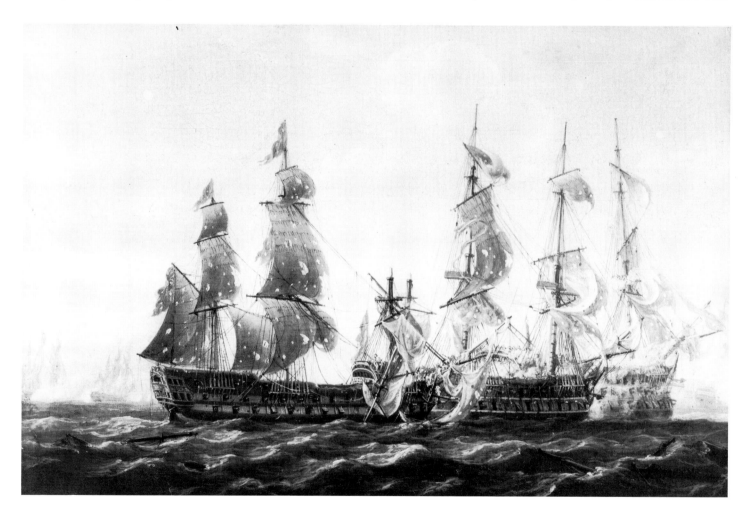

95. Battle of Cape St. Vincent, 14 February 1797.
Nicholas Pocock, 1801

This battle brought Admiral Jervis a peerage and Commodore Nelson a knighthood. Here, the port bow of Nelson's *Captain* is seen up against the starboard quarter of the *San Nicholas*, with the latter's bowsprit inadvertently caught up in the *San Josef*. In the confusion both Spanish ships were boarded and captured under Nelson's direction.

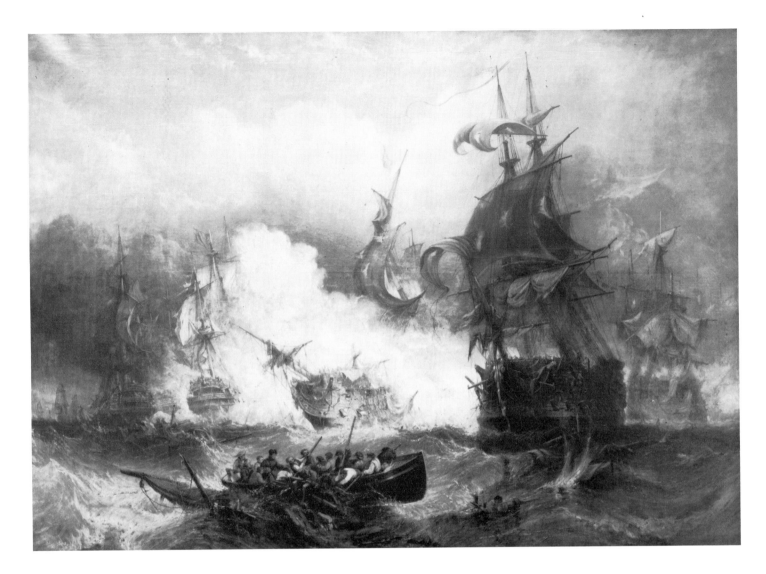

bility of tactical thought progressed during the last few years that Jervis, though pressed by his junior admirals to do so, refused to order a court-martial and instead promoted Nelson to rear-admiral.

With the failure of the Franco-Spanish plan for an invasion of Ireland, France turned to Holland for another fleet to cover the landing of French troops. But even as the Dutch fleet left the Texel, the British struck. This time the attack was in two columns at right angles to the Dutch line, a concentration of force at single points that broke the line into three separate parts. Although the Dutch fleet put up a bitter resistance, they were no match for their opponents and nine of their sixteen ships of the line were taken as prizes. The British admiral was Adam Duncan and the battle was fought off Camperdown [fig. 96].

In May 1798, on a report that Napoleon had sailed from

Toulon with an army of 36,000 troops in 400 transports, Jervis detached Nelson with part of his fleet into the Mediterranean to discover where Napoleon had gone. After a long search the French Mediterranean fleet, which had escorted Napoleon and landed his army in Egypt, was discovered at anchor in Aboukir Bay, close to Alexandria. Once again a new twist was given to the tactics of battle. As he approached, Nelson noticed that the French ships were lying to a single anchor. He realized that if the French had given themselves sufficient room to swing with the tide at single anchor, there must be room for a British ship to pass. This enabled him to concentrate his eleven ships of the line on the head of the French line, attacking them from both sides simultaneously, and gradually work down to the centre and rear as the French ships were silenced. Of the thirteen French ships at anchor, only two escaped, the remaining eleven being

96. Battle of Camperdown, 11 October 1797.
William Adolphus Knell, 1848

The Battle of Camperdown, a furious confrontation reminiscent of the Anglo-Dutch struggles of the seventeenth century, is painted here by Knell with appropriate stylistic nostalgia some fifty years after the event. To the right, the English two-decker the *Ardent* is engaged with the *Vrijheid*; wreathed in smoke, the latter's port-side bow is shattered and her main mast is collapsing.

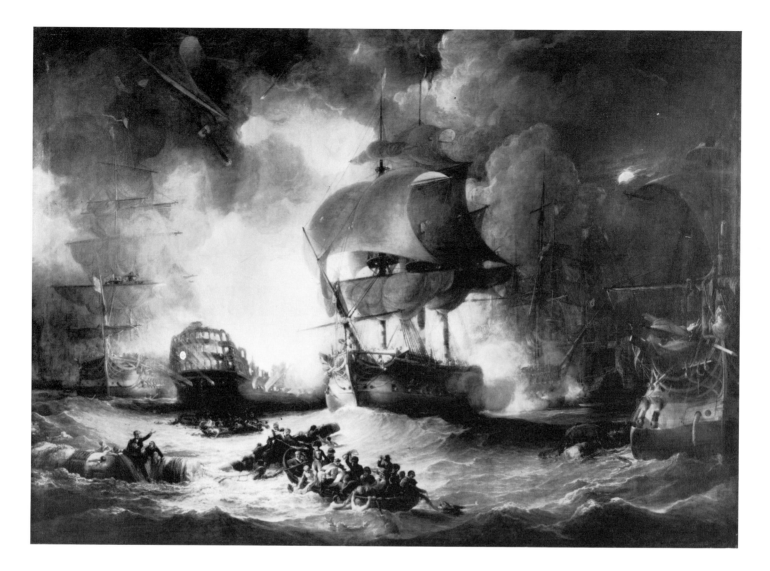

burned or captured [fig. 97]. It was a brilliant tactical success and the strategic results were far-reaching. The French army in Egypt was cut off from home—most of them were captured later—and Britain once again controlled the Mediterranean with her sea power. This was reinforced a few months later by the capture of Malta from the French, with its magnificent and fortified harbour commanding the narrows of the central Mediterranean.

The declaration by France of an Armed Neutrality of the North in 1801 presented Britain with a new problem. This was an alliance encouraged by Napoleon between Russia, Prussia, Sweden and Denmark to enforce a total embargo on all British trade in the Baltic. Britain was still largely dependent on the Baltic trade for the supply of masts and tar for her shipbuilding, and with the Danish fleet commanding the narrow exits from the Baltic to the North Sea, these vital supplies were threatened. Admiral Hyde Parker was sent with a British fleet into the Baltic to persuade Denmark to revoke her armed neutrality and allow the Baltic trade to Britain to pass. Nelson sailed as second-in-command of the fleet and it fell to him to plan and fight the ensuing battle. To avoid the great Trekroner Fortress which guards the northern entrance to Copenhagen, Nelson took his squadron round the middle ground sandbank and approached from the south. After a furious battle [plate 47], the Danish defensive line of ships was so shattered that eleven of them struck their colours. Nelson offered an armistice which was accepted, and the engagement ended with the loss by Denmark of fifteen ships, one of which was taken as a prize. Shortly after the battle Denmark agreed to the British demands and the Baltic trade was allowed to pass freely.

97. Battle of the Nile, 1 August 1798. George Arnald, 1827

This surprisingly powerful interpretation of the famous action between British and French fleets is by an artist better known for his sentimental genre paintings and restrained views of the English countryside. His subject, an episode from Nelson's first victory as an admiral, features the explosion of the French flagship *L'Orient* (left), the rescue of some of her crew (foreground), and, by contrast, the majestic poise of the *Swiftsure* amidst the hectic action.

In March 1802 a peace was signed at Amiens, though throughout Europe there were few who did not recognize that it could only be temporary. Although France had won great victories on land, Napoleon's ambitions were still unrealized. Britain had emerged from this first half of the war paramount at sea, almost entirely as the result of the new battle tactics. She had also been strong enough to blockade the main harbours and ports of her enemies, bottling up their warships and crippling their trade. Neutral ships trading with her enemies were also closely controlled, stopped and searched for contraband.

The resumption of the war in 1803 saw the genesis of another French plan to invade Britain, still the main obstacle to French expansionism in Europe and abroad. Although Napoleon assembled an army of 130,000 men around Boulogne and sufficient transport to ferry it across the Channel, there could be no invasion until a French battle fleet controlled the English Channel for long enough for the troops to cross to Britain.

Opportunities to evade a blockading squadron depended mainly on the weather. A local gale could disperse the blockading ships and present an opportunity to break out into the open sea. The French naval plan depended on this, starting with the fleet blockaded in Toulon. Once at sea it was to leave the Mediterranean, drive off the blockading squadron at Cadiz and release the Spanish ships there. Together they were to cross the Atlantic and raid the West Indies, drawing off the larger part of the British navy to protect the trade in that area. The Franco-Spanish fleet was then to recross the Atlantic, liberate the squadrons blockaded in Ferrol, Rochefort, Lorient and Brest, and thus form the strong fleet required in the English Channel to start the invasion.

On paper, it appeared to be a promising plan though in the end it failed as it took no account of the smaller ships which made up the total strength of the British navy, the sloops, cutters, and brigs, with lieutenants in command as a first step up the ladder of promotion. In 1805 there were 248 of these smaller ships, a figure which, as the war progressed, grew to 411 in 1809, a measure of their value in the overall strategy of the naval war. Their duties were never-ending, a constant stream of them taking orders and appreciations from the Admiralty in London to the admirals at sea, an equal stream bringing home every bit of enemy information gathered by the fleets and squadrons. Others, sighting and shadowing enemy ships to make sure of their position, course and speed, brought the information to the nearest British admiral, yet others stopped merchant ships to enquire whether they had sighted a warship during their passage. Their influence on the whole sea campaign that was to end in the Battle of Trafalgar was immense and it says much for

the training and understanding of their young commanders that they hardly ever put a foot wrong, realizing the sort of information that was required and which admiral most needed to know it.

To begin with, everything worked out as the French had planned. In March 1805 a violent gale forced Nelson and his blockading squadron to leave Toulon and retire to Sardinia to repair damage to the ships. On his return he found that the French fleet, with Admiral Villeneuve in command, had sailed. Nelson sailed east to make sure that the French were not repeating their previous attack on Egypt, and he returned to Gibraltar to learn that Villeneuve had passed through the Straits, released the Spanish squadron at Cadiz, and when last seen had been sailing west. He assumed that their destination must be the West Indies, sent off a sloop to give the Admiralty all his information and intentions, and proceeded in chase.

The Admiralty, appreciating that Villeneuve, as soon as he knew he had drawn off Nelson, would return to release the twelve Spanish ships in Ferrol, ordered reinforcements to join Admiral Calder who was blockading that port and also warned Admiral Cornwallis commanding the blockading squadron off Brest. Villeneuve soon learned of Nelson's arrival in the West Indies and he recrossed the Atlantic for the next step in the invasion plan. Nelson followed him three days later, reached Gibraltar to make sure that Villeneuve had not returned to the Mediterranean and then sailed north to reinforce Cornwallis off Brest, leaving most of his ships there but himself returning to Portsmouth.

Meanwhile, off Ferrol, Villeneuve with twenty ships of the line ran into the reinforced Calder with fifteen. The weather was misty, resulting in a somewhat scrappy action in which two Spanish ships were captured. Villeneuve reached Ferrol to link up with the Spanish ships there and a couple of weeks later sailed to unite with the Rochefort squadron and join the main French fleet at Brest. It was unfortunate for him that the ships in Rochefort were not ready and, in despair, he returned to Cadiz, where Admiral Collingwood, having withdrawn his squadron to let the Franco-Spanish fleet enter the port, promptly reinstated a close blockade.

The campaign at sea was now approaching its end. Nelson, the obvious choice to command the fleet in the coming battle, sailed from Portsmouth to join Collingwood off Cadiz. He would have in his fleet twenty-seven ships of the line and four frigates, opposing him would be thirty-three French and Spanish ships of the line with five frigates. Nelson settled down to wait for Villeneuve to come out, remaining over the horizon and out of sight of enemy eyes at Cadiz.

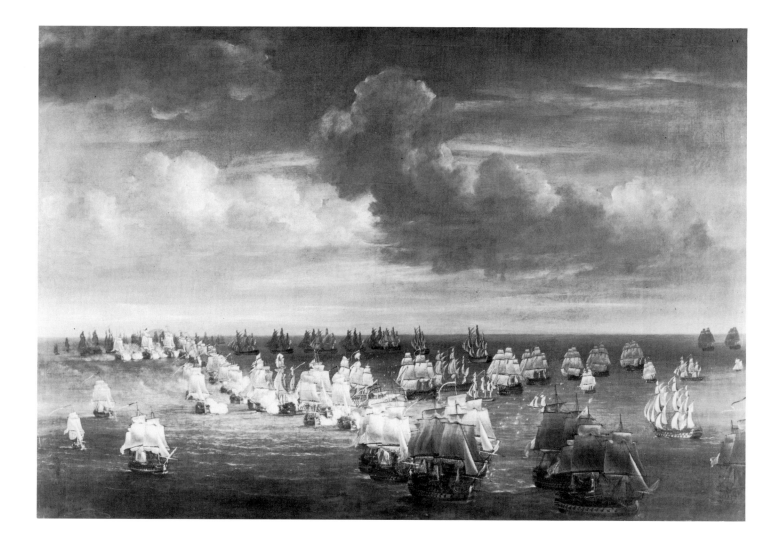

On 19 October the inshore frigate saw signs of movement in
Cadiz harbour. Two minutes later the information was received
on board Nelson's flagship, HMS *Victory*, over the horizon. That
night, to guard against any attempt by Villeneuve to re-enter
the Mediterranean, Nelson set the fleet's course for Gibraltar.
This was indeed Villeneuve's intention, and on 20 October the
two fleets were in sight of each other. Cut off from his goal, Villeneuve reversed course to return to Cadiz but by daylight on
the 21st, he was still at sea off Cape Trafalgar, his fleet in a somewhat disorderly formation. Nelson, who had discussed his plan
of action with all the captains previously so that no further
signals were necessary, led off into battle [plates 48, 49; fig. 98].

The plan was a refinement of the new tactical policy of breaking through the enemy line. The wind was light from the west,
which meant the enemy had to sail close-hauled on the port tack.
The British ships attacked in two divisions in line ahead, running
free before the wind so that, after breaking through, they could
luff up alongside individual ships and engage them with broadsides. The two British divisions attacked the French-Spanish
centre and rear, ignoring the van division completely, which in
the light wind prevailing would take some considerable time to
gain distance ahead, tack, and return to the aid of the centre
and rear ships. Until they could do so, the British fleet would
enjoy a sizeable superiority in numbers of ships, with enough
time to overwhelm the enemy.

And so it turned out. The first shots in the battle were fired
at noon on 21 October and by 4 p.m. eighteen French and
Spanish ships had been lost, of which seventeen had been taken
in prize. It had taken the French van division all this time to
tack and reach the scene of the battle and by now it was too
late. The ships were easily driven off, only to be captured later
by a British squadron.

**98. Battle of Trafalgar, 21 October 1805: Breaking the Line.
Nicholas Pocock**

This is a bird's-eye view, from the north-east, of the Franco-Spanish line being
broken by the allied fleet in two places soon after 12.30 p.m. The lee division
in the distance is led by Collingwood in the *Royal Sovereign*, and the weather
division in the foreground by Nelson's *Victory*.

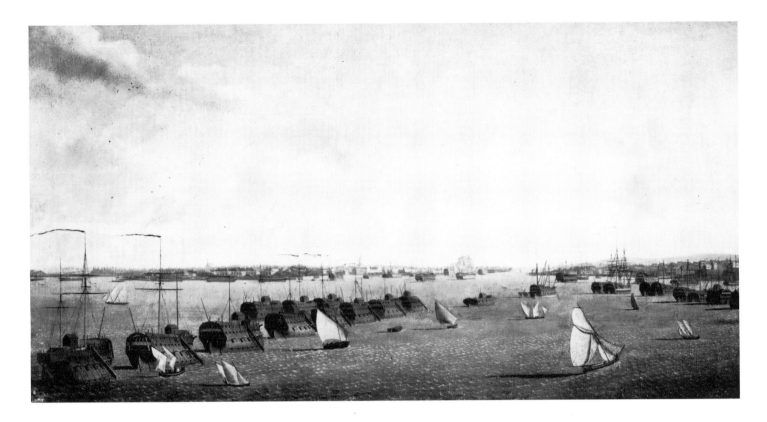

Trafalgar, by eliminating the last organized resistance of the French and Spanish fleets, ensured for Britain unlimited command of the seas. There were sporadic actions in the Mediterranean, Atlantic, and West Indies as small French squadrons escaped from their blockades but they were all quickly run down and eliminated.

Another legacy of Trafalgar was Britain's ability to land and maintain large military forces for campaigns in Europe. With command of the seas firmly in her grip there was no difficulty in landing Wellington and his army in Portugal and keeping them supplied throughout the long campaign in the Iberian Peninsula that was to lead to the final defeat of Napoleon.

18. BIRTH OF UNITED STATES SEA POWER

In 1794 an Act of Congress was passed in North America to form the US Navy. What are known as the 'six original frigates' were laid down under the Act and their names, *United States*, *Constitution*, *President*, *Chesapeake*, *Constellation* and *Congress*, are famous in US naval history. There had been earlier frigates authorized in 1775 by the revolutionary Congress during the Revolutionary War, but these six represent the official start of the American navy. They were built longer and fuller than contemporary frigates of other navies of the same firepower, three

of them mounting 44 guns, the others with 36 guns, later increased to 38. The *Constitution* [fig. 101], built in Boston in 1797, was one of the 44-gun frigates, with a displacement of 2,200 tons, and is perhaps the most famous of all American warships.

These frigates received their first experience of battle during the War of 1812 when the United States, irritated by the stopping and searching of American merchant ships for contraband and particularly for British naval deserters, declared war on Britain [fig. 100]. Of the six, the *Constitution* and *United States*

99. Portsmouth, showing the Prison Hulks. Attributed to Daniel Turner

One of a group of at least nine paintings describing the appearance of the hulks in Portsmouth harbour which accommodated French prisoners of war. The work of Daniel Turner, an obscure artist, has much of the charm but few of the visual errors which characterize 'naive' painting.

100. The Action on Lake Borgne, 14 December 1815. Thomas Lyde Hornbrook

Five American gunboats on Lake Borgne, commanded by Lieutenant Thomas Catesby Jones, provided a formidable obstacle to British ambitions to attack New Orleans. The British solution was to attack with 42 launches manned by 980 seamen. The launches were led by Commander Nicholas Lockyer, who is here seen boarding Jones's gunboat to the right of centre.

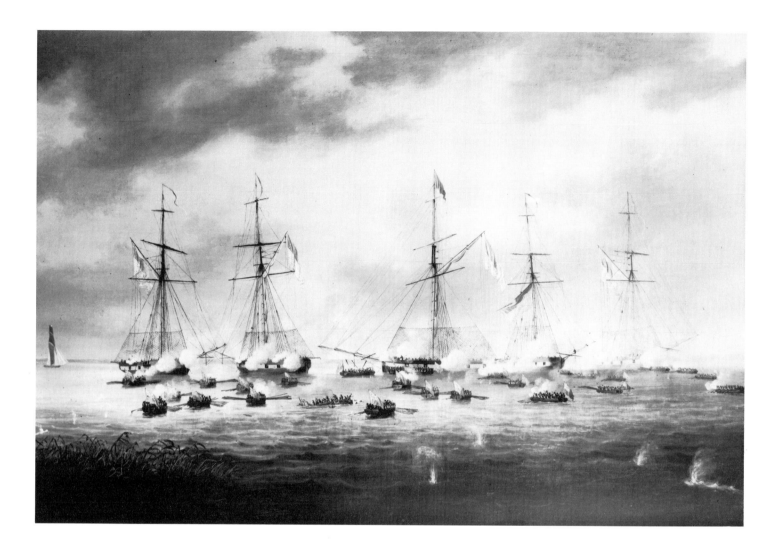

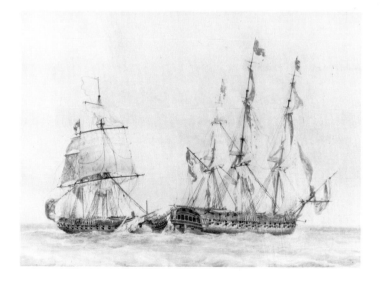

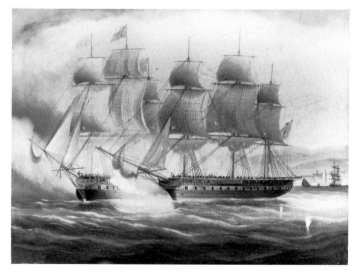

101. 'Java' and 'Constitution', 29 December 1812.
Nicholas Pocock, 1813

In this famous duel between the British frigate *Java*, on the left, and the American frigate *Constitution*, the *Java* was reduced to a wreck and sank after a heroic fight. The *Constitution* ('Old Ironsides') is now a museum ship at Boston.

102. 'Shannon' taking the 'Chesapeake', 1 June 1813
Thomas Buttersworth

Buttersworth, a competent seaman/painter, records a celebrated action off Boston between two frigates captained by notable officers: on the right, the *Shannon* (Captain Philip Bowes Vere Broke) fires her starboard guns into the *Chesapeake* (Captain James Lawrence). In the background, nearer to Boston, is an anchored brig and a cutter that is under way.

had the more impressive records in frigate actions against British ships, due mainly to the British reliance on the carronade, an essentially short-range weapon which forced them to attempt to fight at close quarters. Most of them had their masts shot away while trying to do so. Four British frigates and one sloop were lost in this way. The score was slightly evened in 1813 when the British *Shannon* met the *Chesapeake* and forced her to strike her flag in an action that lasted only fifteen minutes [fig. 102].

19. SHADOW OF THE FUTURE

In March 1802 a wooden vessel of 58 feet in length and a beam of 18 feet made her maiden voyage on the Forth and Clyde Canal in Scotland. She was built to the order of Lord Dundas, a governor of the canal, and named *Charlotte Dundas* [fig. 103] after his daughter. He gave the order for her building to William Symington, an engineer with a workshop on the River Clyde, asking him to design a vessel to replace the horses which towed the barges up and down the canal. Symington designed the ship with a single paddle-wheel in a casing at the stern, driven by a single-cylinder steam-engine which developed about 12 horse-power. On her first trip she towed two 70-ton barges up the canal against a strong headwind at a speed of over three knots. After three or four weeks towing barges up and down the canal she was withdrawn as it was feared that the wash created by her paddle-wheel would damage the canal banks.

On one of her canal trips she carried as a passenger an American inventor named Robert Fulton. He was so impressed with this demonstration of steam propulsion for ships that on his return to America he designed a ship of 133 feet in length to be driven by two paddle-wheels, one each side of the ship. As there were no builders of steam-engines in the United States he ordered one from Boulton and Watt in Britain and had it shipped across the Atlantic. The ship was named *Clermont* and in 1807 on her maiden voyage she covered a distance of 240 miles in sixty-two hours, an average speed of 3·9 knots. She continued in service on the East Hudson River for two seasons, being eventually withdrawn as she was too small to accommodate the crowds that wished to sail in her.

Her financial success as a river ferry inspired Henry Bell, a Scottish engineer, to start a similar service on the River Clyde. He built the *Comet* [fig. 104] in 1812 and his service proved so successful that he extended it up the west coast of Scotland to Oban and Fort William and achieved an average speed of 6·7 knots. Two years later he had five more ferries running a service on the River Thames between London and Margate.

A steamship passenger service across the English Channel between Brighton and Le Havre was opened in 1816 and in 1822

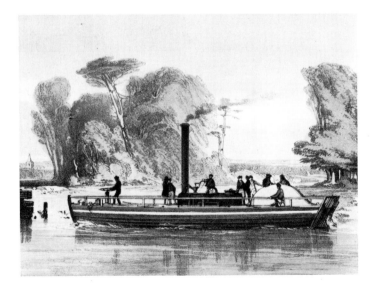

103. The 'Charlotte Dundas'. J. C. Bourne after C. F. Cheffins
It was hoped that the *Charlotte Dundas* would be the first steamship to demonstrate that steam navigation was commercially viable. Built in 1801 by the engineer William Symington (1763–1831), she was capable of towing two barges, each loaded with 70 tons. Such power, however, was her downfall: she was withdrawn soon after entering service for fear that her wash would destroy the banks of the Forth and Clyde Canal on which she worked.

104. The 'Comet'. H. B. Barlow after C. F. Cheffins
Henry Bell's *Comet* of 1812 was to show conclusively that steam was both a practical proposition for coastwise navigation and could be commercially successful. Placed in service between Glasgow, Greenock and Helensburgh, she became the first steamship in Europe to operate a regular passenger service. She drove ashore in 1820 and was lost. Her engine is now preserved in the Science Museum, London.

a ship named *Aaron Manby*, with an engine designed by Henry Bell, opened a passenger service between London and Paris. Like the *Charlotte Dundas* before her, she was a landmark in the development of ships. Her hull was constructed of iron plates instead of the conventional wood, bringing a whole new dimension to the science of shipbuilding.

There was no stopping the advance of the steamship, and in 1838 two of them successfully crossed the Atlantic Ocean, one from Cork to New York, the other from Bristol to the same port. Although the sailing ships, which over the centuries had opened up the world, carried its trade, and fought its sea battles, had a few more years to run, their days were now numbered.

20. THE GREAT AGE OF MARINE ART

From the achievements of the early pioneers, English marine painting moved quickly to maturity. As a branch of landscape painting, it benefited from the remarkable renaissance of English art in the mid-Georgian period. Under the influence of wealthy connoisseurs, who had made the grand tour and who began embellishing their houses with appropriate works of art, English painting flourished. Portraiture had always been popular, but more recondite genres began to find a market. From the mere topographical record, landscape painting moved up the scale of serious art. English patrons might jib at religious works or history paintings, but visions of the English countryside possessed then as now a universal appeal.

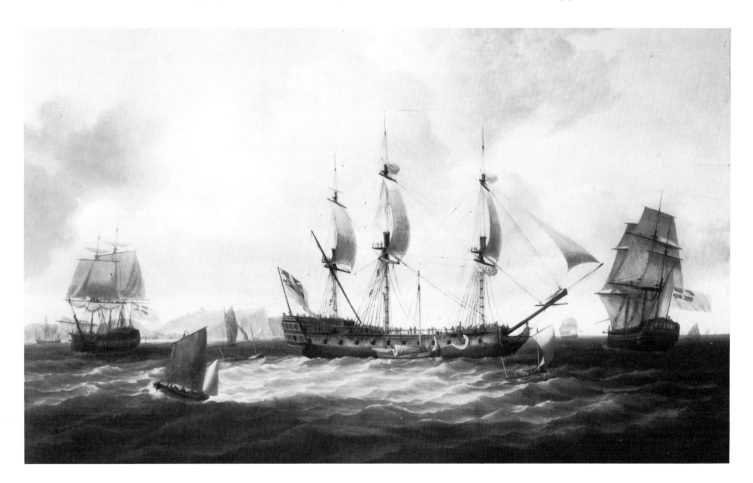

105. The 'Pitt' in Three Positions. Dominic Serres, 1786
The *Pitt*, an East Indiaman launched in 1780, is shown off Dover from three viewpoints (a well-established device in the art of ship portraiture), after her return from China in 1786. The picture was painted late in Serres's illustrious career.

A focus to all this new artistic activity was provided by the foundation of the Royal Academy in 1768. Talk of such an institution had been in the air since the early eighteenth century. Artists needed a settled arena in which to exhibit their works, a well-run school to train them, and an institution of sufficient weight to safeguard standards and promote quality. Inevitably those whose works were not hung, or those whose merits were overlooked, complained vociferously, as discontented artists have always done. But under the distinguished presidency of Sir Joshua Reynolds, the Royal Academy, for all its failings, made possible an expansion of the arts undreamed of by its founders. The growth in the numbers of artists exhibiting, and in the numbers of patrons necessary to support them, was due in large measure to the success of the Academy in providing a discriminating centre and fulcrum. Election to the coveted position of Royal Academician was fiercely contested. To be in the Club

was the aim of every ambitious artist, and it was at the annual exhibition that laurels were won.

Among the founding members of the Royal Academy was one marine painter, the *émigré* Frenchman, Dominic Serres (1722–93) [plate 42; figs. 84, 105]. Over the course of the next half century, he was to be joined by other notable names in the annals of marine art. At the 1769 Academy exhibition only a handful of marine paintings were shown, mostly by Serres. Ten years later he was joined by John Cleveley the Younger [figs. 90, 106], Francis Holman [plates 36, 41], Richard Paton [plate 43; figs. 69, 81, 93] and others.

Most marine paintings were of specific events, battles and ship portraits. A desire to record the great naval achievements of the period led to a thriving trade in battle pictures. English successes in the European and colonial wars which followed each other in such rapid succession were at sea, not on land.

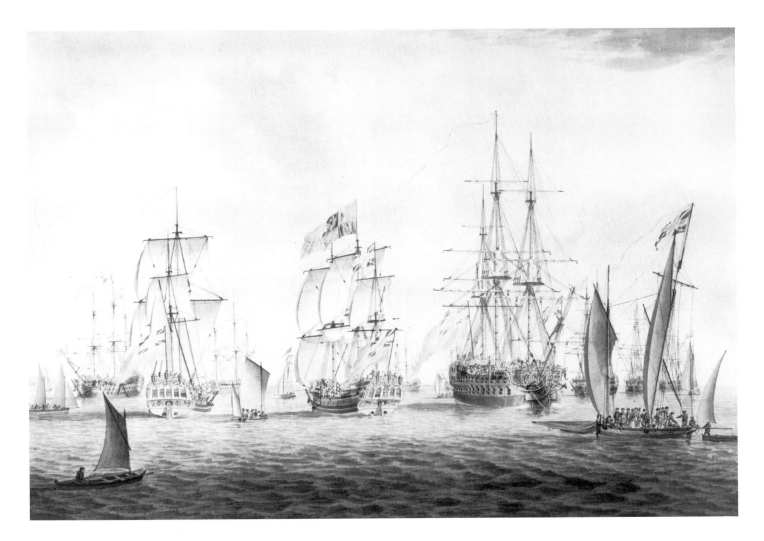

106. Reviewing the Fleet at Spithead, 22 June 1773.
John Cleveley the Younger

In the centre of the watercolour is the *Augusta* with the royal standard at the main. On board is King George III on his way to the naval review. Later he ordered £350 to be distributed among the crew of the *Augusta*, a 'bonus' to mark the event.

From large fleet actions to fierce engagements between two or three ships, from sieges to blockades, marine artists had an inexhaustible supply of dramatic subject matter. Several had served at sea. They had an intuitive knowledge of ships and seafaring, and salt was in their blood. They knew the intricacies of rigging, the set of the sails in particular weathers, the perspective of hull and deck, and the detail of ship decoration. Artists rarely went to war themselves, relying on sketches and reports brought back by officers. They worked out with their patrons what particular incident of an action was to be recorded, selecting a point of view and sketching out the relative positions of ships and fleets at the time. Very often patrons suggested adjustments and corrections to the composition and to the details of the ships.

To the necessity for nautical accuracy was added the need for correct topography, the ability to place ships in correct relation to a foreground of sea and spatial recession often terminating in a coastline. Inevitably the immediacy of an on-the-spot sketch is lost, but these paintings are highly orchestrated seapieces in tune with the formalistic conventions of eighteenth-century landscape art. That is not to say that the pictures lack blood and guts, thunder, or the drama of war, especially of lines of battleships pounding each other to pieces, but that the vision of the artist is conditioned by ideas of balance, rhythm and aerial perspective. Actions are set well back from the front of the picture plane. We see them at a comforting distance, like well ordered elements on a stage. Skies and seas have few of the tactile qualities so memorable in the best Dutch marine paintings, less of the expansive sense of space and atmosphere. Nature, like man, is tamed.

Profits from battle pictures were boosted by the sale of prints. There was a continuous demand for images celebrating the nation's glories, satisfied by engravings after popular battle scenes. In some cases the stimulus for a print preceded the painting. Dominic Serres's famous set of pictures recording the capture of Havana in August 1762 [plate 42] was a speculative venture undertaken in partnership with Lieutenant Durnsford. Durnsford, who served on the campaign, supplied Serres with sketches, from which he worked up twelve subjects, probably on a small scale. The engravings were published by Durnsford

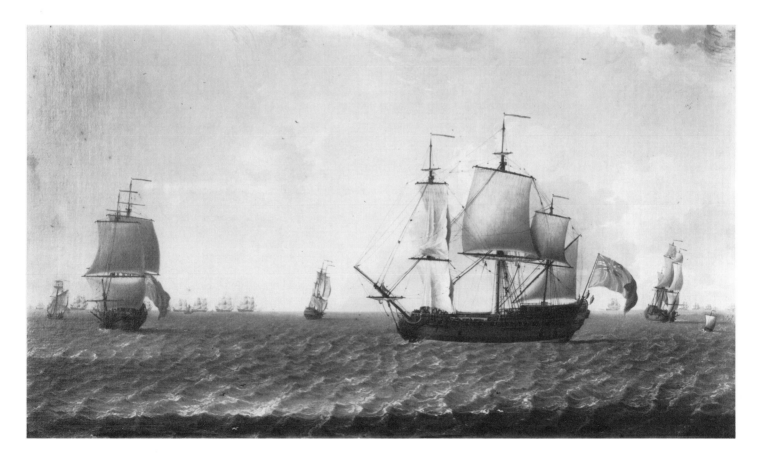

107. An Indiaman in Stays. Francis Swaine

East Indiamen were often rather more opulent in appearance than are the examples portrayed here unambitiously by Swaine. The artist shows the principal foreground vessel in stays. (If, head to wind during the operation of tacking, the head of a sailing vessel fails to pay off on the opposite tack, she is said to be 'in stays'.)

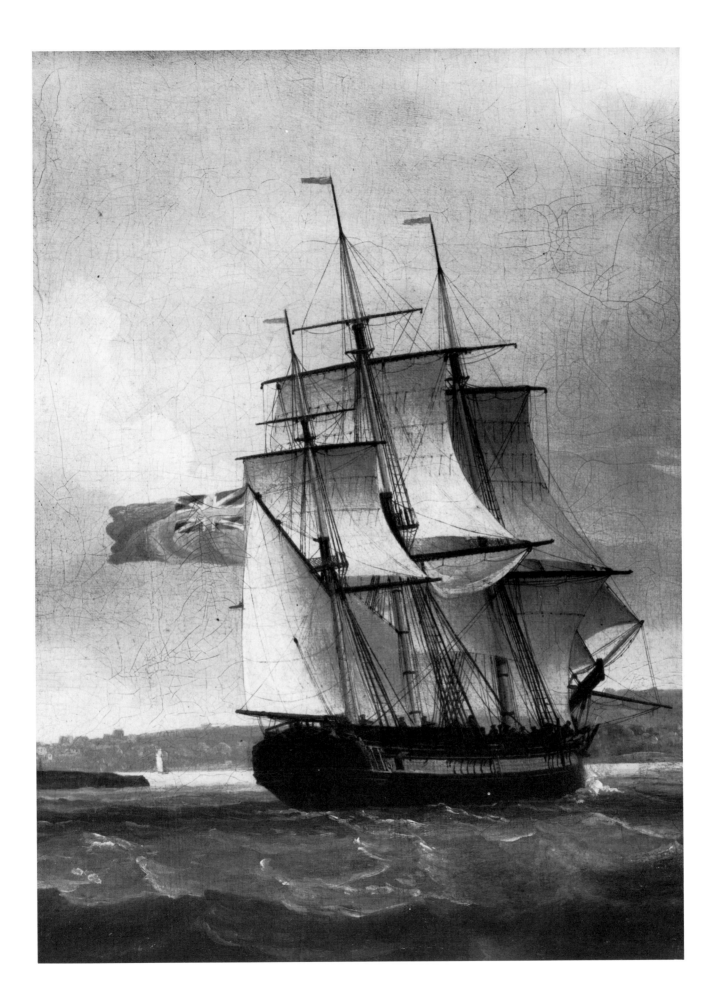

in batches of three or four during 1764–5, as subscriptions came trickling in. After the successful launch of the prints Serres appears to have been commissioned by the Keppel family to paint a number of the subjects on a larger scale. Two of the pictures were exhibited in 1768, another is dated 1770 and a fourth 1775.

The variation in size in the large-scale pictures can probably be attributed to the differing proportions of the rooms in which they hung, although no evidence exists to show that they were displayed as a set. Nor is it clear which Keppel commissioned them, the commander-in-chief George, his second-in-command William, or the commodore Augustus. The campaign made the fortune of all three brothers, and it was appropriate that some of the Spanish loot captured at Havana should go to record the events by which they had gained it.

Serres had earlier depicted the great battle of Quiberon Bay (1759) [fig. 84], and the capture of Belleisle (1761), and he went on to record other victories in the Seven Years War. Patronized

by George III, popular in society, his career demonstrated what could be achieved by a successful marine painter. There was no shortage of rivals. Among the older painters were Francis Swaine (c.1720–82) [fig. 107], Francis Holman (d.1790) and Richard Paton (1717–91). And the coming younger men showed a dash and spirit and sparkle sometimes lacking in the more staid production of their elders.

Nicholas Pocock (1740–1821) [plate 46; figs. 95, 98, 101; frontispiece] had been a sea captain for ten years before he turned professional painter in 1780. His *Battle of Frigate Bay* runs Serres a close second, and his *Defence at the First of June* is fresh and vigorous. Thomas Luny (1759–1837) [plates 52, 53; fig. 110] came out of the studio of Francis Holman, and made his name with repetitive scenes of ships at evening and figures on the foreshore. Thomas Whitcombe (c.1752–1824) [plate 60; figs. 108, 109], almost his exact contemporary, is another masterful ship portraitist and battle painter, whose work contains precision of detail with a liberating sweep in the rendering of sea

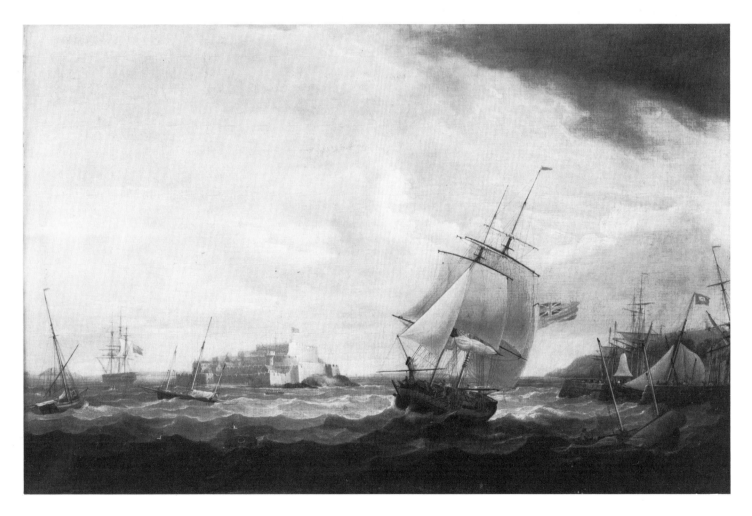

108. The 'Ealing Grove'. Thomas Whitcombe

The *Ealing Grove*, a West Indiaman launched in 1792, is portrayed starboard quarter view off an unidentified strip of coast. The picture is related to another portrait by Whitcombe of the same ship, broadside view, in the National Maritime Museum collections; originally, they were probably both part of the same canvas.

109. Castle Cornet, Guernsey. Thomas Whitcombe

Although Whitcombe produced a large body of work illustrating the actions of the Napoleonic Wars, much of it engraved, he also painted many portraits of merchant ships. Perhaps his most charming works, however, are the rarer general views of shipping and coastal subjects such as this one; although it portrays a wide range of activity, it is nevertheless spacious and atmospheric. The principal vessel in the foreground is a merchant brig.

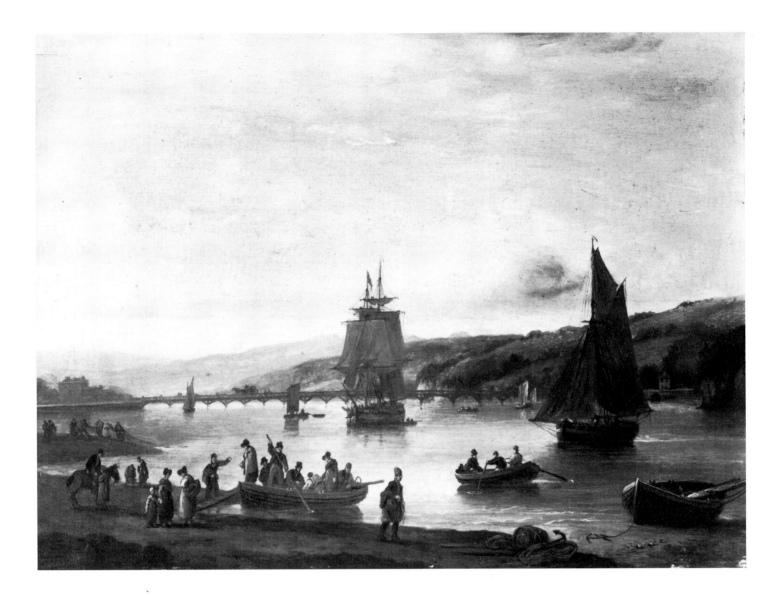

and sky. Like their sporting counterparts, these three artists were versatile journeymen who could turn their hand to any subject required by a patron. Their bread-and-butter work was painting accurate ship portraits, often in more than one position, for captains and owners. But given the right opportunity, they were all capable of higher flights of imagination, expressing subtleties of design and atmospheric effects in grandly conceived compositions.

The boom in marine art was not confined to oil painters. Watercolour was a less prestigious medium, but it was cheaper and equally capable of translation into print form. It had a long and honourable history going back well before the rise of the English watercolour school. Since the seventeenth century naval

officers had annotated their charts, surveys and logs with watercolour views as an aid to navigation. The ability to draw an accurate profile of a coastline or the approach to a port was considered to be a valuable practical skill. While the work of these early amateurs is often prosaic, the more talented were capable of making their scenes come alive, including in them charming incidental details and effects.

A desire for a visual record of unknown places and people led Captain Cook to employ artists on all three of his famous voyages. Like the scientists on board they were there to document discoveries, and to provide drawings that could subsequently be used as illustrations to the official accounts of each voyage. Two of them happened to be painters, William Hodges

110. Teignmouth. Thomas Luny, 1824
Thomas Luny's retirement to Teignmouth, due to a growing physical disability, scarcely marked the end of his painting career. Many of his later works are local subjects of a kind similar to this; here, on panel, he describes with some precision the landing of a party from the Teignmouth ferry.

(1744–97) and John Webber (*c*.1750–93), and from their sketches [figs. 88, 89] they worked up large-scale oil paintings that dazzled the public with an exotic vision of the Pacific. Such pictures, however famous they have become, were secondary to the workaday topographical and survey drawings which both artists were employed to produce. John Cleveley the Younger (1747–86) worked up watercolours of Lord Mulgrave's polar expedition of 1773 from sketches taken on the spot [fig. 90], and William Westall (1781–1850) accompanied Matthew Flinders' expedition to Australasia, 1801–3.

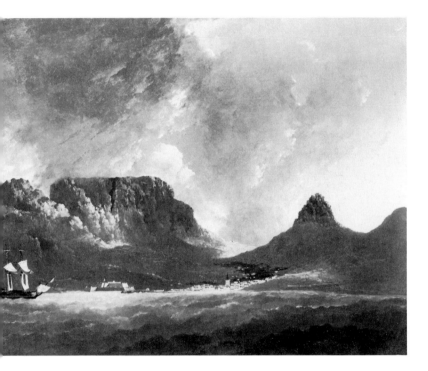

Many of the early marine artists painted in watercolour, sometimes as an aid to the composition of oil paintings, sometimes as a medium in its own right [fig. 106]. Nicholas Pocock had illustrated his logs with vivid pen and wash sketches long before he became a professional artist. He continued to use watercolour throughout his career [fig. 101], often for decorative landscape compositions. A few marine painters worked exclusively in watercolour, such as John Hood (*fl.*1761–72), Samuel Owen (*c*.1768–1857) and Samuel Atkins (*fl.*1787–1808), but the market was evidently more limited than for comparable topographical landscapes.

With the advent of romanticism, a new spirit was felt in the sphere of marine painting. The greatest British artist of the period, J. M. W. Turner (1775–1851), was as much a marine painter as a landscapist. In his early shipwrecks and scenes of stormy weather, he went back to the tradition of the Van de Veldes and the Dutch school, painting a number of works in direct emulation of theirs. His work is suffused by his feelings for the sublime power of natural forces, by the immediacy of his response to the elements of sea, sky and weather, by his genius in the rendering of complex light effects, and by the imposing scale and orchestration of his designs.

We are drawn into vast and visionary spaces, moved by the spectacle of luminous calms, dramatic storms or human disasters. Turner is a great virtuoso, making his spectators experience nature at its most sublime, and then playing on their emotions. To the romantic imagination, the sea is one of nature's greatest forces, all-encompassing, beautiful, wild and terrible, a source of wonder and desolation. Rugged coastlines, storms and shipwrecks enter the vocabulary of romantic landscape art, along with mountain peaks, waterfalls and avalanches.

It would be wrong to exaggerate the dichotomy between the traditional marine painter and his romantic counterpart. In fact, artists like Pocock and Luny were receptive to the new spirit of naturalism and romantic association characteristic of late eighteenth-century art, and they were capable of infusing atmosphere and drama into documentary views of ships and prosaic scenes of shipping. Like Turner, Luny admired the shipwreck scenes of the French artist, Claude-Joseph Vernet (1714–89).

Equally, it would be wrong to characterize Turner simply as a painter of seascapes. The subject matter of the majority of his marine pictures is quite specific: varieties of fishing; packets and passenger boats; the Cowes Regatta; keelmen heaving coals at night; Manby's life-saving apparatus; whalers at work. But Turner was also frequently moved by contemporary issues and events. He expressed his patriotic feelings in several pictures illustrating the Battle of Trafalgar; in noble studies of warships off places famous in British naval history, Spithead, Sheerness, the Medway and the Thames estuary; and in a series of historical works celebrating the great events of the seventeenth-century Anglo-Dutch wars at sea, for example *Van Tromp Returning after the Battle of Dogger Bank*. Turner not only looked back to the heroic past, to the battle pictures of Van de Velde and the classical port scenes of Claude, he also saw the shape of the future in the smoking funnels of steamships, sometimes forcibly contrasted with the traditional shape of sail.

The wars with Revolutionary and Napoleonic France provided an unprecedented opportunity for marine artists to exhibit their skills. Here in the bloody confrontations of rival fleets, pulverizing each other to pieces with broadsides at close range,

111. A View of the Cape of Good Hope. William Hodges, 1772
Hodges, official artist on Cook's second voyage, portrays the Cape from Table Bay from on board the *Resolution*, with the *Adventure* at anchor to the left. This arresting *plein air* work, painted on the spot, was the first major picture in the 'Cook' series and was an important milestone in the career of the twenty-eight-year-old artist.

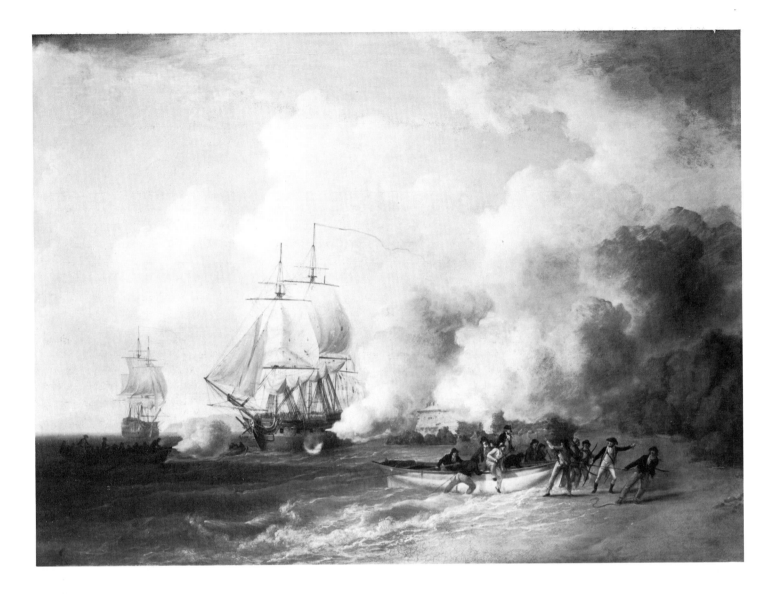

marine painting reaches its apotheosis. All the leading practitioners of the art can be seen in full flow, responding to the magnitude of the conflict with an unprecedented output of work.

The style of battle painting is as varied as the number of artists who practised it: the rather dry renderings of Thomas Buttersworth (1768–1842) and Robert Cleveley (1747–1809), full of accurate detail; the more spirited treatments of William Anderson (1757–1837) [plate 58; figs. 94, 113], Nicholas Pocock, J. T. Serres (1759–1825) [plates 40, 47], son of Dominic, and the idiosyncratic Robert Dodd (1748–1815) [fig. 112]; the great romantic set-pieces by Turner, where human drama is quite as important as that of the ships themselves. It is often difficult to relate the various depictions of a battle to the same

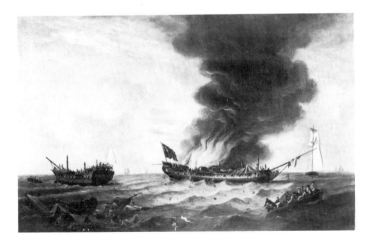

112. A Furious Frigate Action. Robert Dodd, 1781

This scene of devastation records the aftermath of a celebrated three-hour action on 6 October 1779 between two frigates captained by particularly persistent officers. The *Quebec* is shown right of centre, dismasted and with her quarterdeck burning; to the left lies the *Surveillante*, only marginally less damaged. In the foreground a British boat picks up casualties.

113. Capture of Fort Louis, Martinique, 20 March 1794. William Anderson, 1795

A representation of an episode during the lengthy Anglo-French confrontation in the West Indies. From a ship's barge in the right foreground, Commander Robert Faulkner leads his men up a Martinique beach, part of an operation in which the *Zebra* (left of centre, port bow view) and the *Asia* spearheaded an assault on Fort Louis, the key to Fort Royal.

event, so individual is the approach and the parts of the action shown. Nicholas Pocock's bird's-eye view of *Trafalgar* before and after [fig. 98] reduces the ships to toy models, while Turner's *Trafalgar* [plate 48] glorifies a single ship, the *Victory*, which appears titanic in scale.

A clear distinction must be made between pictures purporting to provide an *ad vivum* guide to the course of a particular action, and those more grandiose thematic works which must be classsed as history painting. No one was in any doubt that history painting was the highest form of art, and great efforts were made to promote it in a country generally antipathetical to the claims of serious art.

The American expatriate artists, Benjamin West (1738–1820) and John Singleton Copley (1737–1815), had pioneered the modern history subject, treating the heroic deeds of their own time in contemporary dress, instead of painting more traditional classical subjects. Copley's huge picture of Admiral Duncan receiving the sword of the defeated Dutch Admiral de Winter at the Battle of Camperdown in 1797 illustrates in a heroic figure composition the aftermath of battle.

A work in the same vein shows the deck of Admiral Howe's flagship, the *Queen Charlotte*, at the Glorious First of June in 1794 [plate 45], by another American and follower of West, Mather Brown (1761–1831). Such pictures, celebrating individuals rather than events, emblematic in intention for all their wealth of detail, add a new dimension to the imagery of marine art.

Commissions for such enormous works were not easily come by, and their authors struggled to market them in a number of ingenious ways (including auction and raffle), as well as trying to sell engraving rights. Philippe de Loutherbourg's *Glorious First of June* [plate 44] was exhibited at the same period as Mather Brown's, and was seen as a competitive work. Both pictures were promoted in one-picture shows, both were engraved, but de Loutherbourg, like Brown, had difficulties in finding a buyer.

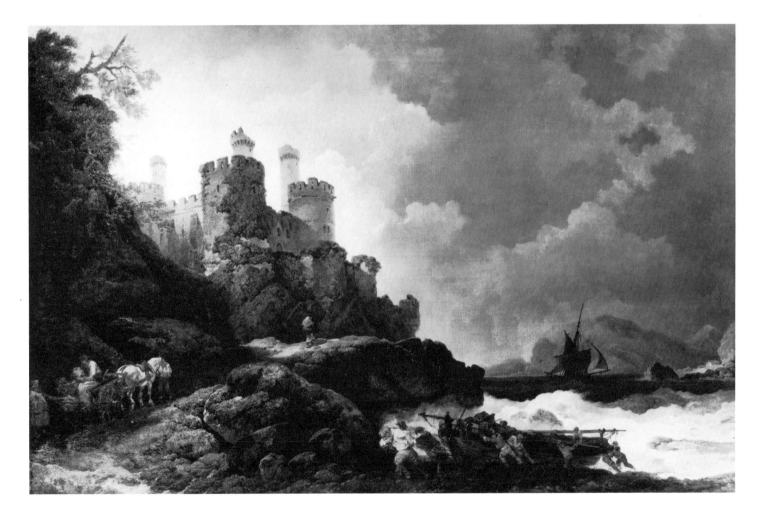

114. Conway Castle. Philippe Jacques de Loutherbourg, 1800

A fishing boat is brought ashore under the walls of Conway Castle in the estuary of the River Conway in North Wales. De Loutherbourg here presents the castle, one of the grandest feudal fortresses in Britain, built in 1284, as a storm-tossed and romantic ruin. The painting inspired Turner to attempt a view of the same subject.

De Loutherbourg (1740–1812) is an underestimated figure in the history of marine art. A Frenchman lured to England in 1771 by hopes of patronage, he made his mark with scenery for the theatre, and paintings of landscapes and seascapes. In his views of rocky castles from the sea [fig. 114], his scenes of smuggling and shipwrecks, he anticipated many of the themes of romantic landscape art. Restless and ambitious, he saw contemporary history painting as a means of exploiting patriotic fervour to extend his painting into the sphere of the monumental. His *Glorious First of June* shows the rival English and French flagships surging dramatically towards the front of the picture space, while in the foreground English seamen, symbols of compassionate humanity, rescue their shipwrecked enemies. All is fire, smoke, blood and thunder, combining de Loutherbourg's high sense of spectacle with brilliant transparent effects of tone, and fine control of well rehearsed nautical detail. De Loutherbourg's example was followed by many later marine artists who con-tinued to record the great events of the Napoleonic conflict long after it had ended. One of the most famous paintings of Tra-falgar, by Clarkson Stanfield, was exhibited in 1836, while two grandiose works commissioned for Greenwich Hospital, Sir William Allan's *Battle of St. Vincent* and George Arnald's *Battle of the Nile* [fig. 97], belong respectively to 1845 and 1827.

The imagery of sailing ships at war comes to an end with the Treaty of Vienna in 1815, and with Napoleon's departure to St. Helena [plate 50]. There were isolated engagements there-after, for example Codrington's victory at Navarino over the Turks in 1827 (which helped to secure Greek independence), and the attack on Russian ports in the Baltic during the Crimean War, but in general Britain maintained her mastery over the seas by peaceful means. The resulting loss of such an important sector of the marine art market did not immediately affect the quality of marine painting, but it did contribute to its long-term decline.

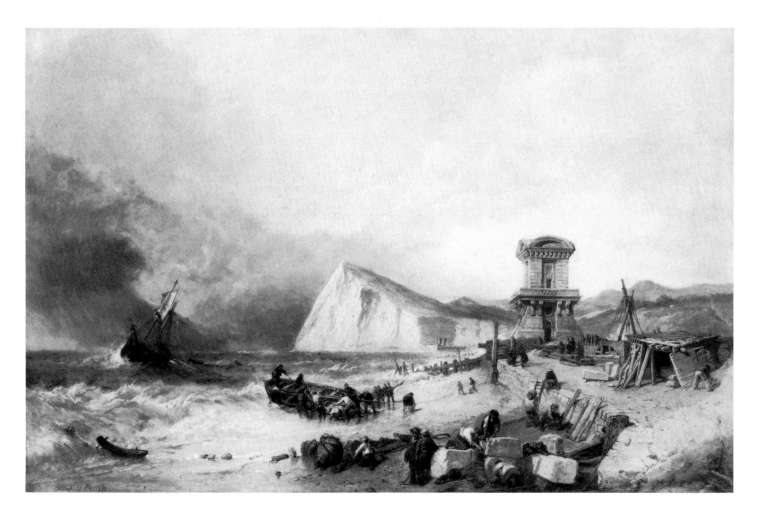

115. Shakespeare Cliff, Dover, in 1849. Clarkson Stanfield, 1862
Stanfield, among the best known marine painters of his day, produced many rather theatrical coastal views of this kind. Here, a brig in distress off Dover is about to be assisted by a group of fishermen and their makeshift lifeboat. The Pilot's Watchtower lies to the right.

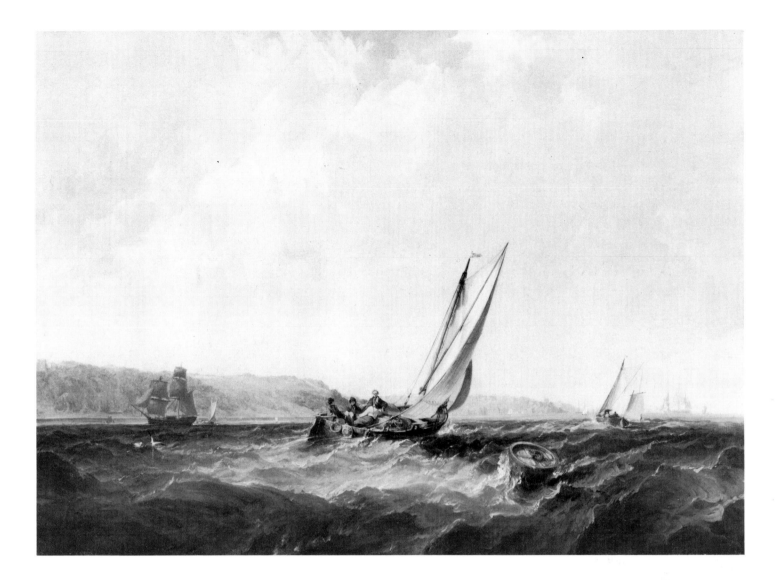

The leading figures of the period from 1815 to the mid-century were painters of considerable power and originality. Two of them became successful Royal Academicians, Clarkson Stanfield (1793–1867) [fig. 115] and E. W. Cooke (1811–80); the third, George Chambers (1803–40) [plates 54, 57; fig. 116], was much less well known, then as now, but is perhaps the most beautiful painter of the three. Cooke's *Beaching a Pink* [plate 51] rivals the achievements of the Dutch school in its dramatic subject matter, sheer immediacy, and brilliance of tone.

Stanfield and Cooke represent marine art with a capital A. Their work can be compared with the marine subjects of their landscape peers, with the stunning beach and coastal scenes of John Constable (1776–1837), Richard Parkes Bonington (1801–28) and David Cox (1783–1859), with the luminous calms of

Old Crome (1768–1821), father of the Norwich school, and the spirited seascapes of John Sell Cotman (1782–1842), another member of that famous school.

If this is the romantic imagery of the sea with which we are all familiar, lower down the scale a new generation of ship painters emerged to continue the tradition of Whitcombe and Luny. Scarcely less talented in their chosen sphere, they were locally based and had no pretensions to academic honours. Robert Salmon (1775–c.1845) [plate 55; fig. 117] and Samuel Walters (1811–82) [plate 56] in Liverpool, John Ward in Hull (1798–1849), Joseph Walter (1783–1856) [fig. 118] in Bristol, William Huggins (1781–1845) in London—their work constitutes a meticulous survey of every type of shipping from Indiamen to the modern paddle steamer.

116. Fresh Breeze off Cowes. George Chambers, 1840

The small coastal vessel in the centre of this direct and invigorating painting was typical of the kind used for lobster fishing. The care with which its crew is described is evidence of the growing taste for human incident in marine pictures, one by-product of the popularity of genre painting in Victorian England.

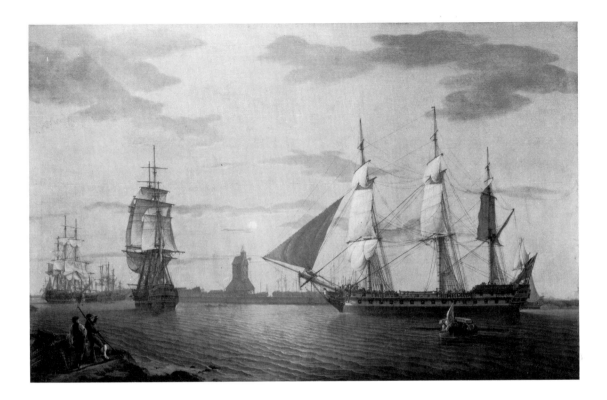

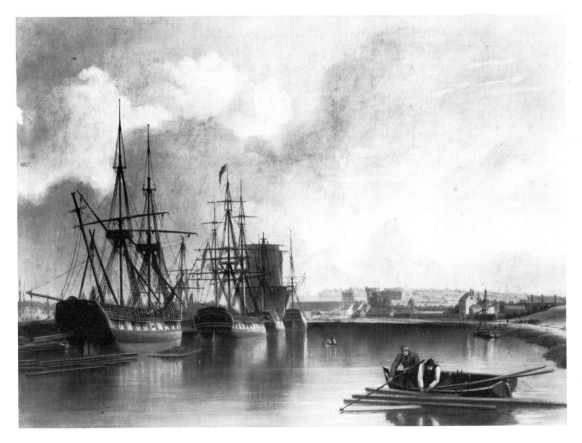

117. The 'Warley', an Indiaman. Robert Salmon, 1804

The *Warley* made six voyages to the East between 1796 and 1807. She was one of the larger of the vessels in the service of the East India Company at this time and was built by John Perry of the Blackwall yard. In the background of this picture can be seen East India ships in the Brunswick Dock, Blackwall, and Perry's mast-house, used for stepping and lifting out the very substantial lower masts of these ships.

118. Bristol. Joseph Walter, 1834

Walter's intimate knowledge of ships might suggest that, like his contemporary Nicholas Pocock, he spent some time at sea; in fact most of his life was spent in Bristol. In this painting, the nearest of the merchant ships moored on the Bristol Avon has had her mizen-mast unstepped—possibly to enable timber to be unloaded through a stern port.

Salmon moved from Liverpool to Greenock, and back again, then to London, Southampton, Boston (1829), and finally home again, in search of work and clients. His pictures of ships, usually with a view of a port in the background, are formidably accurate and quite superb, while no one can miss his strong and stylized wave patterns. His work has long been admired in America, along with that of other *émigré* artists, who helped to found a flourishing school of ship painters.

Though their pictures are often repetitive in type and format, these later painters achieved a high standard of drawing and craftmanship, and they can surprise us with felicities of colour and touch. The decline in the status of such ship painters was largely attributable to three causes: dwindling patronage for art in the provinces; the advent of photography; and the growing philistinism of naval officers and merchant seamen. No longer concerned with artistic quality, they were easily satisfied by the primitive work of pierhead painters, or the more sophisticated records of the professional photographer. From careful shots of

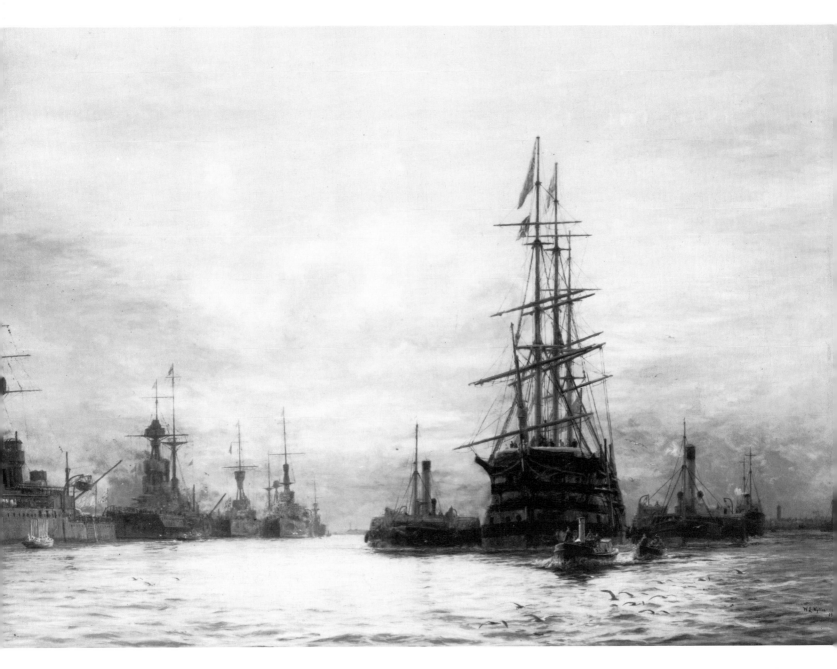

**119. Last Voyage of HMS Victory, 16 December 1921.
William Lionel Wyllie, 1922**

The *Victory*'s last voyage was to No. 1 Dock at Portsmouth, where she now lies restored to her Trafalgar state. Wyllie, himself deeply involved with the restoration project, records this moment with some poignancy: both the sunset and the lurking presence of modern fighting ships signal the final passing of an era.

ships taken from dry land, the camera gradually moved on board to record the realities of life at sea. The gritty character of these close-ups of physical hardship and effort is a moving commentary on what it was like to sail large merchantmen at the moment when their future was threatened by the steamship.

The decline of the sailing ship signalled the end of the classic period of marine art. The sea continued to inspire painters—Victorian painting is rich in examples of seafaring subjects. What went was the tradition of battle scenes and ship portraits treated both as documents and as works of art. Romantic re-creations

of the past, heroic enterprises of the present, human dramas and tragedies, the simple and noble lives of seafarers and fishing communities, picturesque views of coastal towns and estuaries, these are some of the themes with which marine art of the later nineteenth century concerned itself. There was a divorce between the artist painting evocative marine subjects for a general audience at the Royal Academy, and the local ship portraitist plying his trade as a craftsman. The time when the maritime specialist and the marine artist had been one and the same person had passed.

21. INTO THE SUNSET

The successful ending of the Napoleonic War in 1815 had left the British navy supreme in all the world's oceans and seas. It left, too, a feeling of complacency in the British Admiralty, and indeed throughout the navy as a whole, a belief that the British warship, with its masts and sails and its batteries of broadside guns firing solid iron shot was the sole begetter of all this success. Not for them the iron hull or the noisy, dirty steam-engine driving a paddle-wheel. In any case a paddle-wheel was far too vulnerable to be of any use to a fighting navy, and preliminary tests on cast-iron plates with solid shot proved that they frac-

tured when hit. The only concession to modernity that the Admiralty was prepared to consider was a couple of small wooden paddle-steamers, the *Comet* and *Monkey*, used solely to tow sailing warships out of harbour when a head wind made it impossible for them to sail out. They entered the navy in 1822 and 1823 respectively.

Yet the steam-engine had to come, and during the 1830s a few small steam vessels, mainly gunboats, were built experimentally. All were of less than 1,000 tons displacement, with a small armament, and were designed for inshore bombardment of land

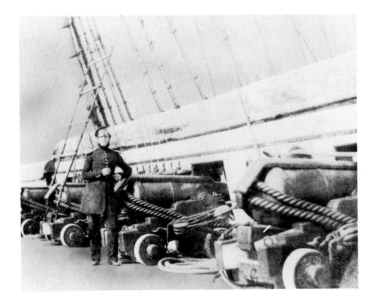

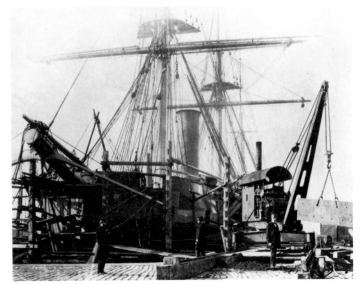

120. HMS Superb (1842)
A calotype photograph, probably taken by Nicolaas Henneman in about 1845, showing an officer on board the second-rate ship of the line, HMS *Superb*. He is standing on the quarterdeck with four of the 32-pounder shell guns which formed part of the ship's armament. The main shrouds can clearly be seen, as can the canvas covers over the hammock stowage. The *Superb* was built at Pembroke Dock and was launched in 1842.

121. HMS Royal Oak (1862)
The wooden broadside iron-clad frigate HMS *Royal Oak* was launched at Chatham Dockyard in September 1862 and is here shown in dry dock during fitting out. One of her 4½-inch thick iron armour plates is being hoisted into position by the dockside crane. As completed she carried a double topsail barque rig but was later converted to ship rig.

targets. Between 1833 and 1836 an underwater propellor was developed to replace the paddle-wheel. As a result the steam-engine was at last accepted as an essential auxiliary means of propulsion and during the 1840s all new warships and many of the older warships were brought into the dockyards to be fitted with an engine. Yet masts and sails were still considered so important that an elaborate arrangement was fitted in all these warships to lift the propellor above the waterline when the ship was under sail so as not to affect the ship's sailing qualities. It was not until 1861 that this difficult and time-consuming exercise was abandoned in the British navy.

On the whole, the navies of the other European nations were as cautious as that of Britain in the adoption of the new technology based on iron, coal and steam. Iron was little used until the early 1860s. The first British iron-clad ship, HMS *Warrior* (1860), currently undergoing restoration, had 4½ inch armour with 18 inch teak backing, and a full outfit of masts and sails [fig. 122]. Yet the end of the wooden warship hull came suddenly and universally. In 1824 a French artillery general, Henri-Joseph Paixhans, developed a naval gun which fired an explosive shell with a flat trajectory instead of mortars fired parabolically. It was first used in battle in 1853 at Sinope in the Black Sea when a Russian squadron of wooden-hulled ships armed with Paixhans guns met a Turkish squadron of wooden-hulled ships armed with normal naval guns firing solid shot. In the action the Russian ships were only slightly damaged, those of Turkey set on fire by the explosive shells and burnt down to the water-line. It was a lesson no navy could afford to ignore and no more wooden-hulled warships were built, those that were, to use up stocks of timber, being completed as iron-clads.

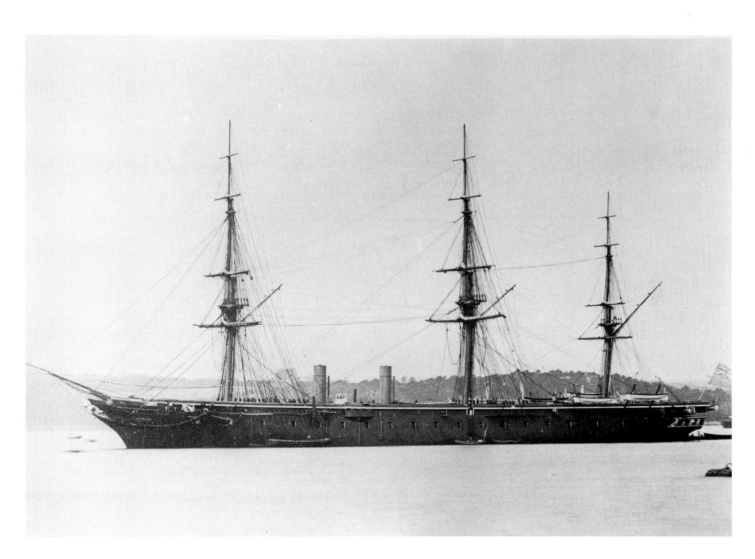

122. HMS Warrior (1860)
The *Warrior* was the world's first iron-built, ocean-going warship. She is shown here at anchor before being paid off in 1864 for re-arming. Her sea-going career ended twenty years later when she was laid up in reserve. It was many years before she found employment, first as a hulk attached to HMS *Vernon* and then as a floating pontoon at Pembroke Dock.

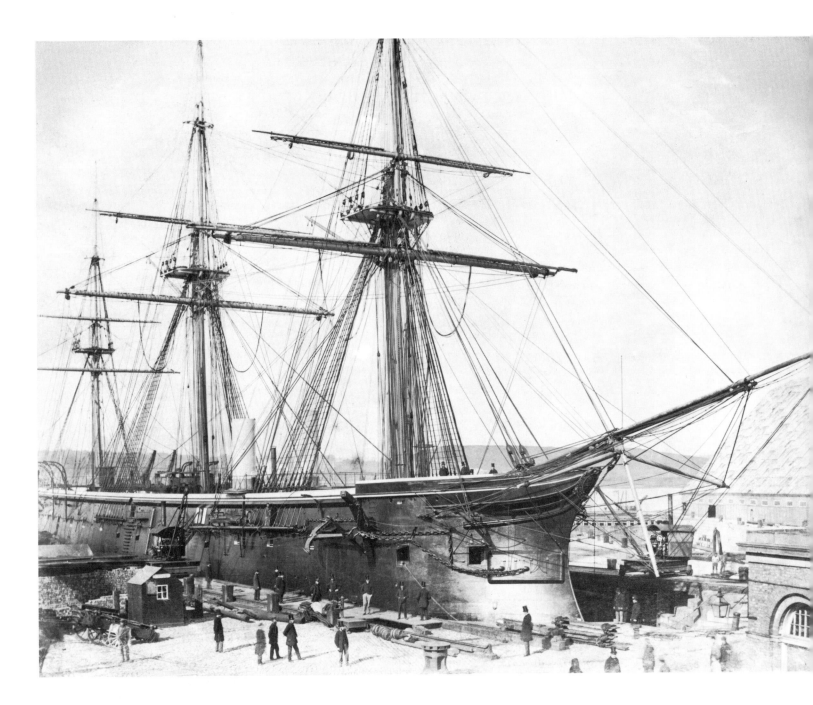

Sail, particularly in Britain, was still preserved, as many senior officers still considered that training in a fully-rigged ship produced the best seamen. As guns increased in size, and armour in thickness, as engines increased in reliability and power, still the British warships were given their three masts and full outfit of sails [fig. 121]. Most other navies realized around 1870 that the sailing battleship was an anachronism and adopted steam as the sole means of ship propulsion, but in Britain masts and sails lingered on [fig. 123]. The last major warships to be built with a full rig of masts and sails were the *Imperieuse* [figs. 124, 125] and *Warspite*, completed in 1883 and 1888 respectively. Yet this was not quite the end of British naval sail. Between 1902 and 1904 a class of six ships, the last of a long line of sloops retaining the elements of sail power, were completed. Although they had modern steam-engines as their main motive power they were also schooner-rigged with square sails on the foremast. Not only

123. HMS Bellerophon (1865)

Shown here in dry dock at Chatham early in 1866, the central battery iron-clad HMS *Bellerophon* displays her ship rig, but so far without her topgallant yards, which have not yet been crossed. Her funnels are raised, although the fore funnel is obscured by the starboard shrouds of the foremast. At the time of her completion the *Bellerophon* was the most powerful ship in the Royal Navy.

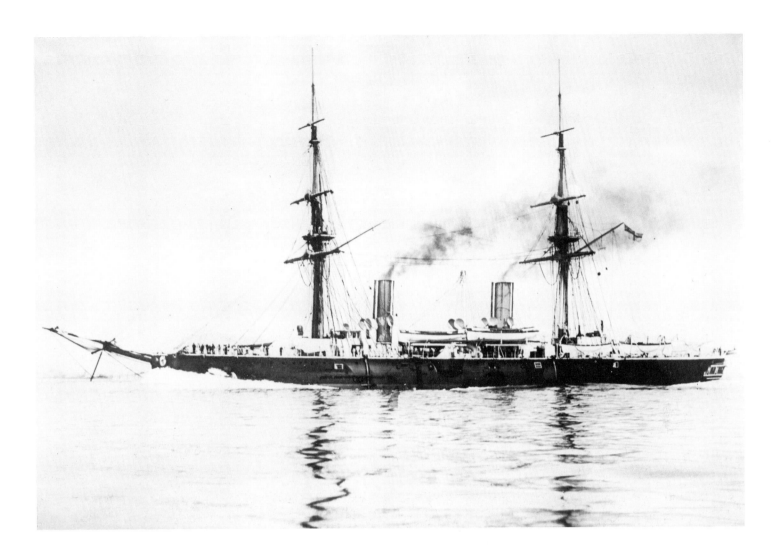

were they the last British warships with masts and sails but also the last to have figureheads and gilded trailboards, the final reminder of the glories of the naval past.

It took the first thirty to forty years of the nineteenth century for the marine steam-engine to make much impression on ship-owners and traders. Where a steam-engine was fitted on a sailing ship during these years, it was invariably as an auxiliary source of power to keep the ship moving when the wind dropped away, except occasionally in coastal trade and for short sea passages. Even in the second half of the century, when the steam-engine had proved itself reliable and had been developed into a power-ful driving force, there were still a number of the longer trade routes which only the sailing ship could serve. The steamship needed to replenish the coal she consumed on passage and as yet there were not enough coaling stations on the long voyages where she could do so.

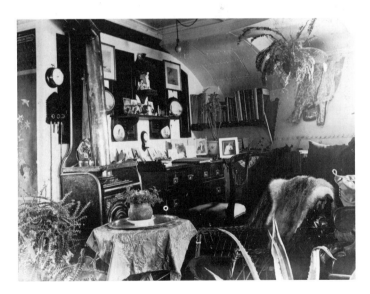

124. HMS Imperieuse (1883)

HMS *Imperieuse* was an armoured cruiser constructed by Portsmouth Dockyard between 1881 and 1886. She was the last major British warship to be completed with a heavy sailing rig. During trials she proved to be a very poor sailer, and within a year her brig rig of some 20,000 square feet of sail area had been removed and replaced by a single military mast amidships.

125. HMS Imperieuse (1883)

This photograph of the commander's cabin on the armoured cruiser HMS *Imperieuse* was taken during the period 1891 to 1894 when she was flagship of the China Station. Note the rather ornate coal-fired stove and the highly polished copper kettle. The soft furnishings and potted plants add a touch of homeliness, in contrast to the stark riveted steel of the ship's side and deckhead.

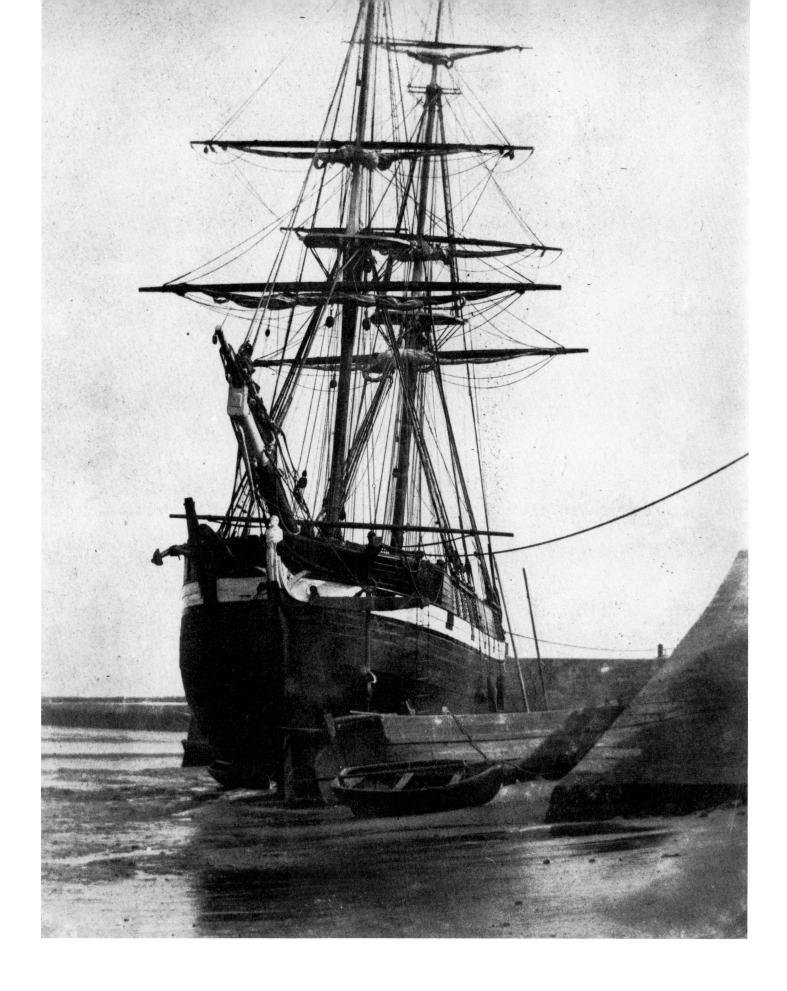

British merchant ships in the early years of the century took as their model the naval frigate. They were strong and sturdy ships [figs. 126, 127], built like the frigate to heavy scantlings, and if a bit slow through the water, they had a big carrying capacity. Even though trade was booming in the years after the Napoleonic War, there was still little urgency as yet for speed.

The challenge to the slow, heavily-laden merchant ship came from North America. During the War of 1812, the United States had built a number of privateers, mainly schooner or brig-rigged, to prey on British merchant shipping, and speed for this purpose was essential. These privateers had a higher length-to-beam ratio than the average British ship and they also had the rounded bottom. It was a disappointment after the end of the war to discover that superior speed was not yet an attraction to shipowners if at the same time it meant a reduction in carrying capacity. But there were two rich trades in which speed was a definite asset, the 'blackbird' trade, which involved shipping tens of thousands of negroes from Africa for sale as slaves to the plantation owners of the southern states of the USA, and the Chinese opium trade. Speed was essential in both cases in order to outrun ships whose duty it was to prevent this disreputable traffic.

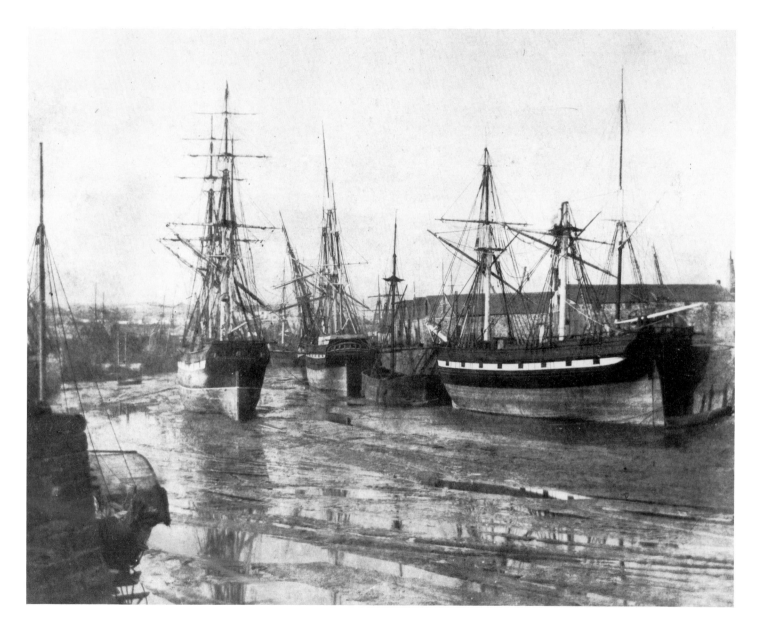

126. A Merchant Brig of the Mid-Nineteenth Century

This early photograph, taken before 1850, shows a trading brig dried-out in a harbour. At this time there were many of these small vessels trading around the British coast and further afield. In particular, scores of collier brigs were engaged in trade between the north-east coast and London, carrying cargoes of coal to supply the capital's demand.

127. Swansea in the 1840s

This photograph of Swansea was taken *c.*1845 and shows deep-sea merchant sailing ships in the River Tawe, dried-out at low tide. The flat bottoms of these vessels allow them to sit upright on the mud of the river bed without further support. The ship in mid-river is the *Countess of Bective*, built at Sunderland in 1843. On the right, alongside the quay, is the barque *Mary Dugdale*, built in 1835 at Hull.

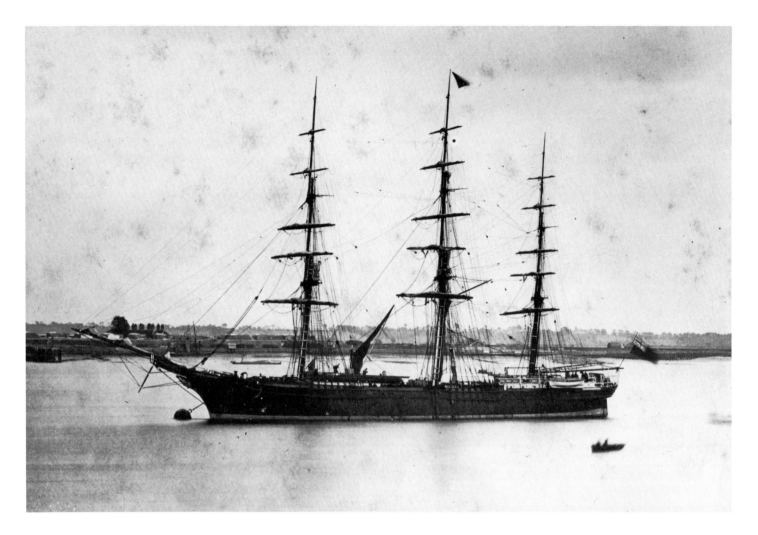

These American privateers were almost all built at ports in Maryland and Virginia and were widely known as 'Baltimore clippers'. Of around 300 tons displacement, they had the sharply raked bow, but not yet the hollow bow which was the hallmark of the true clipper. A larger ship, the *Ann McKim*, was built at Baltimore in 1832 and given a full square rig, and though even she did not have the hollow bow, many people have considered her to be the first true clipper. However, this distinction belongs to the *Rainbow*, built by Smith and Dimon in New York to a design by John Griffiths. She was launched in 1849 and her revolutionary design created a considerable stir. Although her long, deep keel and hull lines were designed for speed through the water, in fact she was not all that fast as her length-to-beam ratio was a little less than 5 to 1 compared with over 6 to 1 of the later clipper ships [fig. 128].

The best of the British merchant ships were known as 'Black-wall frigates' [fig. 129]. They acquired the name because the

major builder of them was Green and Wigram at Blackwall, and they were 'frigate-built'. They were built mainly for the Indian trade—the East Indian Company had lost its monopoly of that trade in 1813—and, with a finer hull form than average, were reasonably fast. The first of them was Green and Wigram's *Seringapatam*, of 818 tons, launched in 1837. She set a new London to Bombay record of eighty-five days. But the performance of these ships did not compare with the clippers, and when the time came to compete with the Americans for the high-paying cargoes, something very much more advanced than the Blackwall frigate would be needed.

The real competition came in 1850 in the China trade. When the East India Company lost its monopoly there in 1833, British ships were still protected by Cromwell's Navigation Act, limiting imports into Britain to those carried in British bottoms or in ships of the producing countries. This Act was repealed in 1849 and the trade was opened to all comers. Tea from China commanded

128. The 'Storm King' (1854)

The American-built ship *Storm King* is shown at a buoy in the Thames at Gravesend, probably in the 1870s. In comparison with the vessels seen in figs. 126 and 127, the hull of the *Storm King* can be seen to have the fine, hollow bow and shapely stern associated with greater speed and characteristic of ships regarded as 'clippers'.

very high freight rates, with a considerable premium each year for the ship which reached London with the first cargo of the new crop. In 1850 American clippers arrived in Canton to compete in the tea trade and the first ship to reach London that year was the clipper *Oriental*. She made so fast a time over the 16,000 miles from Canton to London that the freight rate paid to her was almost double that offered to British ships.

The greatest name in America as a builder of clipper ships was Donald Mackay of Boston, and his ships became the talk of the world. The first was the *Staghound*, revolutionary in design and launched in 1850. She was followed by the *Flying Fish*, *Flying Cloud* and *Sovereign of the Seas*, all of them with reputations as real flyers. When the discovery of gold in California started a great gold rush, the fastest route from the east coast of America to the west coast was by sea around Cape Horn. The profits from this trade were enormous and shipowners could more than

cover the entire cost of building and fitting out a clipper from the freight earned in a single voyage. Everything went by sea, the miners themselves, their tools and equipment, the food, drink, and building materials for the new towns which were springing up almost overnight, and even the girls for the saloons, to separate the miners from the gold they had won from their diggings. Mackay's *Sovereign of the Seas* earned more than $84,000 in freight rates on her maiden voyage to California, well in excess of her building costs. These American clippers for the California trade were built with a length-to-beam ratio of a little over 6 to 1, and were more strongly constructed than average because of the stresses of rounding Cape Horn in very rough seas.

In 1848 gold was discovered in Australia and another great gold rush began. At that time the Australian trade, largely in the hands of James Baines's Black Ball line of Liverpool, was served by British Blackwall frigates, but they had not the speed

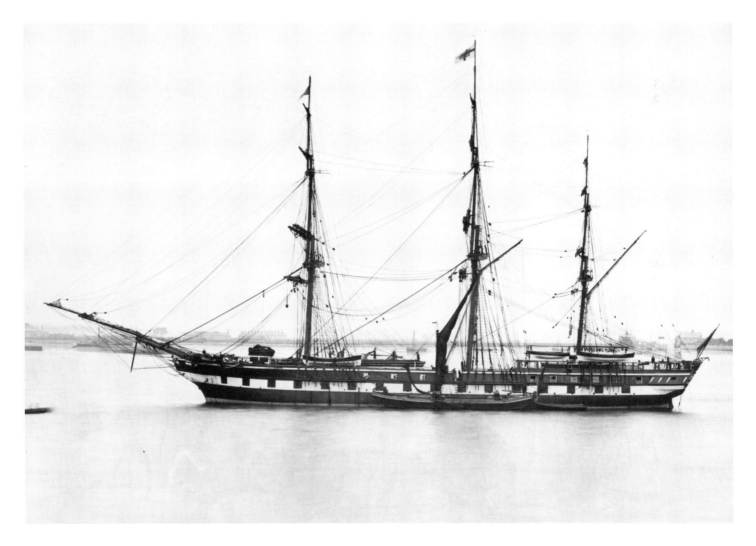

129. The 'Clarence' (1858)

The ship *Clarence*, a Blackwall frigate, was built at Sunderland by W. Pile for the London shipowner Richard Green. Green owned several frigate-built ships and the *Clarence* was one of the fastest of his fleet, being credited with a run of 372 miles in twenty-four hours in 1864.

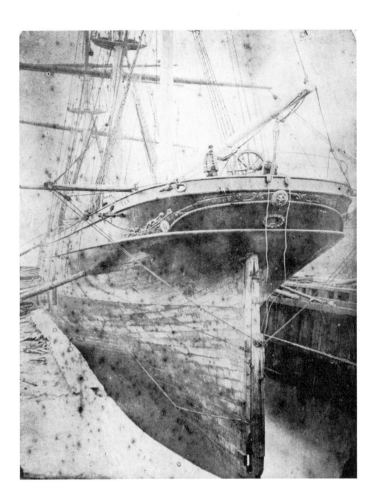

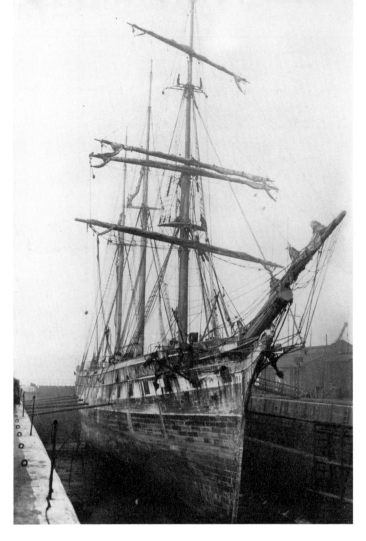

needed for a gold rush. Baines ordered a clipper, the *Marco Polo*, to be built at St. John's, New Brunswick, and in 1852–3 she broke all sailing records to Australia and back. In 1853 he chartered the *Sovereign of the Seas* fron Donald Mackay and in 1854 ordered four big clippers from him, the *Lightning, Champion of the Seas, James Baines* and *Donald Mackay*, and they proved themselves to be among the fastest ships in the world at that time. On her maiden voyage in 1854 the *James Baines*, carrying 700 passengers, 1,400 tons of cargo, and 350 bags of mail, sailed the 14,034 miles from London to Melbourne in sixty-three and a half days; in 1856 her deck log recorded 'ship going 21 knots with main skysail set'. In 1857 the *Champion of the Seas* logged 465 miles in twenty-four hours while running her easting down, a phenomenal average speed of fractionally under 20 knots. It is records such as these that stamp Donald Mackay as a designer and builder of outstanding skill.

The first British reply to the all-conquering American clipper was the small *Scottish Maid*, built by Alexander Hall of Aberdeen.

She was not a true clipper in the traditional design, though she once made the very fast time of thirty-three hours from Leith to London. The first true clippers built in Britain, also by Hall of Aberdeen, were the *Stornoway* and *Chrysolite* for the China tea trade. But the best known of British builders of clippers was Robert Steele of Greenock. When American clipper building declined during the Civil War of 1861–5, he produced some of the best known of all sailing ships of that era. They were by no means just copies of the American design but a distinct type of their own, with a high length-to-beam ratio of between 7 and 8 to 1 with the raked stem rabbeted onto a long, straight keel to give a very good grip of the water. They were smaller ships, of around 1,000 to 1,200 tons, with more delicate lines and a much better balanced sail plan that was just as efficient in a gale as the American clipper but also enabled them to 'ghost' in light airs, while an American clipper would lie becalmed. Steele's ships were usually composite-built, with the wooden hull planking bolted to iron frames, deck beams, and stringers, and

130. The 'Cutty Sark' (1869)
The *Cutty Sark* was a ship-rigged tea-clipper of 963 gross tons, built at Dumbarton in 1869. This photograph shows her in dry dock in 1872, with the jury rudder which had been rigged whilst she was sailing in company with the clipper *Thermopylae* off the South African coast. Heavy weather broke away the *Cutty Sark*'s rudder and this temporary one was fitted at sea. In spite of this, the *Cutty Sark* arrived in London only one week after the *Thermopylae*.

131. The 'Ferreira', formerly the 'Cutty Sark' (1869)
Shown here in dry dock at London is the Portuguese barquentine *Ferreira*, her unfamiliar name and shabby appearance concealing the identity of the tea-clipper *Cutty Sark*. The old ship had been sold to the Portuguese by her owner John Willis in 1895, when she was no longer paying her way under the British flag.

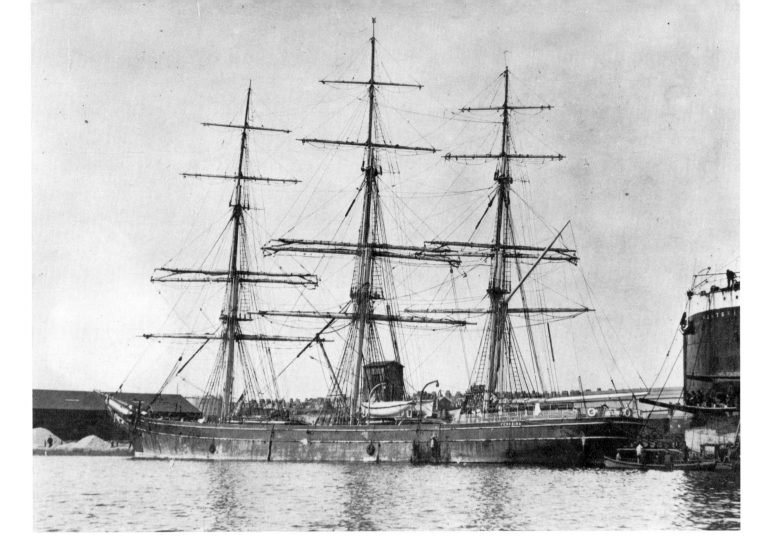

the hull was sheathed with copper sheets below the waterline to protect the timber from wood-boring worms and excessive growth of weed and barnacles.

With the American competition now overcome, the British clippers had the China trade once more in their own hands. Every year they would race home from China with the new crop, the first to arrive assured of a handsome premium. The most famous of these annual races was that of 1866 when five British clippers, their holds stuffed with cases of tea, left Foochow within two days. The first to leave was the *Fiery Cross* on 29 May, the *Ariel*, *Taiping* and *Serica* left harbour on 30 May, and the *Taitsing* followed on 31 May. Ahead of them was a voyage of 16,000 miles round the Cape of Good Hope. At 8.45 p.m. on 6 September the *Taiping* arrived in London Docks. Half an hour later the *Ariel* docked alongside her, and the *Serica* arrived at 11.45 p.m. The other two reached London two days later. A passage of ninety-nine days was remarkable for any ship, that three should accomplish it together was almost a miracle. The average pass-

age time for a clipper was 110 days. And perhaps even more remarkable was that the three ships which arrived first were all designed and built by Robert Steele.

The search for speed continued, and in 1868 Walter Hood of Aberdeen built a clipper of 991 tons to a design by Bernard Waymouth, named *Thermopylae*. On her maiden voyage, with passengers and cargo, she sailed the London–Melbourne passage in fifty-nine days, a record for a sailing ship that has never been beaten. In the following year John Willis ordered from Scott and Linton of Dumbarton a clipper of 963 tons with which to challenge the *Thermopylae*, to be named *Cutty Sark* [figs. 130–2]. She made her first voyage laden with tea from China in 1870, 109 days from Shanghai to Beachy Head, an unremarkable time. But both she and the *Thermopylae* were really too late for the China tea trade. The Suez Canal was opened in 1869 and the steamships, equipped with the new compound engine, and with a much shorter route home through the Canal, brought the tea to London in less time than a clipper.

132. The 'Ferreira', formerly the 'Cutty Sark' (1869)
Her new name did nothing to conceal the clipper's fine lines and she is instantly recognizable as a vessel of some distinction. At the mainmast truck can still be seen the emblem of the 'short-shirt' from which the *Cutty Sark* took her name. Following service as the *Ferreira*, the *Cutty Sark* is today preserved as a museum ship at Greenwich.

With the tea trade now unprofitable, the clippers looked elsewhere to earn their keep and turned to the wool trade from Australia. Voyages to Australia were still beyond the compass of a steamship, partly because of a lack of coaling stations on the route from which to replenish their fuel, and partly because the marine engine itself was still inefficient and wasteful of coal, awaiting the development of higher steam pressures and of triple expansion to bring even the most distant ports within their reach. The wool trade lasted until around the end of the century for sailing ships, though with steadily diminishing returns during the last ten years as the steamships began to take over.

The pattern of the wool trade involved an outward voyage to Australia round the Cape of Good Hope and a homeward voyage round Cape Horn to take advantage of the prevailing westerly winds in the southern latitudes. Its profits attracted very large numbers of sailing ships to the trade and as late as 1891 no fewer than seventy-seven large sailing ships were loading wool at the same time in Sydney harbour for the wool sales in London. They carried immense cargoes, using screwjacks to compress the bales into the holds to make room for more. The clipper *Mermerus* once screwed 10,000 bales worth £132,000 into her holds, and the little *Cutty Sark*, loading at Brisbane, once brought home 5,304 bales, screwing them down until the wool in them was almost solid.

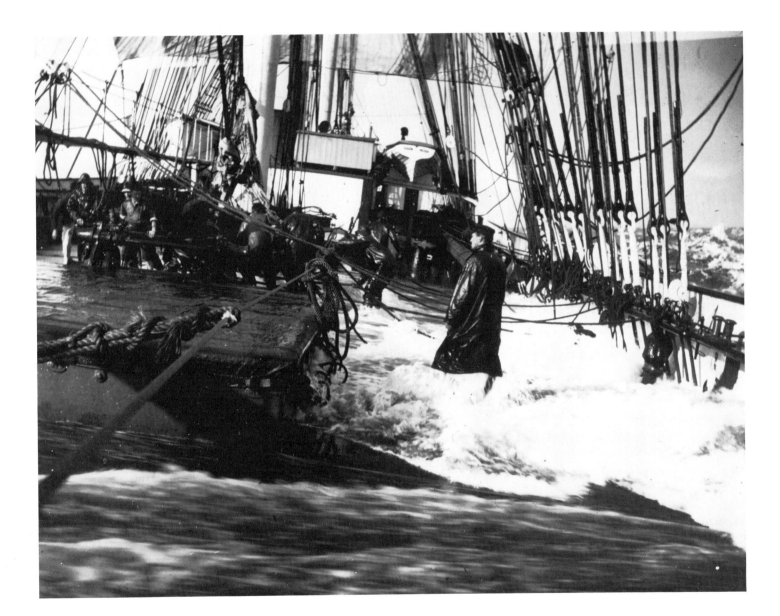

133. The 'Medway' (1902)
This photograph was taken in 1912 and shows a scene which would have been familiar to any merchant seaman of the nineteenth century. The latter-day merchant sailing ships, with their steel hulls, rigging and gear, were driven hard and a big four-masted barque such as the *Medway* might make 14 knots in a stiff blow. Such conditions made severe demands on the crew, who would spend much of their time soaked and near to exhaustion.

134. The 'Kilmallie' (1893)
Bending a lower topsail aboard the British barque *Kilmallie*. The sail has been hoisted, still rolled-up, using a gantline from the head of the topmast. The crew members on the yard will now draw the canvas out along the yard and secure the head of the sail to the jackstay, which can be seen running along the top of the yard. The sail may then be set from the deck.

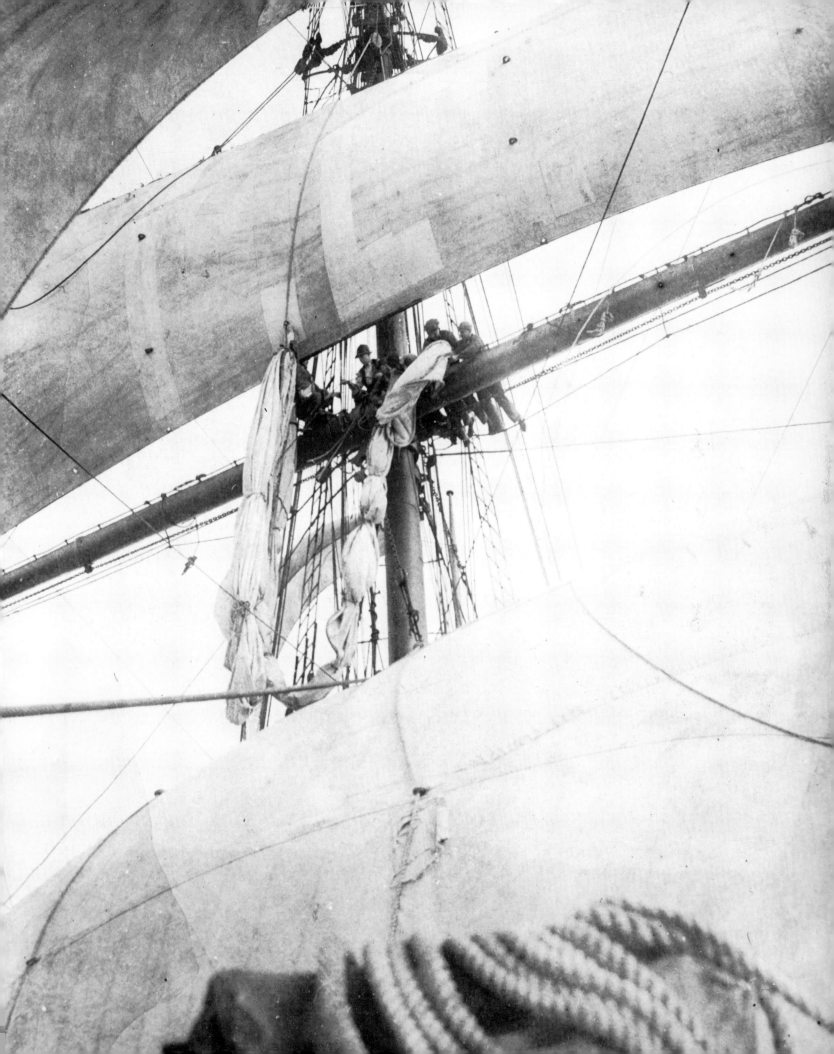

By the end of the nineteenth century the end of the working sailing ship was in sight. One profitable trade that lasted into the opening years of the twentieth century was grain—wheat, barley, and corn—from the west coast of Canada and America to the ports of Europe, sailing round Cape Horn. Well over a million tons were shipped each year. Another trade was in coal and manufactured goods to the west coast of South America and home with hides, nitrates, and guano, using the Cape Horn route both ways. As the traditional sailing ship trades lost out one by one to the steamships, the competition for these last available trades attracted virtually every sailing ship in the world. In the fierce scramble for cargoes the clipper was soon squeezed out.

Only large cargoes paid their way and the clipper, for all her speed, was never designed to carry a large cargo. Her slim lines and rounded hull made that impossible. And so the final generation of the sail trading ship, faced with the growing competition from steamships, was born around 1890.

In their hull form they could not be called handsome ships. To get the capacity required they had to be built to the roughly square cross-section of the steamship and this made them somewhat slab-sided. They made up for their generally unattractive hulls by the beauties of their rigs, barque or schooner, set on four or five masts. They were built of steel, with steel masts and yards, and wire-rope rigging to reduce windage. And they were

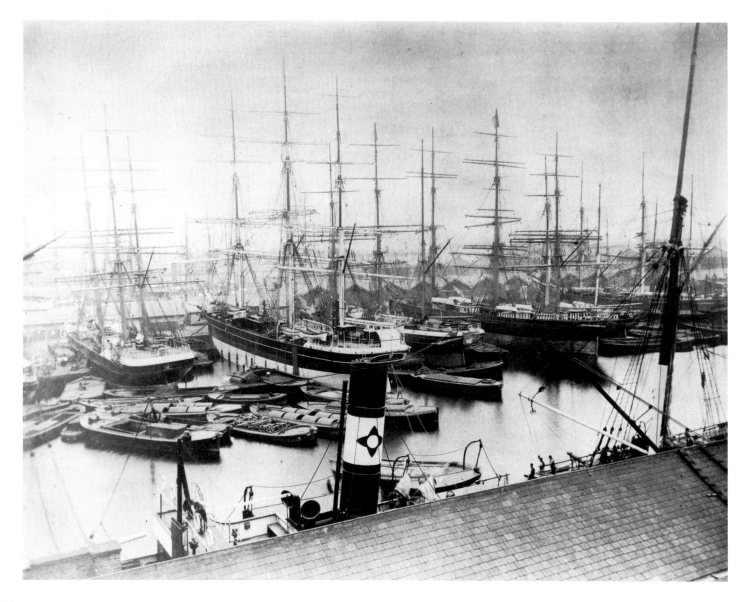

135. The South West India Dock, London, in the 1880s

It was not until 1883 that the tonnage of steamships on the British register overtook that of sailing vessels, and it can be seen from this photograph that sail was still very much in evidence in the London Docks in the eighties. The only steamship in evidence here is the vessel in the foreground, her funnel projecting above the shed roof. By the end of the century the total tonnage of British steamships exceeded that of sailing vessels by more than three times.

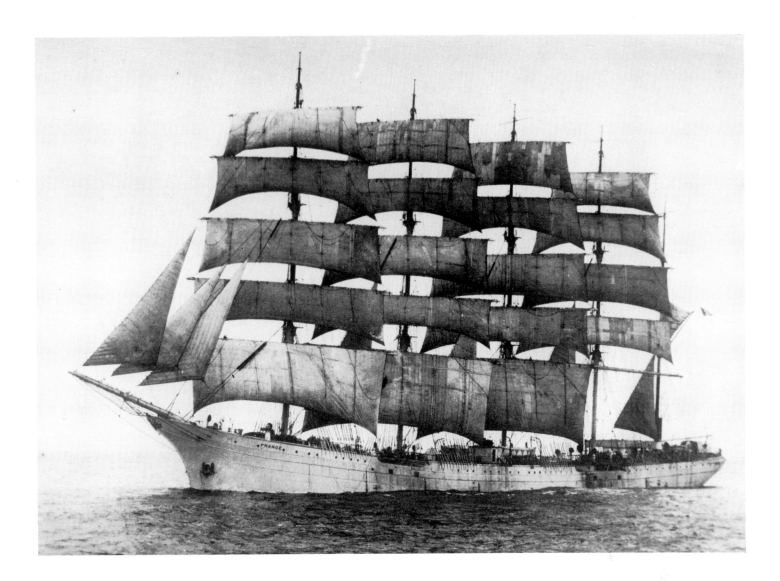

built big. The *France*, built by Henderson of Glasgow in 1890 for the A. D. Bordes line, had a deadweight tonnage of 5,900; her successor, also called *France* [fig. 136], built by Chantiers de la Gironde in 1912 for the Société des Navires Mixtres, was even larger. With a deadweight tonnage of 8,000 she was the largest sail trading ship ever built, fractionally overtaking the German *Preussen*, one of the famous 'Flying P' line of Ferdinand Laeisz of Hamburg, built nine years earlier. The second *France* was a five-masted barque, *Preussen* carried a full square rig on all her five masts, the only ship in the world ever to carry such a rig.

Two events ended their days. In 1897 Lloyds, who handled most of the world's shipping insurance, sharply increased their rates for sail tonnage, making it still more difficult for shipowners to run their ships at a profit in a rapidly declining freight market. Then, in 1914, the Panama Canal was opened to shipping. It killed the South American trade in hides and nitrates, the last stronghold of sail, as steamships, using the new Canal, could carry it more efficiently and more cheaply than the sailing ship using the Cape Horn passage. With no freight left to be earned, and no hopes of new cargoes, most shipowners abandoned their lovely sailing ships in their last ports of call, stripped them of everything saleable, and left them to rot. As an old sailing ship song of the last days has it:

> *But the steam come up and the sail went down,*
> *And them tall ships of high renown,*
> *Was scrapped, or wrecked, or sold away.*

136. The 'France' (1912)
The world's largest merchant sailing ship, the *France*, built for the New Caledonia nickel ore trade to Europe. She was fitted with 295 horsepower oil engines driving twin screws as auxiliary power but the engines were removed shortly before the loss of the ship in 1922 since they made no real contribution to the vessel's performance. Under sail alone the *France* was capable of making 14 knots, and in one twenty-four hour period averaged over 17 knots.

List of illustrations

Pictures are oil on canvas unless indicated otherwise. The abbreviation GH refers to the Greenwich Hospital Collection.

COLOUR PLATES

76 × 139.5 cm. NMM 36–75 Neg. 2461

28. Greenwich Hospital. Giovanni Antonio Canale, called Canaletto (1697–1768). 27 × 42 in; 68.5 × 106.5 cm. NMM 39–1766 Neg. A6700

29. A Vice-Admiral of the Red and a Squadron at Sea. Charles Brooking (1723–59). 14½ × 22½ in; 37 × 57 cm. NMM 62–13 Neg. A3827

30. A Ship in a Light Breeze. Charles Brooking (1723–59). 27 × 27 in; 68.5 × 68.5 cm. NMM 36–73 Neg. A9234

31. A Danish Timber Bark getting under Way. Samuel Scott (1702–72), 1736. 89½ × 86 in; 227.5 × 218.5 cm. NMM 50–282/2 Neg. A6856

32. An English Fleet coming to Anchor. Peter Monamy (1681–1749), c.1715. 34½ × 51 in; 87.5 × 129.5 cm. NMM 27–366 Neg. B2679

33. Wager's Action off Cartagena, 28 May 1708. Samuel Scott (1702–72). 34 × 49 in; 86.5 × 124.5 cm. NMM 37–2061 Neg. B2856

34. Lord George Graham in his Cabin. William Hogarth (1697–1764). 25 × 27 in; 71 × 91 cm. NMM 32–30 Neg. A9156

35. A Sixth-Rate on the Stocks. John Cleveley the Elder (c.1712–77), 1759. 36 × 57 in; 91.5 × 145 cm. NMM 39–368 Neg. 7932

36. Blackwall Yard. Francis Holman (fl. 1767–90), 1784. 37 × 80 in; 94 × 203 cm. NMM 35–49 Neg. 1365

37. A Launch at Deptford. John Cleveley the Elder (c.1712–77), 1757. 48 × 74 in; 122 × 188 cm. NMM 33–47 Neg. 104

38. *Resolution* and *Adventure* in Matavi Bay, Tahiti, c.1773. William Hodges (1744–97), 1776. 54 × 76 in; 137 × 193 cm. NMM 36–17L Neg. A7756

39. A View of Cape Stephens in Cook's Straits, New Zealand, with Waterspout. William Hodges (1744–97), 1776. 54 × 76 in; 137 × 193 cm. NMM 36–9L Neg. 4198

40. The Royal Yacht *Royal Sovereign* (1804). John Thomas Serres (1759–1825), 1809. 54 × 66 in; 137 × 167.5 cm. NMM 40–327 Neg.7032

41. A British Brig with Four Captured American Merchantmen. Francis Holman (fl. 1767–90), 1778. 39 × 59 in; 99 × 150 cm. NMM 46–124 Neg. A604

42. The British Fleet entering the Harbour at Havana, 16 August 1762. Dominic Serres (1722–93), 1775. 47 × 71 in; 119 × 180.5 cm. NMM 48–729/8 Neg. B4011

43. Moonlight Battle off Cape St. Vincent, 16 January 1780. Richard Paton (1717–1791). 40 × 58 in; 101.5 × 147 cm. GH 123 Neg. 1588

44. Battle of the Glorious First of June. Philippe Jacques de Loutherbourg (1740–1812). 105 × 147 in; 267 × 373.5 cm. GH 45 Neg. A9662

45. Lord Howe on the Quarterdeck of the *Queen Charlotte*. Mather Brown (1761–1831). 102 × 144 in; 259 × 365.5 cm. NMM 38–64 Neg. A9663.

46. Nelson's Flagships. Nicholas Pocock (1740–1821), 1807. 14 × 21 in; 35.5 × 53 cm. NMM 38–1274 Neg. A9157

47. Battle of Copenhagen, 30 March–2 April 1801. John Thomas Serres (1759–1825), 1801. 19½ × 32 in; 49.5 × 81 cm. NMM 35–52 Neg. 2099

48. Battle of Trafalgar, 21 October 1805. Joseph Mallord William Turner (1775–1851), 1824. 102 × 144 in; 259 × 365 cm. GH 98 Neg. A7755

49. The Fall of Nelson. Denis Dighton (1792–1827). 30 × 40 in; 76 × 101.5 cm. NMM 47–21/5 Neg. 3205

50. Napoleon on the *Bellerophon* at Plymouth, August 1815. John James Chalon (1778–1854), 1816. 38 × 60 in; 96.5 × 152.5 cm. GH 20 Neg. 1743

51. Beaching a Pink in Heavy Weather at Scheveningen. Edward William Cooke (1811–80), 1855. 42 × 66 in; 106.5 × 167.5 cm. NMM 66–8 Neg. B1735

52. The *Dutton* wrecked in Plymouth Sound. Thomas Luny (1759–1837), 1821. 30 × 44 in; 76 × 112 cm. NMM 46–424 Neg. A1479

53. A Fleet of Merchantmen. Thomas Luny (1759–1837), 1802. 34 × 50 in; 86 × 127 cm. NMM 50–350 Neg. 4163

54. The Bombardment of Algiers. George Chambers (1803–40), 1836. 69½ × 99 in; 176.5 × 251.5 cm. GH 80 Neg. A7215

55. A Frigate coming to Anchor in the Mersey. Robert Salmon (1775–c.1845), 1802. 19 × 24 in; 48 × 61 cm. NMM 65–14 Neg. A7681

56. The *Euphrates*, Indiaman. Samuel Walters (1811–82), 1835. 38 × 60 in; 96.5 × 152.5 cm. NMM 55–2 Neg. B7027

57. Greenwich Hospital. George Chambers (1803–40), 1836. 27½ × 40 in; 70 × 101.5 cm. NMM 36–79 Neg. 4585

58. Return of George IV to Greenwich. William Anderson (1757–1837). 29½ × 42½ in; 75 × 108 cm. NMM 27–72 Neg. A2643

59. The *Charlotte of Chittagong* and other Indian Government Vessels at Anchor in a River. Franz Balthazar Solveyns (1760–1824), 1792. 21 × 24 in; 53.5 × 61 cm. NMM 58–19 Neg. A706

60. Trinity House Yacht and Revenue Cutter off Ramsgate. Thomas Whitcombe (c.1760–1824). 24 × 36 in; 61 × 91.5 cm. NMM 27–286 Neg. 7738

61. Shipyard at Dumbarton. Samuel Bough (1822–78), 1855. 53 × 70 in; 134.5 × 178 cm. NMM 46–248 Neg. A1473

62. A Haybarge off Greenwich. Edward William Cooke (1811–80), 1835. 14 × 31 in; 35.5 × 79 cm. NMM 84–3 Neg. C9912

63. Napoleon III receiving Queen Victoria at Cherbourg. Jules Noel (1815–81), 1859. 65 × 90 in; 165 × 228.5 cm. NMM 59–18 Neg. A1460

64. *Erebus* and *Terror* in the Antarctic. John Wilson Carmichael (1800–68), 1847. 48 × 72 in; 122 × 183 cm. NMM 48–530/2 Neg. 3522

65. Catching a Mermaid. James Clarke Hook (1819–1907), 1883. 36 × 55 in; 91.5 × 139.5 cm. NMM 83–18 Neg. C9636

Glossary

Bowline. A rope attached to the leading edge of a square sail and used to haul it as far forward as possible when sailing close to the wind. A square-rigged ship when sailing as close to the wind as possible is said to 'sail' or 'stand on a taut bowline'.

Bowsprit. A large spar projecting over the stem of a sailing ship to provide the means of staying a foretopmast and from which the jibs are set.

Brace. A rope or tackle attached to the ends of the yards of a square-rigged ship and used to trim them, and the sails they carry, to the wind according to the direction in which the ship is sailing.

Careen, to. The operation in older days of heaving a ship down on one side on a steeply shelving beach to expose the other side for cleaning off weed and barnacles or for repairs. The ship was then floated off on the tide, turned, and careened again to expose the opposite side. The ship was hove down with tackles attached to the mastheads, and relieving tackles, passed under the keel, were secured to convenient points on the exposed side to control the angle of heel and bring her back upright after the side had been cleaned.

Course. The name given to the sail set on the lower yards of the foremast and mainmast of a square-rigged ship. The similar sail set on the lower yard of the mizenmast (q.v.) in a three-masted ship is known as the cro'jack.

Deckbeams. Transverse beams secured to the tops of the ribs of a ship, on which the upper deck is laid. They are an essential element of the basic design of a ship to give her the strength required to withstand the rigours of the sea.

Entry. The form of the fore-body of a ship below the waterline. A ship with a pointed bow is said to have a fine entry, to give an uninterrupted flow of water as the ship thrusts through the sea. *See also* **run.**

Fore-and-aft rig. The arrangement of sails in a ship where the leading edge of the sails is attached to the masts or to stays.

Gaff. The spar to which the head of a four-sided fore-and-aft sail is laced and hoisted on the after side of a mast.

Gantline. A single whip (q.v.) used to hoist the standing rigging of a ship to the masts when fitting-out and for hoisting the sails from the deck in square-rigged ships when required to be bent to their yards. The word is a corruption of the original 'girtline'.

Gunport. The square hole cut in the side of sailing warships through which the broadside guns were fired, one gunport to each gun. When not in use they were closed with a port-lid hinged on the top edge.

Jackstay. A rope, batten, or iron bar fitted to the upper side of a yard to which the head of a square sail is bent.

Keel. The principal timber of a wooden ship extending the whole length of the ship and to which the stem (q.v.) and sternpost (q.v.) are fixed at either end. The ribs, which form the shape of the hull, are attached at intervals along its length. It is a ship's strongest single member and could be called the backbone of the ship.

Lateen rig. A narrow triangular sail set on a very long yard of which the forward end is hauled well down so that it sets obliquely on the mast and produces a high peak to the sail. It is a rig of great antiquity, thought to be pre-Christian and of Arab origin.

Leeboards. An early type of drop keel made of wood and pivoted at its forward end on each side of a flat-bottomed or shallow draught sailing vessel. When sailing close to the wind the board on the lee side is dropped to increase the effective draught and to reduce leeway.

Leech. The after edge of a fore-and-aft sail or the outer edges of a square sail.

Luff. The leading edge of a fore-and-aft sail. When used as a verb it is an order to the helmsman to bring the ship's head closer to the wind.

Lug rig. A four-sided sail with a very wide throat laced to a lug or yard. The lug, with the sail, is hoisted on a mast, and when set up taut virtually becomes an extension of the mast. This rig was first developed during the late seventeenth century and was used mainly for the fishing and coasting trade, or for smuggling.

Mizen. The name of the third, aftermost, mast of a square-rigged sailing ship or of a three-masted schooner or of a ketch or yawl.

Poop. The name given to the short aftermost deck raised above the quarterdeck of a ship (q.v.).

Quarterdeck. That part of the upper deck of a ship which is abaft the mainmast.

Reach. The point of sailing where a vessel can hold her course with the wind free and her sails full.

Ribs. The timbers of a wooden ship fixed to the keel at intervals to form the shape of the hull. The tops of the ribs support the transverse deckbeams (q.v.) to provide extra strength and rigidity to the ship.

Run. The shape of the after part of the hull of a ship below the waterline in relation to the resistance built up as she goes through the water. A ship with a clean run is one in which the shape of the afterbody enables her to slip easily through the water without excessive resistance through turbulence.

Scantlings. The dimensions of the timbers which go to make up the framework of a ship—keel, stem, sternpost, ribs and deckbeams. In modern shipbuilding, scantlings embrace all the parts used in the construction of a ship's hull, and rules governing these dimensions are laid down and followed by most ships of any size built throughout the world.

Sprit. A long spar stretching diagonally from the base of a mast to the peak of a loose-footed, four-sided, fore-and-aft sail, as in the typical barge rig still to be seen today.

Spritsail. A small square sail set on a yard beneath the bowsprit (q.v.) in older square-rigged ships, introduced early in the sixteenth century to balance the lateen mizen (qq.v.). A spritsail topsail was a similar sail but set on a short mast stepped on the end of the bowsprit above the spritsail. It is also the name of the loose-footed, four-sided, fore-and-aft sail extended by a sprit.

Square rig. The arrangement of sails in a ship when they are laced to a yard square to the masts.

Stay. A part of the standing rigging of a sailing ship which supports a mast in the fore-and-aft line.

Stays. The moment during the operation of tacking across the wind when a sailing ship is directly head to wind. If she loses her speed as she comes up into the wind and is sluggish in regaining it after crossing the wind, she is said to be slow in stays.

Staysail. A triangular fore-and-aft sail set by being hanked to a stay. They are set both in square-rigged and fore-and-aft rigged ships and are named from the stay (q.v.) on which they are set.

Stem. The timber, bolted to the forward end of the keel, which forms the bow of the ship. It is normally shaped to take up the designed curve of the bow.

Sternpost. The timber, bolted to the after end of the keel, on which the ship's rudder is hung.

Tafferel. The curved wooden top of the stern of a sailing warship or East India-man, normally carved or otherwise decorated.

Transom. The athwartship timbers bolted to the sternpost (q.v.) of a ship to provide a flat stern. In older square-rigged ships they were usually heavier than other timbers in order to support the overhang of the stern and quarter galleries.

Truck. A circular wooden cap fitted to the top of a ship's masts. They usually carried one or two small sheaves for signal halyards and the hoisting of distinguishing flags, battle ensigns, etc.

Wale. An extra thickness of wood bolted to the sides of ships in positions where protection is needed. Sailing warships had a wale between each row of gunports to prevent the port-lids being damaged when going alongside an enemy ship to capture her by boarding.

Whip. The name given to a single rope rove through a single block and used for hoisting heavy articles.

Yard. A large spar crossing the masts of a sailing ship horizontally or diagonally from which a sail is set.

Index